Diploma in Financial Management

Project text

This project text

BPP is an **approved provider** of training materials for the ACCA's DipFM qualification

In this September 2007 edition

- Explanation of the project requirements and examiner feedback

- Chapters on analysis and research

- Plenty of activities and exercises to demonstrate and practise techniques

- A selection of ACCA 'live' Projects with suggested approach and answers prepared by BPP Learning Media

- Full index

- Layout designed to be easy on the eye and easy to use

FOR PROJECTS FROM AUGUST 2007

BPP
LEARNING MEDIA

First edition 2002
Sixth edition September 2007

ISBN 9780 7517 4282 4
(previous ISBN 0 7517 2594 3)

British Library Cataloguing-in-Publication Data
A catalogue record for this book
is available from the British Library

Published by

BPP Learning Media Ltd
BPP House, Aldine Place
London W12 8AA

www.bpp.com/learningmedia

Printed in Great Britain by W M Print
45-47 Frederick Street
Walsall, West Midlands
WS2 9NE

Your learning materials, published by BPP Learning
Media Ltd, are printed on paper sourced from
sustainable, managed forests.

We are grateful to the Association of Chartered
Certified Accountants for permission to reproduce past
examination questions. The answers to past
examination questions have been prepared by BPP
Learning Media Ltd.

Contents

Introduction

This book has been specifically written to help you to tackle the Project element of each of the two Modules of the ACCA's DipFM qualification.

It contains these features:

- The requirements of the projects

- Advice on how to start the work, analyse the assignment, carry out any necessary further research and write the answers

- Four ACCA 'live' projects for each Module up to and including Autumn 2006, with a suggested approach and a model answer, both written by BPP Learning Media.

In producing this book, we have assumed that most students will complete the Project element of the Module after the relevant exam. You will therefore find technical terms within this book which you will only have encountered once you have worked through the exam syllabus. This is not necessarily an insuperable problem. If you are completing the Project before taking the exam, it just means that you may have to refer to the BPP Learning Media Study Text for the relevant area a little more frequently, for clarification of terms used.

In this book we refer to aspects of, and provide illustrations of, all four subject areas within the DipFM syllabus, so do not be deterred if you find a topic which you have not yet studied. All the material in this book is designed to provide you with illustrations and advice on project technique, not technical content, so you should read material on as yet unfamiliar technical topics with that end in mind.

International terminology

With effect from the December 2006 exam session all DipFM projects and exams have been set using international terminology. This project text has been fully updated to reflect that change.

The DipFM syllabus

The ACCA Diploma in Financial Management has two modules, A and B, each of which covers two subject areas.

Module A has the following two elements:

> Subject area 1: *Interpretation of Financial Statements*

> Subject area 2: *Performance Management*

Module B has the following two elements:

> Subject area 3: *Financial Strategy*

> Subject area 4: *Risk Management*

Subject Area 1 – Interpretation of Financial Statements

Aim

The overall aim of this paper is that candidates should be able to understand and interpret the financial statements produced by organisations for external users. Candidates should develop an understanding of the regulatory framework in which these statements are prepared and of the principles and methods which underlie their preparation.

Objectives

On completion of this paper candidates should be able to

- Describe the role and function of external financial reports and identify their users and the regulatory framework in which they are prepared

- Explain the accounting concepts and conventions present in generally accepted accounting practice

- Explain, supported by simple computations, the presentation, measurement and meaning of the primary financial statements and their contents

- Describe the informational role of the constituent parts of a corporate annual report usually presented in addition to the primary financial statements

- Compute, interpret and appraise financial performance, financial position and adaptability as revealed by financial statement analysis in particular by the use of financial and accounting ratios.

Syllabus content

1 **Regulation of Financial Statements**

The regulatory framework within which financial statements are prepared.

(a) The role of the International Accounting Standards Committee Foundation and constituent bodies

(b) The role of the auditor and the meaning of fair presentation

2 **Financial Information**

(a) The objectives of financial statements and the needs of users

(b) The reporting entity

(c) The qualitative characteristics of financial information

(d) The elements of financial statements

(e) Measurement in financial statements including an appreciation of the limitations of historical cost and the basic nature of current value accounting models

(f) The basic features of accounting for public sector and non-profit organisations

3 **Financial Statements**

(a) The structure, features and content of the primary financial statements:

  (i) Income statement

  (ii) Balance sheet

  (iii) Cash flow statement

  (iv) Statement of changes in equity

(b) The major features, but not detailed contents of other elements of corporate annual reports:

  (i) Notes to the accounts and additional financial statements

  (ii) Management report

  (iii) Chairman's statement

  (iv) Financial reviews

  (v) Environmental reports

  (vi) Interim accounts

  (vii) Preliminary announcements

(c) The terminology and underlying accounting methods and principles used in preparing financial statements in respect of:

  (i) Tangible non-current assets, including depreciation and the impact of revaluation

  (ii) Intangible non-current assets, including goodwill and research and development costs

  (iii) Current assets, in particular inventories and construction contracts

  (iv) Liabilities, including leases, contingencies and provisions

  (v) Share capital and reserves

      (vi)   Events after the balance sheet date

      (vii)   Reporting the substance of transactions

      (viii)   Reporting financial performance, including segmental analysis

      (ix)   Business combinations and other investments

      (x)   Cash flow reporting

      (xi)   The accounting implications of taxation, in particular current and deferred taxation

For all of the above computations may be required to support explanation, appraisal and justification of accounting policies and treatments.

4   Analysis of Financial Statements

(a)   The computation, interpretation and appraisal of financial ratios in respect of:

      (i)   Profitability, earnings, operating performance and efficiency

      (ii)   Liquidity, solvency and working capital management

      (iii)   Asset and capital structures, including gearing

      (iv)   Cash flows and cash flow management

      (v)   Stock market performance including earnings, dividend and price relationships

(b)   Common size statements, trend analysis, inter-firm analysis and failure prediction models.

(c)   The limitations of financial ratio analysis

Excluded topics

The following topics are specifically excluded from the syllabus:

- The detailed process of double entry bookkeeping
- Foreign currency translation
- Accounting for pension costs and retirement benefits
- Related party disclosures
- Reporting for smaller entities
- SICs and IFRICs

Key areas of the syllabus

The key topics are:

- The regulatory framework
- The principles underlying financial statements
- The structure and content of the primary financial statements
- Financial statement analysis

Subject Area 2 – Performance Management

Aim

To develop a good understanding of knowledge required and techniques available to enable managers to measure and manage business performance within their organisation. Both financial and non-financial measures of performance are included in this paper.

Objectives

On completion of this paper candidates should be able to:

- Understand how performance measures should be linked to overall organisation strategy

- Prepare budgets and use them to control and evaluate organisational performance

- Identify and apply techniques that aid making decisions that will maximise financial performance

- Identify and implement appropriate costing systems and business control systems

- Identify and apply techniques to evaluate decisions in relation to: costing, pricing, product range, marketing strategy, purchasing and production strategies

- Identify and apply non-financial performance measures, and understand the inter-relationships between different performance measures

- Understand the behavioural and organisational consequences of using performance measurement and performance management techniques

- Identify and apply techniques for evaluating the performance of divisions

- Identify and understand issues that may cause performance not to meet expectations, such as: actions of competitors, labour disputes, supply problems, foreign exchange movements and late payment

- Demonstrate the skills expected in the Diploma in Financial Management

Position within the syllabus

Candidates are expected to have a good knowledge of basic accounting principles from subject area 1. Knowledge from subject areas 3 and 4 will be helpful but not essential.

Syllabus content

The syllabus considers Performance Management from three broad and overlapping perspectives, namely: planning and decision making, measuring performance, and managing performance. There are also some general issues.

1   General issues for performance management

    (a)   Mission statements, objectives and targets

    (b)   Responsibility centres

    (c)   Information systems and costing systems to provide appropriate information

    (d)   Overall organisation strategy and how performance measurement and management should enable strategy to be realised

2   Planning and decision making

    (a)   Preparing budgets, fixed and flexible budgets, cash budgets

    (b)   Budgets in different contexts, including: manufacturing, sales, service industries

    (c)   Alternative approaches to budgeting, for example, zero-based budgeting and activity-based budgeting

    (d)   Decision making techniques required to determine plans that will maximise financial performance for products, customers, etc, including:

        (i)   Cost-Volume-Profit analysis, including breakeven and margin-of-safety
        (ii)   Relevant costs and opportunity costs
        (iii)   Limiting factors and scarce resources
        (iv)   Decision making under uncertainty, particularly expected values

    (e)   Pricing policies (for example: penetration, skimming) and techniques for setting prices (for example: cost-plus, variable cost-plus, marginal cost, target cost and pricing)

    (f)   Strategic planning and operational planning

    (g)   The future of budgets and alternatives to budgeting

    (h)   Costing data for decision making, and use of activity-based costing data

    (i)   Transfer pricing policies and practices

3   Performance measurement

    (a)   Financial measures of performance, including:

        (i)   Actual v budget and variances, for costs, profit and cash

        (ii)   Standard cost variances, operating statements and appraisal of performance

        (iii)   Measures of shareholder value

    (b)   Critical success factors and key performance indicators

    (c)   Non-financial performance measures

    (d)   Balanced scorecard

    (e)   Benchmarking against world's best practice

    (f)   Divisional performance measures, including:

        (i)   Return on Investment
        (ii)   Residual Income and EVA®

      (iii)   Accounting profit and controllable profit

      (iv)   Cash flows

4   **Performance management**

(a)   Purchasing and production management, including:

      (i)   Supply chain management

      (ii)   E-procurement

      (iii)   Just-in-time production and purchasing

      (iv)   Target costing and kaizen costing

      (v)   Out-sourcing, joint-ventures and partnerships

(b)   Activity-based management and business process re-engineering

(c)   Techniques for ensuring value-for-money, particularly re not-for-profit organisations

(d)   Techniques to ensure continuous improvement

(e)   Use of performance measurement techniques to manage performance

(f)   Management of divisional performance, including transfer pricing issues

(g)   Behavioural and organisational consequences of performance measures, particularly budgeting and other accounting system data

(h)   Understanding of practical issues that may affect an organisation's ability to manage performance effectively, including: actions of competitors, price movements, foreign exchange movements, labour disputes, supply problems, etc.

(i)   Incentive schemes linked to performance measures

Excluded topics

No issues relating to performance management are specifically excluded.

Key areas of the syllabus

The key topics include:

- Decision making techniques to enable managers to maximise financial performance
- Budgeting and standard costing techniques that assess financial performance
- Costing systems and the use of data produced, including activity-based costing
- Techniques to aid performance evaluation of divisions
- Techniques to manage the performance of purchasing, production and sales functions
- Understanding of behavioural and organisational consequences of performance measurement
- Practical issues that affect a firm's ability to manage performance effectively
- Non-financial performance indicators and balanced scorecard

Subject Area 3 – Financial Strategy

Aim

To develop an understanding of the role of financial strategy in the investing, financing and resource allocation decisions within an organisation.

Objectives

On completion of this paper, candidates should be able to:

- Explain the role and nature of financial strategy and its relationship to shareholder value
- Identify the main elements of investment appraisal
- Evaluate long-term decision opportunities through the use of appropriate techniques
- Identify and evaluate the major sources of finance available to an organisation
- Explain the role of capital markets in raising finance
- Discuss the main methods of managing working capital and analyse working capital policies
- Evaluate the motives for, and financial implications of, mergers and acquisitions
- Discuss the impact of taxation and inflation on financial strategy decisions

Position within the syllabus

The paper is directly related to the management decision-making theme of the Diploma in Financial Management and links closely with the other three subject areas within the scheme. Some overlap between these subject areas is inevitable. For example, financial statements and ratios that are considered in subject area 1, fixed and variable costs and relevant and irrelevant costs that are considered in subject area 2, and gearing that is considered in subject area 4, may also be considered in this paper.

Syllabus content

1   The nature and scope of financial strategy
- (a)   Financial strategy and organisational objectives
- (b)   Financial strategy and the role of the finance function

2   Investment appraisal
- (a)   Evaluation of long-term investment opportunities through the use of:
  - (i)   net present value
  - (ii)   internal rate of return
  - (iii)   accounting rate of return
  - (iv)   payback period (including discounted payback period)
  - (v)   profitability index
- (b)   Advantages and disadvantages of each appraisal technique
- (c)   Asset replacement decisions
- (d)   Simple single-constraint capital rationing decisions
- (e)   Sensitivity analysis
- (f)   Methods available to approve, monitor and control investment projects
- (g)   Non-financial issues in investment appraisal

3   Raising finance
- (a)   Key features of the main sources of finance, including
  - (i)   share capital (including forms of share issue and the redemption and repurchase of shares)
  - (ii)   loan capital (including mezzanine finance, junk bonds, securitisation, warrants and convertibles)
  - (iii)   leasing (including sales and lease back) and hire purchase
  - (iv)   invoice discounting and debt factoring
  - (v)   bills of exchange and acceptance credits
  - (vi)   bank finance
  - (vii)   PFI/PPP
  - (viii)   internal sources of finance
- (b)   Use of forecast financial statements and financial ratios to evaluate financing proposals
- (c)   Factors influencing the choice of financing methods
- (d)   The effect of financing decisions on risks and returns to investors
- (e)   The problems of overtrading
- (f)   The cost of capital, including calculation of the:
  - (i)   cost of equity (including a basic understanding of the Capital Asset Pricing Model)
  - (ii)   cost of loan capital
  - (iii)   weighted average cost of capital
- (g)   Finance and the small business

4   Capital markets
- (a)   The nature and purpose of stock exchanges
- (b)   Implications of obtaining a stock market listing
- (c)   The efficiency of the stock markets
- (d)   Implications of market efficiency for managers and investors
- (e)   International capital markets
- (f)   Stock market ratios
- (g)   The nature and role of venture capital

5   **Working capital**

   (a)   The nature and importance of working capital management

   (b)   Methods employed to manage inventories, receivables and cash

   (c)   Main elements of trade credit policy (including the main sources of information available to assess creditworthiness of a credit customer)

   (d)   The management of trade payables and bank overdrafts

   (e)   Financial implications of different working capital policies

   (f)   Working capital problems of the small business

6   **Business combinations**

   (a)   Motives for business combinations

   (b)   Assessing the impact of a proposed combination on financial performance and shareholder wealth

   (c)   Advantages and disadvantages of different forms of bid consideration

   (d)   Methods available to resist a proposed takeover

   (e)   Basic techniques for valuing a business including:

       (i)   net asset approach

       (ii)   income flow and cash-flow approaches

       (iii) dividend based approach

       (iv) price-earnings ratio approach

   (f)   Company restructuring including divestment, spin offs, management buy-outs and buy-ins

Excluded topics

The following topics are specifically excluded from the syllabus:

- Calculations to derive discount factors. Candidates will always be supplied with discount tables
- The mathematical derivation of any formulae
- The use of statistical probabilities for measuring the risk of a particular investment or policy

Key areas of the syllabus

The key topics are:

- Investment decision making
- Raising finance
- Capital markets
- Working capital management
- Business combination
- Share valuation

Subject Area 4 – Risk management

Aims

The aims of this syllabus are

- To develop an understanding of the main frameworks and techniques concerning the management of financial risk and operating risk

- To achieve a sound appreciation of the theory and practical aspects of corporate governance

- To develop an understanding of the key issues surrounding the capital structure and dividend policies of businesses

Objectives

On completion of this syllabus, candidates should be able to:

- Explain the nature of risk and the benefits of risk management

- Identify the main processes of risk management

- Explain the importance of aligning risk management processes to the culture and values of a business

- Identify the main forms of both financial and operating risk and describe the techniques that may be used to manage exposure to these types of risk

- Discuss the frameworks of corporate governance regulations and the key issues relating to these frameworks

- Explain the role of the board of directors and discuss the main issues relating to its composition, responsibilities and functioning

- Identify and discuss the main social, environmental, political and ethical issues that businesses must confront

- Explain the effect of dividend policy on shareholder wealth and discuss the factors influencing the dividend policy of a business

- Explain the effect of capital structure on shareholder wealth and calculate the cost of capital of a business

Syllabus content

1 **Managing risk**

(The risk element comprises 50% of the total syllabus)

– the nature of risk
– risk concepts (exposure, volatility, severity, probability etc)
– the benefits of risk management
– the framework for risk management (including the COSO ERP framework)

2 **Risk management processes**

– risk identification and awareness
– risk measurement and assessment
– risk response and control
– risk monitoring and reporting

3 **Risk and corporate characteristics**

– risk appetite and policy
– risk culture and corporate values
– risk management and the implications for organisational structure

4 **Managing financial risk**

– the nature of financial risk

– the main forms of financial risk (foreign exchange risk, interest rate risk, gearing risk, etc)

– the main techniques to manage financial risk (portfolio analysis, scenario analysis, stress testing, futures contracts, options etc)

5 **Managing operational risk**

– the nature of operational risk

– the main forms of operational risk (process risk, people risk, systems risk, event risk, business risk)

– risk management processes (risk policies, risk identification and assessment, risk mitigation and control)

– the nature and scope of corporate governance

– concepts and theories of corporate governance

– models of corporate governance (including international comparisons)

6 **The framework of corporate governance regulations**

(The corporate governance element comprises 30% of the syllabus)

– the role and nature of the regulatory framework
– voluntary codes
– financial reporting requirements
– auditing and statutory requirements
– issues relating to the regulatory framework

7   **The board of directors**

–   the role and composition of the board of directors

–   theories of boards

–   appraising the performance of the board of directors

–   the role of non-executive directors

–   nomination, appointment and remuneration issues

–   the nature and role of board committees

–   issues relating to the role, responsibilities and functioning of the board

8   **Corporate citizenship**

–   the nature of corporate social responsibility
–   social and environmental issues in corporate governance
–   ethical concepts and issues in corporate governance

9   **Dividend policy**

(The financial management element covers 20% of the syllabus)

–   dividend policy and shareholder wealth (MM v traditional school)
–   the importance of dividends in practice
–   factors determining the level of dividends
–   dividend policy and management attitudes
–   alternatives to cash dividends

10   **Cost of capital and capital structure**

–   costs of different elements of capital (inc. a basic understanding of CAPM)
–   weighted average cost of capital and NPV analysis
–   gearing and the evaluation of capital structure decisions
–   factors affecting the level of gearing
–   the capital structure debate

Key areas of the syllabus

•   Risk planning and the processes for managing risks, including financial and operational risk

•   Key factors and characteristics driving an organisation's attitude towards, and propensity for, accepting risk

•   The framework for corporate governance including the role and the nature of regulatory and voluntary codes, including corporate governance processes and constitution

•   The nature of corporate citizenship and corporate social responsibility

•   Dividend policy and the impact of cost of capital and capital structure on corporate value

Analysis of project topics

Note that all projects set before Autumn 2006 were set using UK terminology and in accordance with UK Accounting Standards. This is reflected in this analysis, but it should give you a good idea of the examiners' main areas of interest.

Live projects: Autumn 2006

Module A

This project is in two parts each of which is worth 50 marks. However, both parts of the project are within the scenario of Exfood.

Interpretation of Financial Statements   *Marks*
Part 1

		Marks
(a)	Identification of ratios or other measures to be used to assess the performance of the company and an explanation of why these measures are significant.	11
(b)	Assessment of the performance of the company using another company performance, Compass plc, as a benchmark	26
(c)	Explanation of how purchased goodwill arises, the nature of impairment and how this might make earnings more volatile.	13

Performance Management
Part 2

(a)	Evaluation of the suitability of Compass plc as a benchmark	11
(b)	Explanation of measures of shareholder value	11
(c)	Discussion regarding improvement of supply chain management	9
(d)	Identification and justification of critical success factors	13
(e)	Provision of specific measures for CSFs identified in part (d)	6
		100

The examiner's comments on students' attempts at this project are with the project itself in Chapter 12.

Module B

One compulsory question covering both subject areas based on the scenario of Kes Pharmaceuticals plc and one of its subsidiaries, Burrator plc.

			Marks
(a)	(i)	Calculation of the cost of capital of Burrator plc	10
	(ii)	Calculation of a share value for Burrator plc under two different assumptions	27
	(iii)	Derivation of another share value using an alternative model	8
	(iv)	Assessing the effect on shareholders of the demerger of Burrator plc	11
(b)		Explaining the criteria to be used in the annual appraisal of a non-executive director	16
(c)		Identification and assessment of key risks faced by Burrator plc after the demerger and how these risks should be managed	28
			100

The examiner's comments on students' attempts at this project are with the project itself in Chapter 13.

Live projects: Spring 2006

Module A

The entire project is based upon the financial performance and information provided about Motorsayles plc.

Interpretation of Financial Statements   *Marks*

(a)	(i) Discussion of the information needs of shareholders in a plc rather than a private company	4
	(ii) Discussion of the implications of shareholders' needs in a plc on the company's managers	4
(b)	Assessment of the company performance	34
(c)	Discussion of effect of introducing an employee share ownership trust	8

Performance Management

(d)	Proposing an updated statement of strategic intent and mission statement	8
(e)	Discussion of responsibility centres and proposal of organisation structure	12
(f)	Identification and justification of critical success factors	30
		100

The examiner's comments on students' attempts at this project are with the project itself in Chapter 10.

Module B

The entire project is based upon the scenario of Centaur Communications plc and its two subsidiaries.

     Marks

(a)	Calculation of annual financing costs for two subsidiaries	24
(b)	Comment on assumptions and results of calculations in part (a)	10
(c)	Factors to consider before agreeing to divestment of subsidiary	10
(d)	Evaluation of proposal to buy one of the subsidiaries using IRR	28
(e)	Discussion of information that would be gathered in a due diligence investigation and advantages and disadvantages of either a main market or AIM listing	28
		100

The examiner's comments on students' attempts at this project are with the project itself in Chapter 11.

Live projects: Autumn 2005

Module A

This entire project is based upon the 2004 annual report of Stagecoach Group plc together with a number of key ratios and other measures of performance for the last five years for both Stagecoach Group plc and a key competitor from the same industry group.

Interpretation of Financial Statements   *Marks*

(a)	Discussion of the importance of relating performance management to the organisational mission statement, strategy and objectives	4
(b)	Selection of six ratios from the appendix that can be used to assess group performance from the perspective of a potential investor and explanation of why these are appropriate measures.	12
(c)	Assessment of group performance based on the ratios selected in (b) in the context of the stated strategic objectives.	30
(d)	Limitations of using information available in the published financial statements for assessment of performance	8

Performance Management

(e)   How internal management can improve performance management through the use   10
        of a balanced scorecard

(f)   Possible content of a balanced scorecard for use in the Group   36
                                                                          ───
                                                                          100
                                                                          ═══

The examiner's comments on students' attempts at this project are with the project itself, in Chapter 8.

Module B

One compulsory question covering both subject areas based on the scenario of a cake and confectionery manufacturer and retailer, Plutus, and a potential joint venture into the coffee shop market for the next five years.

                                                                                                Marks

(a)   Preparation of forecast annual cash flow statements for potential investment for   12
        the next five years

(b)   On the assumption that the joint venture is entered into, preparation of forecast   16
        annual cash flow statements for the investor and discussion of any financing
        issues that the investor must confront. Suggestions as to how financing problems
        may be overcome.

(c)   Calculation of the net present value of the investment in the joint venture and   12
        associated sensitivity analysis.

(d)   Discussion of possible benefits and problems of joint venture.   8

(e)   Discussion of possible reasons for suspicions/tensions between non-executive and   15
        executive directors and how these should be managed.

(f)   Benefits and potential problems with use of risk consultants to identify and manage   10
        risk, and criteria for selecting a suitable firm of consultants.

(g)   Identify the key risks associated with the proposed joint venture and how these   20
        should be managed.

(h)   Outline your own views concerning the proposed joint venture and whether you   7
        believe the company should agree to the proposed joint venture.
                                                                                            ───
                                                                                            100
                                                                                            ═══

The examiner's comments on students' attempts at this project are with the project itself, in Chapter 9.

Live projects: Spring 2005

Module A

In line with other recent projects the assignments for both subject areas were based on the same scenario, the 2002/2003 annual report of New Look, which was provided in the supplements to the project.

Interpretation of Financial Statements   *Marks*

1   A briefing paper to be provided for investors contemplating investment in a retail
        group with a similar profile to New Look which covers the following areas:

        (a)   Comparing and contrasting the needs of:
                (i)   institutional investors   3
                (ii)   private shareholders with a long term perspective   3

        (b)   Assessment of the performance of New Look from the perspective of both   32
                institutional investors and private shareholders. A maximum of five ratios/
                measures to be used for each group and the choice of each ratio/measure
                to be justified

        (c)   The limitations of such assessments based on published financial   12
                information

Performance Management

2   A presentation to be prepared, on the basis that the investors have completed their acquisition of the company, with regard to a management reporting package. Appropriate visual aids were required as part of the presentation. The presentation was to cover:

(a)	How shareholder value could be measured and its relevance for investors	8
(b)	Identification and explanation of the significance of a range of non-financial performance measures for monitoring the performance of the company	24
(c)	Explanation of how benchmarking can assist in managing performance and the identification of activities which should be benchmarked.	18
		100

The examiner's comments on students' attempts at this project are with the project itself, in Chapter 6.

Module B

One compulsory question covering both subject areas based upon a single scenario, that of Emmanuel Hire plc, which runs a chain of tool and equipment hire branches throughout England and Wales.

		Marks
(a)	Evaluation of the potential acquisition of a small company in the same line of business	18
(b)	The factors to be considered when deciding between ordinary share capital or loan capital to finance the potential acquisition	7
(c)	Showing how a suggested interest rate swap arrangement would work and suggesting an alternative method of managing interest rate risk. Comparison of this alternative with the swap arrangement	10
(d)	Preparation of a forecast cash flow statement and forecast income statement under each financing option and evaluation of the effect on profitability and gearing under each option	25
(e)	Detailing the main advantages of a risk-based management approach to decision making and the key tasks that are required to implement such a system	20
(f)	Identifying the key operational risks as a result of the acquisition and how these might be managed	20
		100

The examiner's comments on students' attempts at this project are with the project itself, in Chapter 7.

Live projects: Autumn 2004

Module A

This project continued the trend established by the current examiner of basing the assignments on both subject areas on the same set of accounts, those of Ted Baker plc. Candidates were also provided with an article from *The Times* on the retail sector.

Interpretation of Financial Statements		*Marks*
1	Assessment of the performance of the Group, based on the stated strategy of the Chairman and the information in the Annual Report	40
2	Discussion of the extent to which the influences outlined in *The Times* article could be expected to impact on the performance of the Ted Baker Group for the next two years	10

Performance Management		
3	The incorporation of environmental uncertainty into the Ted Baker Group's planning and budgeting systems	15
4	Identification and justification of appropriate Critical Success Factors (CSFs) to monitor in managing the strategic direction of the Group	20
5	Discussion of whether the CSFs identified in Question 4 would remain appropriate in the event of the Group being adversely affected by a slowdown in the retail sector	15
		100

Module B

One compulsory question covering both subject areas on the scenario of Barra Airways, a typical low cost airline, planning expansion.

		Marks
(a)	Preparation of a report for the Board of Directors on proposed expansion plans, including calculation of NPVs and the payback period, calculation of NPV and payback using an alternative approach to predicting the incremental cash flows and sensitivity analysis	18 18 6
(b)	Comment on the results of the calculations in part (a)	6
(c)	Identification of additional information required to make a final decision	8
(d)	Identification and assessment of the risks associated with the proposed plan	16
(e)	A risk map for the proposed expansion plans and suggestion of policies for dealing with the identified risks	18
(f)	Commentary on the role of internal audit in the company in the context of recent changes in corporate governance	10
		100

Part A
Background to the projects

The DipFM Projects

Introduction

This chapter provides the basic information about the DipFM projects: format, deadlines and comments made by the examiners.

It is important that you fully understand the ACCA's requirements for the projects before you start work, especially the absolutely inflexible deadlines for submission.

1 The background

The introduction of a requirement for a project or assignment was a radical departure in the ACCA Diploma in Financial Management qualification. The ACCA appreciates that the students taking the DipFM qualification are usually accomplished in their field, often already working in management roles, and that therefore the traditional examination-based structure may no longer be appropriate and some form of **work assessment** is also required. Although the examination is still regarded as critical, students are now being given the chance to **demonstrate other skills**, such as IT, analysis and problem-solving as part of the route to obtaining the qualification.

The Module A examiner has commented that 'the purpose of the project is to provide candidates with an opportunity to **investigate part of the syllabus in a fair degree of detail'**. Students are able to demonstrate what they have learned outside the formal constraints of a three hour exam. The Module A examiner hopes that as a result 'many candidates will use the opportunity to develop their thinking and submit imaginative arguments and conclusions'.

The DipFM qualification is structured around two modules. The modules are:

Module A	
Subject area 1:	Interpretation of Financial Statements
Subject area 2:	Performance Management
Module B	
Subject area 3:	Financial Strategy
Subject area 4:	Risk Management

Each module is assessed by means of one three hour examination covering both subject areas within the module, and one project, which contains an integrated assignment on the two subject areas. The maximum word count for the entire project is **5,000 words**. This word count includes appendices and tables but excludes references and any bibliography.

However, **you do not necessarily have to restrict yourself to 2,500 words for each subject area**. The balance will depend on the structure of the project. The Module A examiner in particular has stressed the fact that your word count to answer each question in the project should be in proportion to the marks allocated to that question. So for example if the question carries 10 marks, ie 10% of the total, you should use about 500 words (10% of 5,000) to answer it. You should be aware that when drawing up tables of figures, six figures (eg $123,456) count as one word.

1.1 Form of the projects

Unlike the exam, there is no precise structure or form of project. Each project could consist of one very large question or a number of smaller questions. Guidance issued by the ACCA indicates that no project will have more than eight questions in total, with no one question exceeding 50 marks.

1.2 What order shall I do them in?

The ACCA does not specify the order in which you must complete the elements of the qualification. You will not have passed a module until you have passed both the exam and the Project for that module. You will be credited with the pass in whichever element you do first, and you cannot lose that credit.

It is anticipated that most students will do Module A before Module B, but this is not compulsory.

You should consider whether you would prefer to:

- pass the Module A exam and then complete the Module A Project, thus finishing Module A completely, before moving on to Module B; or

- pass both the Module A and Module B exams and then complete the two Projects. This option enables you to take your time over completing the projects, although it means that you will not be able to describe yourself as having passed a Module, and therefore a tangible part of the qualification, until later on.

Another alternative is to take the whole of Module B prior to Module A. This is quite unlikely and you would probably only do this to fit in with timetabling at your college. Although the two Modules are intended to be 'stand alone', some Module B topics do assume a degree of elementary knowledge acquired in Module A, such as basic company accounting and ratio analysis.

1.3 The skills required

Completion of the projects will require skills that are very different from those needed to pass a traditional examination. These will be explored in depth throughout this book, but they can be summarised as the skills of

- Understanding and **analysis**
- Additional **research**
- **Writing reports** and **presenting information**

The work you do to research and complete the project will enable you to practise the financial management skills that you have acquired within your own work, and from your studies of the four subject areas of the DipFM qualification. You will also put these skills to good use should you move on to a further qualification such as an MBA.

2 The administration of the projects

The projects will be operated in cycles by the ACCA, with the process starting each time the results of the traditional DipFM exams are published. Each time exam results are published, the ACCA will send out the forthcoming project details to the relevant candidates, according to this table.

Exam results date	Project submission deadline	Project results
February	31 May	August
August	30 November	February

You will therefore have a period of just over three months to complete the project. Any project title will expire when the next set of titles is issued. If you miss the deadline you will have to start again on the newly-issued project for the next period.

Candidates also have to declare to the ACCA their intention to submit a project by completing the appropriate examination entry form (sent out by the ACCA with the projects) and returning it to the ACCA by the date specified on the form. If you submit a project without having indicated that you intend to submit, it will not be accepted.

You can only submit the current, valid project, ie the one sent to you by the ACCA in either the February or August prior to your submission date of 31 May or 30 November respectively. If you submit an out of date project it will not be marked. If you declare your intent to submit a project and pay the entry fee and then do not submit the project, for whatever reason, you will not be entitled to a refund.

We think that you should plan to submit your project for each module **after** you have taken and passed the relevant exams. This is because the project titles will be based around topics in the syllabuses and study guides, and you will only have acquired the necessary degree of technical knowledge if you have fully studied and understood the syllabus.

You will have about three and a half months in each case to complete and submit the project. In this time you will have to complete the entire assignment for both of the relevant subject areas within the Module. If you miss the closing deadline, the project title will be void, as the next one issued by the ACCA will replace it. The ACCA will not mark out of date projects. You will then have to complete and submit the new project. This will mean that all the work you have done on the initial project will go to waste, and it is therefore essential that you plan your time carefully. Planning and timetabling skills will be covered in Chapter 2.

You do not, however, have to carry out the project in the timespan immediately after the results of the exams are published. **It is up to you when you submit**, and you may want to leave an interval after completion of the exams, before you start work on the projects. The time constraint only relates to the period within which a project title remains valid, from its issue, for example in February, to its final deadline on 31 May.

2.1 The pass mark

The pass mark for each of the two projects is 50%. In the Pilot Projects and most of the 'live' projects issued so far, 50 marks are available for each subject area, giving a total of 100. However, in the spring 2004 project for Module A there was only one question of five parts, ranging from 6 to 40 marks, testing both subject areas. The same approach was taken by the Module B examiner.

You must achieve 50% for the project as a whole: it is possible (but not desirable!) for you to achieve less than 50% (or half marks) in one part of the project, but to compensate for that by achieving more than 50% in the other part. You would still pass, as long as the total is 50 or more. You must also achieve 50% in total for each module to pass, ie 50% in the project and 50% in the exam.

2.2 Example

In the Module A project you score the following marks on the questions relating to each subject area:

Subject area 1 (Interpretation of Financial Statements)	24 out of 50
Subject area 2 (Performance Management)	27 out of 50
Total	51 out of 100

The average for the whole project would be 51% and you would pass, even though you have scored less than half marks on subject area 1.

2.3 Example

In the Module B project you score the following marks on the questions relating to each subject area:

Subject area 3 (Financial Strategy)	16 out of 50
Subject area 4 (Risk Management)	33 out of 50
	49 out of 100

In this example you would fail, despite the fact that you have scored highly in Risk Management, as the overall mark falls below 50%.

It is important therefore that you concentrate equally on both subject areas within the project. Even if you produce a brilliant response to the questions on one subject area, it will not be classified as a pass if your performance in the other subject area drags you down to less than 50% overall.

2.4 Presentation

Your project must be

- Typed in black ink on A4 paper
- One-sided
- Double-spaced
- In a minimum 12 point font size (although you can choose which font to use)
- With one inch margins on each side.

Handwritten projects will not be accepted by the ACCA.

The ACCA is hoping that in the future electronic submission may be possible (which may be particularly helpful for overseas students) but at the moment **projects must not be submitted electronically**.

You must complete a **Project Submission Form** for each project, and attach it to the front. These forms are distributed by the ACCA with the titles, so please contact the ACCA if you don't have one.

2.5 Word count

The maximum word count for each project is 5,000 words. This figure includes appendices and tables, but excludes references and the bibliography. Some past projects have included a requirement for you to produce slides or a PowerPoint presentation, and the word count for these should be included in your overall word count. When you are preparing tables of figures, the ACCA have stipulated that six figures should be counted as one word, eg $541,203 would constitute one word.

As well as indicating the entire word count on the front page of your project, you should also show the word count for each particular question clearly at the end of that question.

If you exceed the total of 5,000 words, the ACCA will send you an email telling you that the marker will mark your project up to the 5,000 word point but will then ignore the remainder. You should obviously try to avoid this, as if the marker stops marking right at the beginning of a critical appendix showing your key calculations, it may detract significantly from the rest of your project.

3 Interaction with the exams

The examiner for each module also sets and oversees the marking of the projects. The projects are subjected to the same scrutiny prior to their issue as the exams themselves, in that they are thoroughly checked and moderated by the examiner and the moderator for the subject area.

The content of the questions will fall within the scope of the syllabus and study guide. It is possible that the questions will examine issues which are more on the fringe of the syllabus, or more topical, as candidates will have time to research and think through the subject matter. The ACCA have said that extensive research will not be required, although you may find that you need to do some background reading. However, in his comments on the Spring 2005 Module A project, the examiner remarked that 'a number of candidates produced observations and analysis which demonstrated that they had read (and more importantly, understood) material from relevant publications beyond the basic texts.' So if you have the opportunity to read around the subject, it would be sensible to demonstrate that you have done so.

The examiners have said that they may use the projects to re-examine topics that have been handled badly by students in the exams. You should read *Finance Matters* (previously named the *Diploma Newsletter*) for articles by the examiners and for their formal comments published after each set of exams and projects. This is available on the ACCA website. This will highlight areas of particular concern for the examiners, and may provide you with some ideas as to a starting point if they do adopt this policy. Some of these sets of feedback are extremely detailed, and very helpful to students.

It is possible, on the other hand, that the examiners could use the assignments to dovetail with the formal exams, so that in one examination cycle they have greater scope for examining more of the syllabus. The fact that they have the ability to cover large-scale and broader issues within the context of the assignment could mean that they take the opportunity to cover more specific or complex issues in the formal exams.

When the DipFM qualification was launched, the pilot projects and the first projects set under the scheme kept the two relevant subject areas completely separate. However since Spring 2003 the Module A project has been basing questions on both subject areas on a common scenario, always supplying a detailed set of accounts, and since Spring 2004 the Module B project has followed suit.

In some cases, although there is a common scenario the questions set have been under the two separate headings within the Module. However it now seems increasingly to be the case that there is one large question on the scenario consisting of several component parts. No clear delineation is made between the subject areas and there is considerable overlap of subject areas. This has been the case with both Module A and Module B. The examiners therefore seem to be attaining what was stated as their ideal at the outset, ie a truly integrated project examining the entire Module. This pattern seems set to continue.

3.1 The need for research

The examiners have said that students will gain credit for carrying out **research** into the topics within the assignments, but it should not be regarded as compulsory. Certainly there is no need for extensive research. The most useful type of research will probably be background reading around a subject area, for example reading around the company whose accounts are used in the Module A question. Similarly, the assignments will not generally be related to the student's workplace, as this could discriminate against students who are not currently in employment.

4 Differences from exams

In order to approach the projects successfully, you have to cultivate a different mindset from that you have used for the exams. Think about the requirements of the assignments in the two Projects you have to complete, and the skills you will have to demonstrate. They are very different from traditional exams, which are focused on satisfying the examiner in a three hour exam.

Exercise   **Key differences**

Write down the key differences between a project assignment and a DipFM exam.

Answer

DipFM exams	Project assignment
Questions are precisely defined.	The topics chosen may be broader.
You only have three hours.	You can take as long as you like (within the three month timescale).
Pen and paper.	You have to demonstrate familiarity with IT, such as use of word processing, spreadsheets etc: your assignment must be word processed.
You are working to a syllabus.	Topics will arise from the syllabus, but possibly the fringes of it.
Exam technique (timing; allocation of time to questions) is vital.	Report writing technique is the key.

DipFM exams	Project assignment
For many of the questions, the data is given. All you have to do is read a question and answer it.	You will have to draw conclusions from reviewing the data, but this depends on: • Identifying the right data in scope and depth • Asking the right questions of the data Your conclusion may not support what you set out to prove.
Exams are taken under exam conditions: no notes or books may be used in the exam room.	You are encouraged to use research resources, textbooks and your own notes in formulating your answer.
Exam questions, especially in numerical topics, tend to have a 'right' answer.	Project questions may not necessarily have a 'right' answer or even a 'right' approach. Different students may interpret the material in different ways, and not necessarily be wrong. The examiners are looking for the ability to investigate, and the use of imagination.

5 What the examiners say

The examiners for each of the subject areas have given a few initial indications as to their likely approach to the assignments. It is highly likely, however, that the structure and content of the assignments will evolve over time. It is essential that you read *Finance Matters* carefully for articles by the examiners, which may give further information as to their proposed approach. There is a detailed article on the approach by the Module A examiner in issue 56 of *Finance Matters*.

5.1 Module A

The examiner for Module A has made a number of points on his perception of the project and the role of the assignment within it. The main point to notice is the increasingly **integrated nature of the projects**. The examiner has made it clear that the two subject areas in the project are now definitely to be based on the same scenario.

When the current examiner for Module A took over, with effect from the June 2003 exam, he wrote an article outlining his approach. Previously there were separate examiners for the two subject areas, both adopting a different approach.

5.1.1 Key points

(a) The examiner commented that any assessment of performance, whether in the context of interpretation of financial statements or performance management, should '**take account of the context**, ie the general business environment, the **specific industry** and the **organisation's strategy and objectives**'. It is essential that you appreciate this point right from the outset when you are tackling the project. Time and time again the Module A examiner has said in his feedback on each project that **the candidates who fail are those who just make general comments and do not relate their answers to the precise scenario in the question**. If you make comments in your answer that could apply in more or less any situation, they will not earn many marks. You must always keep the precise context of the project in mind and relate your answer to it as much as possible.

(b)   The examiner takes the view that the strategy and objectives of an organisation are important as a basis for managing performance.

'Few organisations make a public disclosure of internal data – most published financial statements provide a statement of strategy and objectives. It therefore seems logical to consider how managers may seek to manage performance to achieve these objectives. The internal planning and reporting systems will be developed to ensure that performance is measured to assist in achieving the stated objectives, or to assess what action ought to be taken to improve performance. Based on this premise, the assignment for Subject Area 2 is likely to require candidates to consider the implications of the organisation's strategy and objectives for internal processes.

The basic approach to the project as a whole will be for Subject Area 1 to consider how performance can be assessed from the perspective of an external user of financial statements, while Subject Area 2 will consider the implications for an internal manager.'

5.1.2 Standard of analysis

A high standard of analysis is required, probably higher than that you are expected to demonstrate in the formal exams. For example in an assignment requiring ratio analysis, you would be expected to pick out and use the trade receivables figure in certain computations, rather than just using the figure for total receivables. This may mean that you have to calculate trade receivables by deducting other forms of receivable, such as prepayments and loans due from the total, to derive trade receivables. Even then, the calculation of the ratio may not earn you any marks; you have to discuss what it tells you.

Exercise	Cruikshank

The assignment mentions that the total payables of Cruikshank Ltd are £854,209. Elsewhere in the information supplied you learn that accruals total £51,703, debenture interest payable is £10,000 and there is an outstanding PAYE liability of £17,757.

As part of the assignment, you want to calculate and comment on the trade payables payment period. You therefore have to calculate trade payables.

Answer

	£	£
Total payables		854,209
Less: accruals	51,703	
debenture interest	10,000	
PAYE	17,757	
		79,460
Trade payables		774,749

You would be expected to use the figure for trade payables only.

The examiner for Module A said in the feedback for the Spring 2003 project that candidates who failed often did so due to inadequate analysis.

5.1.3 Use of a supplement

The use of a supplement in the Module A project is now well-established, and there has been one in every project set to date. Generally the supplement consists of most, if not all, of the annual report of a UK listed company. Examples to date have included:

- Dorling Kindersley, the publisher

- T J Hughes plc, which operates a chain of specialist discount stores

- Britax plc, an international company producing specialised aircraft interiors and vehicle and safety systems

- Thorntons plc, the chocolate manufacturer and retailer

- EasyJet plc, the low-cost airline

- BOC Group

- Ted Baker Group plc, a clothing company

- New Look, a high street retailer

This enables the examiner to set a 'real life' scenario, which means that students can demonstrate their skills in a truly practical situation.

With effect from the projects issued in August 2006, the DipFM exams and projects are now expressed using international terminology and accounting standards. At the time of writing it is not clear whether the Module A examiner may use foreign company accounts in the supplement or UK accounts produced using IFRSs. You should keep an eye on *Finance Matters* for any articles by him that may clarify this.

The examiner has specifically stated that **students are not to contact any company which is used as the subject for a project**. The project will be assessed only on the basis of your use of information in the supplement. The examiner has said 'Candidates are expressly requested not to seek clarification, explanation or additional information in respect of the subject company', although it may be sensible for you to do some background reading on the company concerned.

Questions in the project will also identify areas within the financial statements which are to be used as the basis for a critical discussion of specific accounting issues. Such a discussion will probably go beyond the confines of the information contained in the supplement. For parts of the project, therefore, the supplement should be regarded as a starting point, and you should be able to demonstrate your wider knowledge of the issues involved.

5.2 Module B

5.2.1 Subject Area 3: Financial Strategy

The examiner plans to adopt as far as possible a 'case study' approach to the project for subject areas 3 and 4. The project itself could be as much as 6 or 7 pages long, although the Pilot is only three pages long. Some of the live projects set to date have been 5 or 6 pages long. It could have these features:

- Open-ended (ie more than one way of tackling the project, and not necessarily any one 'correct' answer)

- A need for evaluation of data

- A requirement for some calculations, usually in conjunction with discussions

The examiner has said that marks will be awarded for the quality of both the analysis and reasoning demonstrated in arriving at a solution or conclusion.

The assignment included in the Pilot Project reflects the 'real world' in that there is insufficient information available in order to conduct a more thorough analysis. This lack of information may mean that any conclusions you reach have to be tentative, and you may have to make various assumptions to reach a conclusion. This is perfectly acceptable, but it would be sensible always to state your assumptions.

The examiner offers the following advice to candidates in an article on his approach that can be found on the ACCA's website

- 'Where your answer involves calculations being carried out, any formulae used or key assumptions should be included as part of your answer. The markers must be able to trace the main steps you have taken towards a solution.

- Where recommendations are being made, they should be linked clearly to your analysis of the problem. You should avoid producing recommendations at the end of a project that cannot be supported by earlier analysis and discussion.

- Ensure that your answer to the project is logically structured: it should have a beginning, a middle and an end.

Although these rules may seem fairly obvious, they are often forgotten.'

The Financial Strategy examiner often contributes articles to *Finance Matters* and you may find it useful to refer back to these when you are thinking about the project, as they may shed further light on the examiner's views and interests. For example, in issue 50 the examiner wrote an article on working capital and financing in the context of the small business. In issue 52 he contributed an article entitled 'What every financial manager needs to know about market efficiency'.

5.2.2 Subject Area 4: Risk Management

In the project questions devoted to subject area 4, students will be expected to demonstrate an understanding of the financial risk management techniques that they have learned about in their studies for the exam. The examiner for Module B deals with both subject areas and has now started to link the projects together in the way that the Module A examiner has. Both projects set in 2004 used the same scenario for both subject areas, and the questions are becoming increasingly integrated. This trend continued in 2005 and 2006.

The examiner has said that the assignment will include a mix of theoretical and practical issues, and will highlight issues facing both large and small organisations.

Marks will be allocated where students have demonstrated an understanding of the main areas of responsibility for risk management from all angles, as well as an understanding of the implications and limitations of the application of the codes and guidelines specified within the syllabus. This indicates that in subject area 4, further independent research could be beneficial.

The Module B examiner frequently contributes very useful articles to *Finance Matters* on both Financial Strategy and Risk Management. In issue 56, for example, he contributed an article on the role of non executive directors.

In July 2005 he contributed articles on valuing company shares and the revisions that were made to the Risk Management syllabus. In October 2005 he contributed an article on the risk associated with venture capital, and then in February 2006 (issue 66) an article on the corporate governance issues affecting many companies.

6 Characteristics of the assignments

Doing the projects will be a very different experience from studying for DipFM exams. Hopefully, you will find it an interesting – if challenging – experience, one which will equip you with forensic skills in the world of work and which will broaden your horizons.

To some degree it will involve original work, not based on learning from Study Texts (no matter how good they are), nor is it based on rigorous and repeated question practice from Practice & Revision Kits (no matter how good they are). The foundation and basic technical knowledge, however, will be provided by the syllabus for each subject area.

Moreover, you will have to drive yourself. If you are used to a taught course, you may miss the structure of course exams, mocks and so forth – although you do have the May or November deadline to adhere to. It is **your** project, it is open-ended and, to an extent, you can follow your interests within the parameter of the topics covered within the assignment.

7 Marking the assignments

The ACCA has issued some guidance as to how the projects are marked. Skills in six key areas are assessed:

7.1 Presentation

Projects should be **organised logically and expressed clearly**. Spelling, grammar and punctuation should all be accurate. The Module A examiner has commented on the number of spelling mistakes that he sometimes sees.

7.2 Knowledge

Candidates should demonstrate a comprehensive **knowledge** of the areas being tested.

7.3 Numerical analysis

The study of Annual Reports or financial appraisals will inevitably require numerical analysis. If required to perform ratio analysis, for example, candidates should state clearly the ratios they are using, with the relevant formulae. The main emphasis in most cases, however, will be on candidates' ability to **interpret and analyse results**, rather than on their ability to perform a large number of calculations.

However, at least one question in each project usually requires some form of arithmetic calculations, and some, for example, on Financial Strategy, require a great deal of computation. Although, as mentioned above, emphasis will often be placed on the ability to **interpret and analyse** results, candidates should show competence in calculations, avoiding errors due to inaccurate rounding or mis-specification of equations (for example, putting brackets in the wrong place)'. (**BPP note:** You are not doing these calculations in the rush of the exam room, so there is no excuse for careless mistakes.)

'Marks will not be awarded for careless arithmetic or inappropriate analysis and interpretation. However, marks will be given for feasible assumptions and explanations. Candidates should take care not to simply include numbers without allowing the marker to see where the numbers came from. Candidates should avoid leaving numbers with an unnecessary number of decimal places.

7.4 Critical evaluation

Candidates should be able to analyse situations using appropriate techniques, models and frameworks. Candidates should demonstrate the ability to take raw data and synthesise these to support the decisions and recommendations within the project.

7.5 Real-life examples

Where appropriate, credit will be given to candidates who cite real-life examples which are relevant to the areas being tested. This may reflect the candidate's own experiences or be found in the financial press, relevant publications and websites.

7.6 Conclusions

Conclusions should follow logically the evidence contained in the main body of the question. They should be stated clearly and concisely.

The marks attached to each of these areas will vary for each project.'

(Source: Tackling DipFM Projects, Finance Matters, Issue 53)

8 What you need to do

For the project assignments the **technical knowledge** you need is covered in the rigours of your DipFM exams. Let us examine the skills that the project assignments are designed specifically to deal with.

8.1 Critical examination of arguments and evidence

Consider the following scenario.

Exercise	Key factors

Let us say you are doing an assignment involving the identification of key factors or indicators in the motivation of employees in an organisation. As part of your research, you want to assess the relationship between reward schemes and motivation.

Four months ago, the sales manager at Saramago replaced a salary based scheme for 30 sales staff with a commission only scheme. He says: 'The new scheme has been a big success for the company and staff: they seem a lot happier. I mean, Bill came to see me last week and said he was really looking forward to his bonus, after all the work he'd put in. Money talks doesn't it?'.

How would you **critically examine** the arguments and evidence in this statement?

Answer

By **critical**, this does not mean saying to the sales manager 'That's rubbish, you're no good'. It means that, tactfully, you hold up the statement for review; you do not take it at face value. By **examine** it means that you have to inspect the data, tease out its meaning, test it and so on.

(a)   What does the sales manager mean by **'big success' for the company**? This is his argument. He has not presented you with any **evidence**.

(i)   More **sales revenue** for the company? Is this quantified or measured? Are there sales reports? You'd need to see some figures.

(ii)   Has this been accompanied by problems of credit control and bad debts?

(iii)   Has the increase in revenue over the past four months **really** been affected by the bonus scheme?

- What about seasonal factors? Compared to a similar period last year, is the increase really so wonderful?

- Was revenue significantly up **before** the scheme was introduced?

- Has volume of sales increased or just prices?

(b)   **'Big success'** for staff? Are they earning more? In fact, is the company paying more than is really warranted by the increase? Are they happier?

(c)   His **argument** 'money talks' is that people are motivated mainly by money. Quite possibly, this is true in this case, but you need to put this in a context. His staff may be motivated by other factors, as suggested by a whole host of motivation theories.

(d)   His **evidence** about staff feelings is impressionistic: nothing wrong with that as such, but given he only mentions one person – Bill – this seems anecdotal. (Furthermore, Bill could have been complaining.)

(e)   The sales manager has every reason to praise a system he introduced himself.

If the sales manager were to unveil a detailed report with all the variances explained, proof that bad debts were not increasing and so on, you would see this in a different light.

8.2 Structured/unstructured problems

You may have already learnt about structured and unstructured problems earlier in your DipFM and other studies, but here is a recap.

(a)   A **structured problem** is one in which there is a defined number of elements, and it is possible to go about solving the problem in a systematic way. Exam questions tend to focus on structured problems, and there is normally the opportunity to provide an 'answer'. Some elements of a project assignment may present you with a structured problem, although not necessarily all.

(b)   An **unstructured problem**, on the other hand, is less easy to analyse as it appears to lack any obvious logic, underlying procedures or rules for solving it.

A project assignment may set you an unstructured problem, whereby you discuss an issue without necessarily finding an answer.

An example of a relatively **structured** problem might be as follows.

8.3 Example

A sole trader decides to incorporate his/her business as a limited company and asks your advice as to whether this is a good idea and how to go about it.

(a)   Is it a good idea? It is relatively easy to model the effect of the change on:

- The legal position of the business
- The tax position

and so on, as there are defined rules as to how companies work.

(b)   How to go about it? Incorporating a company is a relatively routine procedure and the legal steps are easy to identify.

An example of a relatively unstructured problem is one for which there are no simple steps to reach a result: it cannot simply be deconstructed into its components, if people disagree fundamentally as to the nature of the problem.

8.4 Example

Many organisations draw up a **mission statement**. This aims to describe what the organisation is 'for' and its aspirations. The mission statement is used as a communication tool to employees, shareholders and customers and so on.

Drawing up a mission statement is an 'unstructured' problem because:

(a)   There are no clear rules as to what a mission statement should be.

(b)   Many 'stakeholders' have completely different perspectives on what organisations are for. These perspectives are not always easy to incorporate in one over-arching mission.

8.5 Ability to locate, extract and analyse data from various sources

8.5.1 Locate data

You have decided that you need to carry out further research on the topic included in an assignment, which is perhaps on the very fringe of the syllabus. Where should you look to find what you want? Obviously, this depends on the type of data that you need to find.

8.6 Example

Let's say, for example, that you are carrying out an assignment which requires an analysis of the effects of the introduction of an International Accounting Standard on the financial statements of a listed company. Where would you find data?

(a)   Some of the data may be necessary **theoretical background**. You would need to find out where the standards are. You could for example, obtain them from a library or from the International Financial Accounting Standards Board. (You would also find DipFM-relevant explanations in the appropriate BPP Learning Media Study Text.)

(b)   Some of the data may be specific to the entity under review. Some firms have shares listed on two stock exchanges (eg London and New York) and the reported financial performance may vary (eg according to US and UK GAAP). The Financial Director may have a particular view as to the value of IASs in this context (not least on the work involved in preparing two sets of accounts).

(c)   Some data could be provided by a review of relevant professional journals, such as *Finance Matters* – accounting standards are the subject of some debate, and even hit the business pages of some of the major newspapers on occasion. You could certainly expect to find information in the *Financial Times* or *The Economist* both of which have very good websites.

Exercise   Extracting data

Jot down as many ways you can think of to **'extract'** data in relation to the items (a) to (c) in the example above.

Answer

Just to give you an idea:

(a)   Taking notes (eg from a Study Text covering accounting standards)

(b)   Discussing the matter at an interview with the Finance Director of your company in which he/she describes his/her opinions in full and details in broad terms, the costs involved of preparing two sets of accounts.

(c)   Inputting data on to a spreadsheet for further analysis

(d)   Articles can be obtained by library visits or visits to relevant websites where a 'search' facility might enable you to review and print out certain articles

8.6.1 Analyse data

Here is an example of what we mean.

- Make sense of the data
- Apply theoretical concepts to it
- Compare it with other data for consistency

Exercise   Data analysis

You have a set of published financial accounts of a company for the past three financial years and copies of relevant International Accounting Standards. What initially could you do to analyse the data?

Answer

The most obvious tool would be ratio analysis which should be familiar from your DipFM subject area 1 Studies. From such data, you can easily calculate receivable, payable, and inventory turnover, the total cash cycle and related trends, the proportion of working capital to total net assets, gearing and so on. You could then get an idea of the total performance of the company.

Of course the **significance** of your calculations will depend on other matters gleaned from other areas of your research. If, for example, different potential treatments for non-current assets could apply, you would want to conduct your analysis with a purpose.

(a)   Effect on reported profits and earnings per share.

(b)   Your research must reveal industry peculiarities that lead to some treatments of non-current assets being preferred over others.

8.7 Analyse and draw reasoned conclusions from

Effectively, this means that you have, as suggested earlier, to review your data, analyse it and come to a judgement about what the data may actually mean. A simple example may be correlation. But many examples are not so simple.

You are shown a graph showing sales of product X in the summer and autumn of 2004.

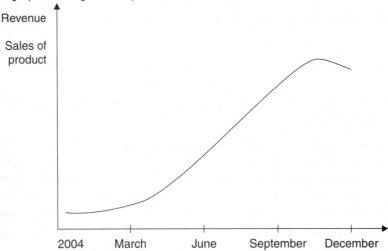

More of product X is sold in the autumn and winter of 2004 than in the summer. Without, for the time being, knowing what product X is you might **assume** that product X is sold when the temperature gets colder.

(a)   If product X is coats, then you can draw a reasoned analysis that high sales volumes relate to cold weather.

(b)   If product X is however, a Harry Potter figure, (a children's toy) then their release may not relate to the hot weather, more to the fact that there is huge demand for these anyway, and some **new** toys were issued in the autumn, to coincide with the related film and Christmas.

Other examples in a business context, are these.

(a)   If a company invests in new technology, and if labour productivity increases soon afterwards, you could reasonably conclude (all other things being equal), that the new technology enabled the workforce to become more productive.

(b)   One company's managers may invest in a high-risk project which offers a high reward if successful. In another company, managers are more cautious. A reasoned conclusion is that managers' attitude to risk depends on various different factors.

8.8 Capacity for independent and self-managed learning

Independent and self-managed: this effectively means that you have to have the necessary skills to complete the project by yourself; in other words, you have the resources you need to learn without being spoon-fed by a tutor, and that you have to plan and manage your learning.

If you are one of the many students who have no tutorial support, you will by now have had plenty of experience in this. We will cover some scheduling techniques shortly.

You should be able to show that:

- You can identify what you need to learn
- You can plan your learning time
- You will identify techniques to help you learn

8.9 Numeracy skills, including the ability to manipulate financial and other numerical data

The Projects are not designed to test these skills as such: the work you have done sitting the DipFM exams so far is evidence that you have these skills in abundance. However, the Project is an opportunity to demonstrate that you can apply these skills or use them.

Look at the business situation below

Exercise	Sources of capital

You are doing an assignment involving an **analysis of different sources of capital on investment decisions**. The company is Iolinda, and you have a lot of data to use.

Iolinda is a biotechnology company about to be listed on a stock market. It has used genetic manipulation (GM) technology to generate a species of rose that is impervious to aphids. The company is very confident that the new rose will be a huge market success, but needs to conduct trials in plant nurseries. Of course, these trials may fail or have unintended consequences: there is a risk that the trials may fail and/or that environmentalists will disrupt them. Iolinda does have some other valuable patents, in GM technology for farmers, but this is the first time it will market directly to a consumer products industry (not food). Consumers and the gardening public will be propagating GM plants.

The venture capital firms that have financed Iolinda want to recover their investment by selling shares. Other biotechnology companies have no difficulties in raising equity. However, the share prices of biotechnology firms have been quite volatile in relation to the market as a whole, with some spectacular successes and failures. Iolinda intends to float whether or not the rose project fails or succeeds.

Required

What **numerical analysis** could you do on data items (1) to (6) below?

(1)   Historic data on likely success/failure of trials of GM products (ie failure rate pre launch)

(2)   Cash flows required for the trials pre-launch

(3)   Proposed pricing strategy (eg penetration or skimming strategies) and sales forecast; distribution and marketing costs assuming launch is successful; comparative volumes in relation to other products

(4)   Projected earnings per share for the company as a whole, or similar information from the prospectus

(5)   Interest rates

(6)   Market values, dividend levels and yields, and betas of similar companies

Answer

Here are some ideas.

The **historic success rate** for GM product trials can be used to develop **probabilities** of the success of the trials, and so you can then calculate **expected values** of the future cash flows. These might give an idea of **risk**. However, you may also need to consider the risk that the **political climate** opposed to GM products may significantly reduce the sales revenue. All this will be relevant to **investment appraisal**.

If significant cash flows are involved, you may be required to prepare **cash budgets** and to monitor **working capital.**

The proposed pricing strategy will give an idea of what cash flows might be expected and hence you could estimate the significance of the rose trial in the **overall product portfolio**.

With suitable information you might analyse the **risk** of the project, and use the **beta**, if it meets the relevant tests.

8.10 Communication skills

Communications skills are covered later in this Study Text. The projects test your skills in report writing.

You may have to present analysis, argument and commentary.

    (a)   **Analysis**: in the answer, you need to be able to explain the analytical work you have done on the data supplied in the assignment, and to describe your method. In fact, thinking how you would explain and justify your analytical work to an audience (eg friends) is a good way of testing whether you have done enough work.

    (b)   **Argument**: stating a case, and justifying it with reasoned argument, often derived from additional research you have carried out.

    (c)   **Commentary**: a commentary could include adding detail, adding context and so on.

 Exercise   **Analysis and argument**

The data below is taken from an unpublished undergraduate dissertation project.

Required

Each sentence is numbered. The ten sentences below contain a mix of **analysis**, **argument** and **commentary**.

Pick **one** example of each type of sentence.

(1) Sales people rarely consider a car as a perk; instead it is a pre-requisite for accepting a job. (2) However, the potential for a company car to motivate a sales force can be considerable if structured thoughtfully and is most powerful in satisfying higher social needs. (3) Within X plc cars are given to all sales staff and better models are allocated according to the progress a salesman makes. (4) Some managers felt that a set of standards should be disclosed so that sales people know on what basis cars are allocated. (5) Survey results revealed that a car signifies financial status and social standing. (Packard, 1980). (6) Therefore, company cars have a significant motivational capacity, as well as being a cause of contention or jealousy especially taking Equity theory into account. (7) Hence this perk must be controlled with integrity and firmness. (8) A survey showed that for some sales people in London a car is of little practical usefulness in the selling task, as the London Underground is more practicable. (9) At present all X plc's sales staff are still issued with a car. (10) With reference to the Cafeteria (or Pick and Mix) reward system mentioned earlier, it may be more satisfactory for sales people to have a choice of a higher salary, a car or some other benefit.

Answer

(a) **Argument** Sentence (2): says why a car can motivate a sales force. Sentences (6) and (7): sentence (6) is based on facts described earlier.

(b) **Commentary** Sentences (3) and (4): descriptive about X plc

(c) **Analysis** There is little analysis in the extract given but it does confirm some of the data. Sentence (5) applies theory to reported results of a survey.

Chapter Roundup

- This chapter has set out the requirements for the completion of the DipFM projects.

- You can spend as much time as you like on the projects, subject to the ACCA's timetable for issue and submission.

- The project will cover both the subject areas within the Module and questions on both will be based on the same set of data.

- You do not need to submit both Module A and Module B projects at the same time, although you can if you wish to do so.

- You may need to carry out further research into the topics included in the project.

- The projects will test skills that cannot be tested by traditional exam methods.

Getting started

2

Introduction

This chapter concentrates on aspects of planning for the projects. Planning is an essential part of any large-scale activity like completing a DipFM project, and successful planning will make the whole procedure much easier.

The chapter suggests a number of techniques for project planning, some of which you may already have encountered in the work environment. It also stresses the importance of adequate timetabling.

1 Project management skills and the assignments

1.1 The DipFM Projects

Any project - whether it is developing a new software package, or constructing a new building – is, in many ways, a unique, one-off task. But all **projects** have:

- A defined start. By choosing to do the project, you have started already.

- A defined project objective. This is given to you in each assignment.

- A number of activities that need to be co-ordinated – some of them depend on earlier activities, some may depend on other people.

- A budget (of money, hours, or whatever).

- A defined endpoint – in this case the submission of your answers to the project to the ACCA.

In commercial projects, a project is successful if it is completed to the client's objectives, is on time and within budget. Even with commercial projects, this is often easier said than done. A construction project might be delayed by unexpected problems, financing problems or just poor project management.

A research project, whether it be a PhD, an undergraduate dissertation, or the Project modules of the DipFM, is a special kind of project.

(a)   **Issues of breadth** – you may find that the field is much broader than you thought, and you need to set up some clear boundaries (see below).

(b)   **Issues of depth**. You may find that you need to go into more detail, if matters are not clear (see below).

The Project is not an exam.

We've made this point already in the previous chapter. But this difference is just as crucial for **how** you **plan** and **manage** your work.

1.2 Deadlines and time pressure – how it differs

Here are some key contrasts about deadlines.

A DipFM exam	Project assignment
- Takes three hours, typically - You have to plan your time carefully in the exam room	You can take as little or as long as you like to do your research, and write the assignment
- Sat on one particular day - You have to plan your time carefully in the run up to this date: learning, practice and revision	You can submit it whenever you like – up to the deadline. You will have a period of up to three and a half months.
- Cannot be put off; if you miss one day, you have to resit.	You can put the work (but not the deadline) off; the time it takes is up to you.
- Exam and studying are done outside the work environment	Depending on the assignment and the views of your employer, some of the work **might** be done at work.

You ought to conclude from this that **your deadlines on the project are for you to manage**. You have to set them, especially when they involve others. You have to police them. This is - in part - what is meant by independent and self managed learning.

1.3 Realistically, how much time am I likely to need?

The answer to this question can – if you are not careful – be another question: 'How long is a piece of string?' But this is not good enough, is it? One important way of approaching this issue is by **analysing the work** involved and developing a realistic schedule based around it. There are a number of ways of doing this.

- Analysing the tasks
- Estimating the time you will need
- Developing schedules

The Module A examiner commented in his feedback on the Spring 2003 project that 'many of the projects which did not meet the pass standard conveyed the impression that they had been completed in a short space of time'. If you do not allow adequate time for the project, you will probably not plan it properly, and may therefore miss some critical aspect. The examiner went on to say, 'There is little doubt that the best submissions came from candidates who had developed their final version over a period of time'. Doing this enables you to reflect on the issues involved and come to a reasoned conclusion.

This is not to say that you must devote every waking hour to the projects for weeks on end. What it does mean, however, is that you should allow yourself sufficient time to absorb all of the material and let ideas percolate through your mind.

1.4 Two subject areas to every project

Remember that each project (which will cover either Module A or Module B) will contain material relating to both subject areas. Initially, they were to be regarded as completely separate and stand-alone, but the Module A examiner moved towards setting both assignments in the Project on the same set of real company accounts and now both examiners have established a pattern of setting assignments, albeit of several parts, which cover both subject areas simultaneously.

You must decide which questions to do first. You can either do them in sequential order, or, if you feel more confident about one of them, or one looks more straightforward, do that one first. This will boost your confidence, rather like doing your best question first in an exam, and make you feel that you have got a significant part of the project under your belt. However, it may well be the case that each question leads sequentially to the next, so it may not be possible to treat them in isolation.

2 Analysing the tasks

Having decided which part of the assignment to do first, **identify each task you have to do** and note it down.

For example, if you are cooking a meal, there are a number of different tasks, such as 'prepare vegetables' and 'make sauce'. Each of these tasks can be further subdivided. 'Prepare vegetables' can be subdivided into 'Prepare tomatoes', 'Prepare onions' and so on. 'Prepare onions' can be subdivided into 'Peel onions' and 'Chop onions'. Finally, you will reach a point where you cannot subdivide the work any further. There is little point in going any further. This technique is called **Work Breakdown Structure**.

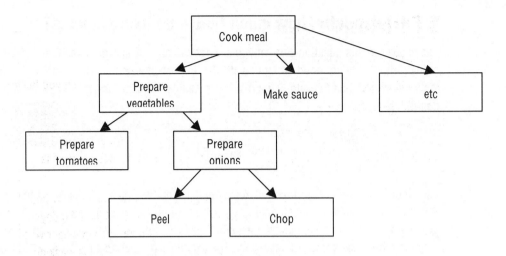

Such a Work Breakdown Structure could be created for the ACCA's Pilot Project for Module A which includes subject area 1, Interpretation of Financial Statements and subject area 2, Performance Management.

2.1 Example

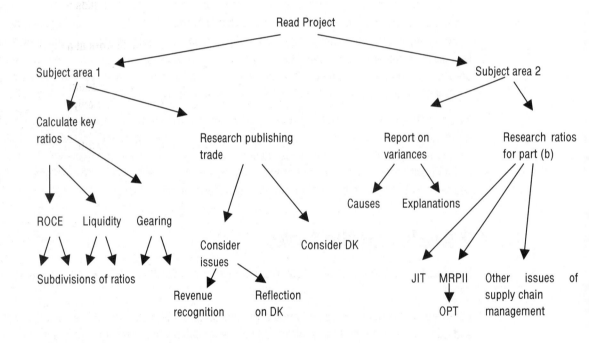

3 Estimating time

How good are you at estimating your use of time?

We suggest there are four types of estimators. How do you find out which you fall into?

Type	Key vice and its cause	How do you know it's you?
1 Over-promiser	Vice: promises things can be delivered sooner than is possible Cause? Unwillingness to sit down and plan hour by hour – 'a month' seems a long time ahead; 20 working days is, in fact, a lot less. Too willing to please a manager who may only be asking for information. Doesn't like asking people to wait for a response. Consequence – unnecessary stress, especially if other people rely on you; reputation for unreliability Cure? Keep records of how long tasks have taken you in the past (eg reading an article) and use these to plan your projects. Give yourself time to plan.	Your manager routinely makes allowances for the fact that you miss deadlines. You constantly fail to meet deadlines you have set yourself. At least you are consistent in your ways.
2 Budgetary slacker	Vice: over estimates volume/difficulty of work; builds in budgetary slack to everything Cause? Excessive fear of pressure; refusal to work at a faster pace than you are capable of; inefficiency Consequence – fewer learning opportunities; boredom; reputation of being slow or lazy, even though the only problem is estimation Cure? Set yourself targets to build confidence. Learn speed reading techniques?	Your manager gives you more work than you think you can cope with, even though you get it done and you are given no more work than others.
3 All over the place	Vice: over- or under-estimates time spent Cause? Cannot relate tasks to time. Consequence: frustration Cure? Try the over-promiser's cure	The most frustrating as others cannot predict a pattern of behaviour, and nor can you. Nobody believes anything you say.
4 Never gets it wrong	The best position to be in. You're perfect.	

(a) If you are an **over-promiser**, you will set yourself unrealistic deadlines for completing the Project. Failing to meet them will depress you – you do not have other people to check your progress. If you do struggle to meet your self-imposed deadlines, you might rush or do the work inadequately. The Module A examiner has made this point: the less successful projects often appear to have been completed in a hurry.

(b) If you are a **budgetary slacker**, this is less of a problem, except that you might take longer on the Project assignment than you really need or you might be insufficiently ambitious.

(c) If you are completely **inconsistent** in your time estimation, you will face both problems at once. Arguably, you should not set yourself a time limit, but plan your work breakdown structure meticulously.

Even if the project assignment you are currently doing only involves reading around the issues identified (eg Just in Time techniques for Performance Management) you will find that reading, taking notes and summarising the results will take far more time than anticipated.

3.1 Dealing with your estimation problems – particularly for over-promisers

The best solution is to keep a **record**, on an experimental basis, of the time you spend on the activities below. They are related to the assignment.

Activity	Relevance	Note down how long you spent doing this
Read, absorb and **take notes** of an article in *Finance Matters* on a subject that is unfamiliar to you – count the words first.	The assignment may involve research, and you will have to do reading – skim reading may not be enough. Furthermore, the data you have to read and absorb may not be written or structured in a way you are familiar with. Directed to an academic or business audience, there may be new terminology to absorb	
Next time you **access the world wide web**, search for a business relevant website, and note how long it takes to access the information you want.	Some searches take a long time; you might have to use a number of different search engines to get what you want; you may want to download files – the speed of this depends on your internet connections.	
Next time you set up a spreadsheet model at work or at home, time yourself – make the model reasonably complex, containing formulae and a graph.	The assignment may require you to set up a spreadsheet and use it to model or manipulate data and present it in a different form.	
Next time you **write a long letter or email** to someone, or a detailed report at work, time yourself and count the words. Note when you started and when you finished to account for distractions. Make sure that this is **word processed.**	Writing the assignment will take a **lot** longer than this, as you will have to think about what you must do. If you **word process** a report, you may be surprised at the time you might spend formatting, printing out, editing what you have written and so on.	

We have chosen the activities above, because reading, surfing the net, spreadsheets, note taking and writing are typical activities you may do in the course of the Project.

When you have identified the tasks you have to do, you might **classify** them as:

- Reading
- Web-searching
- Writing and word processing
- Data manipulation
- Spreadsheets

4 Building up a schedule

The Project assignments are projects with an end in view, the DipFM qualification. You may have heard of people – perhaps friends (or friends of friends) from university - who have stayed on to do a further research qualification, such as a PhD, and whose research programme has drifted off. This can be prevented by adequate planning.

Furthermore, unlike someone doing an undergraduate degree, you will almost certainly have to do your Project work around your job and other social commitments – but you should already have experience of this in doing your DipFM exams to date. Careful planning should help you to maximise the use of your time.

4.1 Deadlines

Your deadlines and schedules are basically up to you. Again, you need a different mind-set to what you are used to for your normal DipFM exams. Studying for your DipFM exams, you made a decision to attend a particular exam sitting and then, perhaps, worked backwards from this, identifying that you had so many available hours to study for those subject areas. You may also have attended courses which would therefore have focused your studies on to specific dates.

For the assignments, rather than working backwards from an exam date, you may be better advised to work **forwards** from a start date. This is because the assignments will involve work you are unfamiliar with. You may not know precisely the result you will come up with; you do not know exactly what the ramifications of the research will be, and how long the whole process will take you.

Step 1   **Decide on a start date. Simple?**

Yes, but have you briefed your partner, friends, family, and work colleagues that you are engaged on a final step to getting a highly-respected professional qualification? They will support you if they know how important it is to you, and it will help them to be understanding – we hope – of long hours spent in the library, or even temporary increases in phone bills as a result of searching the net.

Step 2   **Review your programme of work**

The next section and chapters will describe in brief some of the typical tasks you will encounter in the Project. You may already have some idea as to the number of hours needed.

Step 3   **Identify the learning resources you will need and when available**

Unlike DipFM studies, where you may have used the BPP Study Texts and Practice & Revision Kits as your principal learning tools, the Project may require you to hunt around and discover things. It may simply not be possible to do everything in the evenings – you might need to do some of this work during the week, for example, if you have to visit a specialist library.

4.2 Resources

(a)   **Library**: how far do you have to travel? Opening and closing times? Are there days when it is closed? Do you need a library pass? How will you get there? Walking distance? Bus and train times?

(b)   **Local ACCA student society or centre**. You could enquire if there are facilities for you to use.

(c)   **Computing power** – do you have access to a PC? If you do not have one at home, you may be able to use your office PC after hours or at weekends, for spreadsheet work and word processing your assignment. If you have to go into the office for this, this again affects the time you have available.

       (d)   **Internet.** If you have Internet access at home, all you need worry about is timing and cost. Otherwise consider:

            (i)   Are you close to a cyber-café? When is it busy or cheap? Can you print from it?

            (ii)   Does a friend have net access?

            (iii)   Could you obtain permission to use facilities at work to research via the net – always ask first!

Step 4. Identifying other lead times

4.2.1 The ACCA's timetable

Although you are under no pressure to submit a specific project, you should note that the ACCA will change the titles of the projects after each deadline has passed. The next title will be completely different.

4.3 Lead times

Some of your research, as you will see, may involve primary data (the data that you generate yourself) as well as secondary data. With the possible exception of the World Wide Web, you must also build in lead times from when you ask for something to when you receive it. Here are some indicative examples.

Example	
Reserving a book from the library if it is not in stock	Two weeks? Perhaps longer if someone else is using it. You might have to wait until the weekend to collect it.
Ordering a book over the internet (eg from amazon.co.uk; bol.com)	Amazon.com delivers worldwide, but a local internet book supplier might have better access to local materials. Depends on closeness to wholesalers.
Ordering a book from a bookshop	A quick phone call will establish if one is in stock.
Obtaining articles	Hopefully, your library will have relevant business or academic journals, or you have retained copies of *Finance Matters* (which is also available on the ACCA's website).
Web searching	In theory, if material is downloadable you should be able to do this immediately - a matter of minutes.

4.4 Other planning aids

Useful planning tools are Gantt Charts (or Bar charts) and Network analysis.

You thus need to **schedule the activities** or tasks in the most efficient way given these two factors.

       (a)   The **dependency** of some activities on others. In other words, job B may need to be done before job C. For example, you may need to read articles before, say, discussing them with your manager at work.

       (b)   **Constraints on resources and their availability.** Some resources may not be available at the ideal time.

You will have a broad-brush time estimation for any activity. For this you need, in addition to the **duration** of each sub-unit of work:

       (a)   The **earliest time** work on a particular unit **can** be started

       (b)   The **latest time** it must be started – less of an issue unless you really are working to a tight deadline or around people's holidays

4.5 Gantt charts

A simple plan for a project is based on a **bar line chart**. This is sometimes called a **Gantt chart**.

(a)   It can be used as a **progress control chart** with the lower section of each bar being completed as the activity is undertaken.

(b)   A delay in a particular piece of work and its 'knock on' effect on other work can be shown in a **linked bar chart**. This shows the links between an activity and preceding activities which have to be completed before this particular activity can start.

Here is an example, from a construction project for a garage. We can see the delays to the work on the excavation of the foundation.

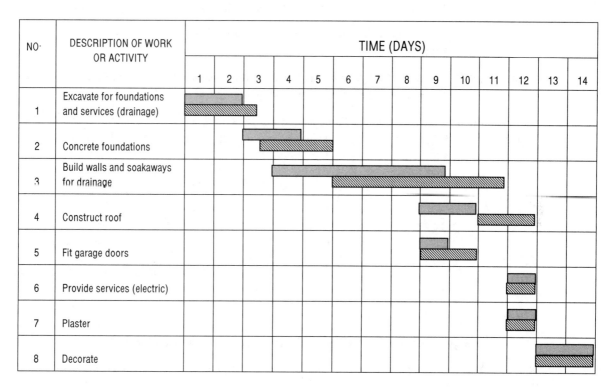

Key

   budgeted time

actual time

(a)   Advantages

- Easy to understand

- **Flexible**: you can draw it on paper or on a spreadsheet – perhaps use colour coding for different jobs

- You can add other things, such as holidays or work commitments

- You can see at a glance where you are, by showing 'actual' performance against plan

(b)   **Disadvantages**: none, really, as far as the Projects are concerned, although for larger more complex projects its main drawback is that it does not specifically show how aspects of work are linked together.

4.6 Critical path analysis (CPA or network analysis)

To overcome this problem, there is a more sophisticated technique known as network analysis or critical path analysis. You are **unlikely** to need this, but you **may at work have access to project management software** and if for some reason you need to use it, here is the underlying method.

Network analysis is a project planning technique which aims to map the activities in a particular project, and the relationship between them. CPA describes the **sequence** of activities, and how long they are going to take. These diagrams are drawn left to right.

(a)   **Events** (1 and 2) are represented by circles. Activities (eg A) connect events.

(b)   The **critical path** is represented by drawing an extra line or a thicker line between the activities on the path. It is the **minimum amount of time** that the project will take.

(c)   It is the convention to note the earliest start date of any activity in the **top** right hand corner of the circle.

(d)   We can then work **backwards** identifying the **latest** dates when activities have to start. These we insert in the bottom right quarter of the circle.

A completed network diagram would be as follows. The **critical path** is AEG. Note the **float time** of five days for Activity F. Activity F can begin any time between days 4 and 9, thus giving the project manager a degree of flexibility.

(a)

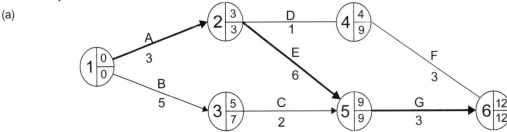

4.7 Use of network analysis in the project assignments

(a)   Use it if **lots** of activities **depend** on others and you can do things in parallel. For example, you can develop your spreadsheet model after you have, say, reviewed and analysed several sets of accounts (providing you know what you are looking for).

(b)   It is less good at helping you **schedule** your project work with other areas of **your** life.

So what should my main planning aid be?

We strongly recommend that – whether on spreadsheet or paper – you draw up an overall schedule on a day-by-day basis, from the start until you intend to complete the project, analysing your time between:

(a)   Work
(b)   Weekend/holiday
(c)   The Project

Submit your plans to a **reality check.**

(a)   Your **partner and/or family** may feel that your plans to work 12 hours on Saturday and Sunday may not be conducive to personal happiness or family life; or that your plans to rise 2 hours earlier every morning are unlikely to meet fruition if you are a notoriously late sleeper.

(b) Your **boss and work colleagues** may be able to advise you of busy times you have not already thought of, for example when you will be expected to provide cover for someone else on holiday.

(c) **Lecturers** at your college will have had years of experience dealing with undergraduate and postgraduate dissertations and research projects.

5 Using IT to help manage the project assignments

Although it is not the purpose of this book to provide you with a guide to various IT software packages on the market, here are some hints and tips.

5.1 Using spreadsheets to plan your project

Although spreadsheets are designed for numerical analysis, they do offer a number of useful features that can be adapted for planning. Below is a simple example using Microsoft Excel. Let us assume that Task 1.1 is library research; you intend to spend 12 hours on this and you commence it on April 8.

		Plan (hrs)	Actual (hrs)	Week beginning 08-Apr							Week beginning 15-Apr						
				Mon	Tues	Wed	Thurs	Fri	Sat	Sun	Mon	Tues	Wed	Thurs	Fri	Sat	Sun
No. of hours																	
Work					8	8	8	8	2		8	8	8	8	8		
Holiday				8													
Shopping																	
Cousin's wedding									6								
Project																	
Task ref																	
1.1	Library	12		5					5	2							
			12	3					3	0						6	
1.2	Etc																

5.2 Dates

You can easily **format cells** to show the **dates**, and you can do this automatically by using the **drag** command. If you are doing a Gantt chart, you can therefore set up the dates very easily. You could use the top cell of each column to signify dates.

5.3 DipFM Project tasks and other commitments: time available

You can input your commitments down the side – as you see we have shown your work commitments at the top, as well as other calls on your time, and have given an hourly approximation.

You can use a **formula** to add up the total hours you plan to spend, and, in the row below, how many hours you have actually spent. You can use the Format/Cell/Pattern command to add colour or shades to each row of cells. You can see that you were over-optimistic in planning to do two hours work on the day of your cousin's wedding.

With time for experimentation and practice, you can do a lot more than this, for example flagging up if some tasks are overdue – but you will need to experiment yourself.

5.4 Scheduling and diary software

If your office operates a network system, such as **Microsoft Outlook** or Lotus Notes, it is quite possible to use this to plan your work.

(a) Microsoft Outlook has a **calendar** facility. You can book up time in your calendar by clicking on the date and 'booking' the time as 'busy' or 'tentative' for your project work. You can print off your calendar by day, week or month.

(b) When you are planning a meeting or activity, you can book **reminders** to yourself that something needs to be done.

(c) Microsoft Outlook also has a 'task' list – this has the advantage of identifying automatically when something is overdue by turning it red.

Note that Microsoft Outlook is not designed to manage a project – but it can be a big help in managing your working life into which the Project must fit.

5.5 Project management software

Specialised software is available to help you manage projects, for example Microsoft Project. This is almost certainly far too sophisticated and complex for the DipFM projects, but if you are familiar with it anyhow, and, for example, it is available at work, you could use this to plan.

Here are some overall guidelines on using IT in planning and managing the project assignments.

Subject	Comment
1 Garbage in, garbage out	No IT application is better than the data you put into it. If you do not think about **what** you have to do and **how long** it will take, and if your plan is fundamentally **flawed**, no amount of tinkering with IT will help you.
2 IT is a servant not master	If you feel that the project is taking shape in a different way from how you had planned, then you will need to change your plan; it will have to be flexible.
3 IT can waste time as well as save it	If your model is more complex or too sophisticated, and the stages in your project are quite simple, then maintaining the model may eat up time which you could more usefully spend on the project content.

6 Setting up your project file

6.1 Setting up your file

One important planning task is **setting up a file for you to manage your data**. You may need two or more but if you start to order and record your paperwork from the outset, this will help you control and keep track. The abilities the project assignments seek to test are not only the content and thought but how you organised the process.

6.2 What you've read

Furthermore, you MUST keep a record of where you obtained your data as you may need to reference it in your assignment. So, if you read an article about the logistics industry in the Economist, say, or the business section of the **Middle Eastern Economic Digest** or the **New York Times**, and if you have used this, then always note down:

- Article source
- Date
- Author, if attributed
- Page references

This is **evidence** of what you have done – and will enable you to find it again – DON'T RELY ON MEMORY. DON'T FORGET TO NOTE REFERENCES DOWN AS YOU USE THEM.

We suggest you obtain an A4 ring binder, with twice as many file dividers as you think you can possibly need. Here are some subdivisions.

Planning section	Your schedules
	Any related correspondence
The project	Detailed analysis of the requirements, probably divided into sections for each part of the project
Details of any additional research	Research design
	What you did
	Notes and references
Analytical frameworks	Where you got them from
	Why you obtained them
Analysis	What you did
	What tools you used
	Spreadsheet models you drew up – show the model first, and the formulae underneath it, in case the worst happens and you lose your model
...and so on	

Chapter Roundup

- When you receive the project, you must decide which part of it to do first or whether you must do the questions in sequential order.

- It is helpful to analyse the required work down into its component parts. This will help you with planning the work.

- It is vital to try to estimate the time that you will need. You have a maximum of three and a half months to complete each project covering two subject areas.

- There are all sorts of techniques which can be used in planning, such as Gantt charts and network analysis. You can also produce a spreadsheet showing how you have scheduled the work.

- Make sure you set up a project file, so you record everything and know exactly where it is.

Part B
Working on the project

Analysing the project

Introduction

You may find it rather daunting when you receive a project from the ACCA and consider that you must complete and submit all the questions in it within a period of about three months or so at the most.

This chapter explains how you should read and then analyse the assignment in depth. In this way you will really get to grips with the information in it and create a firm foundation on which to build in order to proceed to writing an answer.

1 Outline procedure

1.1 Dates

You will receive details of the projects that you are eligible to submit each time results and exam entry forms are despatched by the ACCA, in February and August each year.

Projects issued in February have to be submitted by the following 31 May. Projects issued in August have to be submitted by the following 30 November. In each case, this gives you three to three and a half months to complete the project. Each project, remember, consists of questions covering each of the subject areas within the Module.

The project for Module A will contain:

- questions on Interpretation of Financial Statements (subject area 1) and
- questions on Performance Management (subject area 2).

The project for Module B will contain:

- questions on Financial Strategy (subject area 3) and
- questions on Risk Management (subject area 4).

1.2 Factors to consider

Remember that you do not have to submit a project in any particular period. If you do not think that you will have time to complete a project given your other commitments, or you do not feel happy with the project topics issued by the ACCA, you can choose to wait until a later period to complete your project. However, once you have notified the ACCA of your intention to submit a project in a specific time period, you will not be able to recover any fees paid.

You should think carefully therefore, before embarking on a project, whether it is sensible to complete it in the current phase, or whether it would be better to do it later. Given the importance of the project as an essential part of the Module as a whole, if in doubt about your academic or practical ability to complete the project, we suggest that you wait until the next period.

Remember that you must complete and submit all the questions in a project simultaneously: it is not acceptable to submit the sections for one subject area in a Module but not the other. You must feel that you are competent to do both.

This chapter suggests how you should approach the project once it arrives. Remember that you have got far more time available than in a traditional exam, so it is important that you take your time to familiarise yourself with the content of the project and the implications for the work that you will have to do.

1.3 An integrated exercise

The examiners both now seem to have established a pattern of issuing projects which integrate both of the subject areas within their module. Although the Module A examiner has said that he cannot rule out completely reverting to the 'separate assignment' approach, it seems that the integrated approach will continue for the foreseeable future. You will therefore need to read, analyse and complete each project as an integrated exercise, covering both subject areas simultaneously.

2 Approaching the project

2.1 Objectives of stage 1: Approach the project

- Absorb the project scenario without getting bogged down in detail
- Provide a sound basis for further analysis
- Identify information needs and deficiencies

Step 1.1 **Read the project quickly twice without taking notes**

Don't panic when the project comes in the post or you download it, but **don't ignore** it for weeks. You have to get **to know** the project situation, and the best way is to get started now. You do have up to three and a half months, however, and BPP can help you. Before you do anything, however, **TAKE A PHOTOCOPY**, in case you lose the project, spill tea over it, your computer crashes or whatever. We advise you to photocopy the project on to large A3 paper (this book is A4) so you will have plenty of space to write on it, read as many parts of it together as possible and get to grips with the content.

(a) Book a **quiet, uninterrupted hour** into your diary, when you know you can read the assignment. (You might find that **gentle background music** makes your brain more receptive. Scientific tests have shown that for many people certain types of music – baroque classical, mainly – can relax the brain.)

(b) **Read the project scenario twice**, **quickly, without taking notes**. Speed-reading twice can improve memory retention, and you do not want to get overwhelmed by the detail. So, do not take notes at this stage – sit in an armchair, rather than at your desk, if you need this discipline. At this stage, skim through the supplement that is provided with the Module A project (and sometimes Module B), just to get a feel for the contents.

(c) Now put the project aside for a day or so, and get on with your other work.

Step 1.2 **Quickly re-read the project after a day**

Briefly reviewing information on a regular basis can help you absorb and remember it – scientific fact. Don't take notes this time. This re-reading session is just to refresh your mind.

Step 1.3 **Mark up the project slowly, taking notes**

Read the project (and the Module A supplement) more slowly, highlighting key points, introducing numbered paragraphs or drawing a mind map. The purpose of this stage is still to help you get a broad overview, and the **result of this will be a précis**, summarising the data in the assignment to fix it in your mind.

(a) At your desk, take your A3 copy. This will give you a lot of space to mark up the material or make notes.

(b) Give each paragraph of the project a **separate paragraph reference – you will find it easy to refer to later.**

(c) With a **highlighter** pen, highlight key facts – **do not analyse them for the time being**. Alternatively, you can write down the side of the paper if a fact is important.

(d) Another technique is to do a **spider diagram** or **mind map**. Starting from the centre of the page, you can link things in stages. Mind maps are excellent for linking different items of data together or fixing them in your brain.

Step 1.4   Summarise the data in a précis

What is a précis? A concise summary of essential facts. In other words it is short, comprehensive (it summarises), focused, relevant (essential) and based on facts. **It does not incorporate analysis or opinions.** So what's the point of writing out a summary of a project you have read several times, taken notes on, and by now you know fairly well? There are two reasons for doing a précis.

(a)   You will start testing your **written communication skills** – as you have seen already these are a major part of how you will be assessed in this project.

(b)   It is a scientific fact that putting things into your own words **can help you absorb and understand the data.**

Exercise   Halifax

Here is some data from a newspaper. Précis it into 100 words.

Financial Times	Précis
Halifax, the mortgage bank, yesterday agreed to pay £760m for a controlling stake in St James's Place Capital (SJPC), the holding company for J Rothschild Assurance, in a deal designed to pull the upmarket life assurer into the internet age.	
Halifax bought 17 per cent of the company from Prudential late on Tuesday at 300p a share, a premium of 70p to Tuesday's closing price. It will now extend the offer to up to 60 per cent of the shares, leaving SJPC with a separate listing.	
The bid is the latest move in Halifax's aggressive internet strategy, begun earlier this year when it poached Jim Spowart from Standard Life bank to set up Intelligent Finance (IF), an online bank due to launch this summer.	
It hopes to add £5bn of assets to IF by selling a St James's-branded private banking service, run by IF, through SJPC's 1,000-strong salesforce.	
'This is an absolutely cracking business,' said James Crosby, Halifax chief executive. 'It increases the scale of our distribution operation in long-term savings and will assist our drive for diversification (away from mortgages).'	
Sir Mark Weinberg, chairman of SJPC, said the company had decided last year to seek a strategic partner to help it use the internet to extend its product range, and began talks with Prudential, which then owned 29 per cent of the shares. 'It became clear that their vision and our vision were not parallel to the extent that there wasn't the opportunity for a value-creating partnership,' he said.	

BPP
LEARNING MEDIA

Financial Times	Précis
Analysts said the deal, which is expected to be earnings-enhancing in the first year, would help IF as long as the product, still under wraps, is as exciting as the bank claims.	
The SJPC salesforce own about 8 per cent of the company and have options on another 8 per cent.	

Helping hand

Financial Times	Précis
Halifax, the mortgage bank, yesterday agreed to pay £760m for a controlling stake in St James's Place Capital, the holding company for J Rothschild Assurance, in a deal designed to pull the upmarket life assurer into the internet age.	Halifax, the mortgage bank, has spent £760m to control St James's Place Capital (SJPC), a life assurer with internet potential.
Halifax bought 17 per cent of the company from Prudential late on Tuesday at 300p a share, a premium of 70p to Tuesday's closing price. It will now extend the offer to up to 60 per cent of the shares, leaving SJPC with a separate listing.	Halifax acquired the controlling stake from Prudential Insurance in two stages.
The bid is the latest move in Halifax's aggressive internet strategy, begun earlier this year when it poached Jim Spowart from Standard Life bank to set up Intelligent Finance (IF), an online bank due to launch this summer.	The bid forms part of Halifax's strategy to develop internet businesses, such as Intelligent Finance (IF) an on-line bank.
It hopes to add £5bn of assets to IF by selling a St James's-branded private banking service, run by IF, through SJPC's 1,000-strong salesforce.	In addition, there will be cross-selling opportunities.
'This is an absolutely cracking business,' said James Crosby, Halifax chief executive. 'It increases the scale of our distribution operation in long-term savings and will assist our drive for diversification (away from mortgages).'	There are economies of scale in distribution and opportunities for diversification.
Sir Mark Weinberg, chairman of SJPC, said the company had decided last year to seek a strategic partner to help it use the internet to extend its product range, and began talks with Prudential, which then owned 29 per cent of the shares. 'It became clear that their vision and our vision were not parallel to the extent that there wasn't the opportunity for a value-creating partnership,' he said.	SJPC had been looking for a partner to develop its internet business for some time.
Analysts said the deal, which is expected to be earnings-enhancing in the first year, would help IF as long as the product, still under wraps, is as exciting as the bank claims.	The deal will help IF and it is expected to increase earnings.
The SJPC salesforce own about 8 per cent of the company and have options on another 8 per cent.	

Answer 1

Here is a possible précis

Halifax, the mortgage bank, paid £760m (in two stages) to Prudential Insurance to control St James's Place Capital (SJPC) a life assurer with internet potential. The bid formed part of Halifax's strategy to develop internet businesses, such as Intelligent Finance, an on-line bank. The deal offered cross selling opportunities, economies of scale in distribution and opportunities for diversification. SJPC had been looking for a partner to develop its internet business for some time. The deal was intended to help IF as it was intended to increase earnings.

What do you think? Could it be improved? It appears a bit unstructured.

Answer 2

1   Halifax paid £760m to Prudential to acquire St James's Place Capital.

2   Rationale

    (a)   Halifax and SJPC both wanted to develop an internet business and felt they would make good partners.

    (b)   Other benefits included cross selling opportunities, economies of scale in distribution, and diversification, and increased earnings

2.1.1 Debrief

Answer 2 is probably too concise. It misses out the fact that Halifax is to launch an on-line bank, a key area of its strategy. However, it is clearer in terms of structure, because it adopts report format and has a heading ('rationale').

Whatever your précis, you have summarised the initial assignment situation in your own words, and you will then be in a position to analyse it further.

Step 1.5 **Carry out an information audit**

Now that you have summarised the project, you have an idea of what information you **have** and any information you **do not have**, which may have to be the subject of further research.

If the project supplies you with a wealth of information, you may find it helpful to prepare a checklist like the one on the next page. It will make you focus on the information that you have got and its likely impact in your work on the project.

Given that the project for Module A will almost certainly include a supplement (which has been as much as 60 pages long) and the examiner for Module B has said that his assignment data may run to 6 or 7 pages, it will be critical to analyse what information you have got.

Orientation

Focus		Historic	Future
	Internal	*Internal historic* For example: past financial data, existing corporate culture, past decisions, sunk costs, operating constraints, existing customer contracts	*Internal future* For example: new products planned, new projects, projected future costs or investments, forecasts
	External	*External historic* For example: past trends, history of regulation	*External future* For example: market trends, likely economic outturn, potential competitors

Notes about the checklist

(i)   It is organised **according to business function**: however, the data may not be presented in this way. We suggest you clarify it by identifying where your data lands on the grid below. (Many decisions need to be taken on the basis of **forecast events** or performance. You may be given forecast balance sheets and income statements, or only forecast market data.)

(ii)   We also suggest you add paragraph references as you go through, especially useful when making connections between different areas.

	Focus		Orientation		Notes (eg links, implications, possible calculations)
	Int. ref	Ext. ref	Hist. ref	Fut. ref	
Date of case scenario					
Managing director					
Your boss					
Financial data					
Balance sheet					
Income statement					
Cash flow statement					
Notes to accounts					
Further management accounting data					
Product/service costs					
Revenue details					
Contribution					
Performance measures					
Budget vs actual data					
How the firm appraises projects and investments (eg payback, DCF)					
Operations data					
Location					
Plant and equipment					
Capacity					
Outsourcing					
Planning					
Mission and objectives					
Planning process					
Organisation					
Structure					
Culture					
Power					
Key personnel					
Management assumptions					
Systems					
Management info systems					
Management reports - content and format					
IT deployment					
Funding data					
Equity shares					
Long-term debt, and repayment schedules					
Working capital					
Cost of capital					
Interest rates					

	Focus		Orientation		Notes (eg links, implications, possible calculations)
	Int. ref	**Ext.** ref	**Hist.** Ref	**Fut.** ref	
Product/service					
Range					
Features					
Competitor					
Quality					
Demand					
Marketing mix					
• Product					
• Price					
• Place (distribution)					
• Promotion					
• People					
• Processes					
• Physical evidence					
Performance measures					
Customers					
Market share					
Market size					
Key customers					
Market research					
Marketing strategy					
Environment					
Political					
Legal					
Economic					
Social					
Cultural					
Technological					
Ecological					
Stakeholders					
Competition					
Current					
Potential					
Suppliers					
Current					
Potential					

Step 1.6 Research the industry and company

Researching the industry is a vital component of your **business awareness**. Very soon you should be able to get an idea of recent developments, key issues and so on. This will add authority to the points you make in your answer to the assignment.

So far the Module A project has been based on the accounts of:

- an educational publisher (Dorling Kindersley: pilot paper)

- a chain of specialist discount department stores (T J Hughes plc: spring 2002)

- a manufacturer of aircraft interior systems, specialised vehicle systems and childcare safety systems (Britax International plc: autumn 2002)

- a manufacturer and retailer of chocolate (Thorntons plc: spring 2003)

- a low cost airline (EasyJet: autumn 2003)

- BOC Group: spring 2004

- two fashion retailers (Ted Baker Group: autumn 2004 and New Look: spring 2005)

- a transport company (Stagecoach Group: autumn 2005)

- a retail motor sales group: spring 2006

- a catering group (Compass plc: autumn 2006)

It would be worth researching similar businesses or indeed the company itself for further background information. Do not, however, approach the company directly for further information, as the examiner has requested that candidates do not do this.

2.2 Research the industry

In all of the questions you should get marks for **business awareness** – there is nothing to stop you researching the industry. Here are some pointers.

www.ft.com

You may have to register for this, but it gives you a wealth of information about the industry (and other industries).

www.economist.com

Downloadable surveys and articles

www.londonstockexchange.com

For UK listed companies

www.business.com

An American website, with companies arranged by industry sector and subsector.

Note down – or suggest – critical success factors for the industry. You may need them later.

Step 1.7 **Identify relevant knowledge**

The questions in the projects are intended to be based around the knowledge you have acquired by virtue of studying the syllabus for each subject area. So the themes and topics covered should be familiar, even if the precise detail is not.

You have to apply your knowledge and a good way is to **jot down**, as you go through the project, any areas of knowledge that come to mind. Do **not** try to **shoehorn** all the knowledge you have acquired into the assignment – not everything you know will be relevant. The examiners cannot cover everything in the syllabus in one assignment.

2.3 Conclusion

In this stage, we have covered a lot of ground. You've read the project without taking notes, you've read the project while taking notes, and you've marked up the project and written down the information – without doing any other work.

This preparation has been essential. There is a lot of data to absorb, and, as stated earlier, the purpose of this stage is to get you familiar with the project data in outline. Then you can analyse it.

3 Exploring the project scenario

3.1 Objective of stage 2: Explore the Project Scenario

You should have soundly assessed the fundamentals in Stage 1 *Approaching the Project*

Now you need to start to apply your knowledge, analytical techniques and lateral thinking skills to what you know, so as to tease out more information from the project scenario.

We suggest a number of models you can consider to help you analyse the data. Again, you need to do this systematically.

REMEMBER: EVERY PROJECT SCENARIO IS UNIQUE SO YOU MAY HAVE TO ADAPT THE TECHNIQUES SUGGESTED HERE.

Step 2.1 **Analyse the numbers**

Why should you do this now?

(a)   Unlike projects or case studies offered by other professional bodies, the ACCA's DipFM projects aim to integrate what you have learned in a **financial management** context. In your career, one of the skills you will have to offer to future employers is numerical literacy, and the ability to present, mark up and explain the implications and significance of financial data.

(b)   Unlike some aspects of the formal exams, especially, for example, **Financial Strategy**, the financial data in the project is only **part** of the story, although it is an important part. It will enable you to put other aspects of the project in context. For example, if you work out the cost of capital, you will be able to use it as a discount rate for project evaluation, perhaps.

(c)   As a financial manager, don't be tempted to solve everything by numbers, to the exclusion of other analyses – but numerical analysis may well underpin your conclusions.

(d)   If you have access to a spreadsheet program such as Excel or Lotus 123, you may do some **simple financial modelling**. How sensitive, for example, is profit to changes in assumptions as to inflation or to any new projects envisaged?

(e)   You may find numerical data in a number of contexts.

Step 1. Review your information audit for the numerical data you have.

Step 2. From **internal company data**, calculate key ratios if possible, and identify trends in past, current and forecast data.

Step 3. Apply numerical analysis to **external data** where available, eg market growth rate.

Step 4. Analyse your data for reasonableness. Are internal growth objectives realistic in the light of market and competitor conditions? What about the cost base needed to generate these revenues?

Step 5. Write a summary on the financial position. You will write a summary because you **need practice** and you need to tease out the **meaning of the data.**

Below is a possible checklist you could use. Only calculate relevant ratios, and **invent your own if they are meaningful.** If you do invent ratios, note down what you are calculating and what you are trying to prove and explain this clearly to the examiner. Whose viewpoint are you taking: the managers'? Shareholders'?

Note that * on the checklist = ratios associated with Altman's Z-score predictor of **corporate failure**.

Analytical tool	Issues	Other areas
Actual vs forecast	Identify trends: will they continue?	Comparable companies Competitors
Revenue	Price, volume and mix of products Limiting factors	PEST, business environment Pricing Market share (eg output volume) Forecast market share
Cost of sales	Step costs Learning curve impact Operational gearing (fixed and variable costs)	Production capacity Labour rates Suppliers Money-saving opportunities
Gross profit percentage	Useful marker – given market conditions	Competitor costs for comparison
Expenses	Activity based costing	Can relate to advertising costs used to purchase market share
Net profit	Useful to help forecast cash flows Sensitivity to changes in revenue, and costs	Company valuation (eg discounted future profits) if a take-over target
Interest cover	Cost of borrowing Project appraisal	Bank, investors, PEST analysis
Dividend cover	Shareholders' expectations Policy	
ROE (Return on equity)	Gives the investor's viewpoint	
ROCE* (Return on capital employed)	Accounting measures, easy to manipulate You may need to take a balanced approach to 'capital' employed for a company financed in part by long-term debt; reviewing **operating** performance by reference only to equity shareholders may not be 'helpful'.	Other firms
Retained profit/assets employed*	Future investment in the business	
Non-current assets (gross and net)	Age and valuation (eg at cost) Valuation (historic vs market)	Capacity utilisation
Revenue/non-current assets*		Compare with other firms
Turnover periods • Inventory • Receivables • Payables	Establish operating cycle, as cash can be released from working capital if managed more tightly	

Analytical tool	Issues	Other areas
Working capital/assets employed*	Liquidity? Financing costs?	
Current and quick ratio	Working capital cash flows and timing	
Gearing	Can be calculated in a number of different ways	
Debt/equity*	Timing of cash flows	
Earnings per share	Shareholders	
Price/earnings ratio	Company valuation	
WACC	Project appraisal financing	

Exercise

Music societies

(**Note:** In the project, you will be required to present financial information, which may well have to be written for a non-financial manager, for example, if you have to write a report to the Board of Directors or the shareholders of the company. You will need to avoid jargon or making too many assumptions as to what the manager might know. You will also need to explain what it means and what implications it has.)

In a number of cities, music societies, which are charitable organisations, provide classical music concerts by operating concert halls and supporting orchestras employing full-time musicians. Earned income arises mainly from giving concerts, with additional earned income from catering activities, ancillary sales programmes, CDs and cassettes, souvenirs, and hiring out the concert hall facilities. The earned income is much less than the cost of running the orchestras and concert halls, which are also supported by subsidies in the form of annual grants from local government authorities and the central government, and from business sponsorship, which is a form of corporate public relations expenditure.

The broad aims of the music societies are to provide the best possible standard of live performance of classical music in their home cities (supported by grants from their local government authority) and in other areas of the country (supported by grants from the central government), and to encourage new music and musicians.

As they are charities, music societies do not aim to make a profit. Any surpluses are invested in improvements to the concert halls and spent on additional musicians.

Costs are largely fixed and are broadly 75% orchestral and 25% concert hall and administration (mostly staff). Levels of remuneration, especially for musicians, are low, considering the skills and training required.

The scope for increases in income is very limited. Grants will not increase, and may decrease. The orchestras (allowing for rehearsal time) are fully occupied. Fees for engagements elsewhere in the country and abroad are falling due to the competition from orchestras from other countries.

The chairman of the manufacturing company for which you are a management accountant has recently become a non-executive director of the local music society (X Music), which owns the concert hall and employs the orchestra. His first impressions are that the music is probably excellent, though he is no expert, but that the data available on operations is very limited.

Some comparisons are available with another music society (Y Music) in a smaller city: these are given below.

Required

On the basis of the available data, prepare a report for the Chairman, comparing the key features of the business and financial performance of X Music with that of Y Music.

3.1.1 Comparative data

Number of performances	20X7		20X2 (5 years ago)		20W7 (10 years ago)	
	X	Y	X	Y	X	Y
Concerts in home city	74	84	77	91	75	91
Other concerts in home country	63	26	88	38	81	52
Overseas concerts	8	8	15	-	11	-
TV/radio/recording	5	11	9	5	14	9
Total	150	129	189	134	181	152
Income	$'000	$'000	$'000	$'000	$'000	$'000
Concerts in home city	698	1,043	540	717	410	459
Other concerts in home country	916	762	697	361	518	371
Overseas concerts	282	333	154	-	100	-
TV/radio/recording	70	210	72	128	53	118
Other earned income	466	133	76	41	56	22
Business sponsorship	397	607	141	135	56	44
Total earned income	2,829	3,088	1,680	1,382	1,193	1,014
Grant – central government	1,300	1,500	900	1,000	500	900
Grant – local government authority	655	950	150	750	400	500
Total income	4,784	5,538	2,730	3,132	2,093	2,414
Total costs	4,872	5,356	2,703	3,147	2,059	2,402
Surplus/(deficit)	(88)	182	27	(15)	34	12
Cumulative surplus/(deficit)	(686)	311	80	(26)	141	62

Answer

REPORT

To: The Chairman
From: Financial Manager
Date: 3 July 20X8
Subject: Comparison of the performances of X Music and Y Music

This report provides a comparison of the key features of the business and financial performance of X Music and Y Music.

1   EXECUTIVE SUMMARY

1.1   **X Music's** results for **20X7** show a **marked deterioration** in financial performance. The society reported a **deficit** of $88,000 in 20X7 (compared with surpluses of $27,000 and $34,000 in 20X2 and 20W7 respectively) and a worrying **cumulative deficit** of $686,000 (compared with cumulative surpluses of $80,000 in 20X2 and $141,000 in 20W7).

1.2   **Y Music**, on the other hand, was **more successful** and reported a **surplus** of $182,000 and a cumulative surplus of $311,000 in 20X7. A deficit of $15,000 in 20X2 and a surplus of $12,000 in 20W7, and a cumulative deficit in 20X2 ($26,000) and a cumulative surplus in 20W7 ($62,000) point to the possibility that the society's **results have been fluctuating widely** over the last decade, however.

1.3   An analysis of business and financial data for the two societies highlights a number of factors which may well have played their part in these results.

2 NUMBER OF PERFORMANCES

2.1 Since 20W7, the **number of performances** given by **X Music** has **dropped** by 17% (from 181 to 150), while the number given by **Y Music** has **dropped** by 15% (from 152 to 129). The similarity in these figures tends to suggest that both societies have been **affected to a similar degree by competition from foreign orchestras**. Despite this fall, however, Y Music has reported both a surplus and a cumulative surplus in 20X7.

2.2 The **number of performances of all types of concert** given by **X Music** in **20X7** have **dropped** from those in 20W7 and 20X2. The number of concerts in other areas of the country (not the home city) in particular has dropped by over 28% to 63 from the 88 reported in 20X2. The number of performances in the home city has remained fairly constant (75 in 20W7 and 74 in 20X7).

2.3 **Y Music** has seen a significant **fall in the number of concerts played elsewhere in the home country** (a drop of 50% from 52 in 20W7 to 26 in 20X7). From playing no concerts abroad in 20X2, Y Music played 8 in 20X7 (as did X Music), and made 11 TV/radio/recording appearances in 20X7, compared with only five in 20X2.

2.4 In 20X7, **Y Music** gave 84 **concerts in its home city**, 10 **more than** the number of performances by **X Music** in its home city. This is **surprising** given that Y Music is based in a smaller city with, one assumes, a smaller concert-going population. **Overall**, however, **X Music** gave 150 performances in 20X7, 21 **more than Y Music**, principally because it made 63 performances in other areas of the country. X Music's disappointing results cannot therefore be attributed to the number of concerts it performed.

3 INCOME

3.1 **Both societies** have reported a **significant increase** in total earned income over the ten-year period. X Music's earned income was 137% higher in 20X7 ($2,829,000) compared with that in 20W7 ($1,193,000). Y Music's was 205% higher ($3,088,000) compared with $1,014,000). It is, however, the **income per concert** that has **led to X Music's poor financial performance**, as illustrated by the following figures for 20X7.

	20X7	
	X Music	Y Music
	$	$
Income per concert in home city	9,432	12,417
Income per concert in home country	14,540	29,308
Income per overseas concert	35,250	41,625
Income per TV/radio/recording event	14,000	19,091

3.2 X Music achieves a significantly lower income per performance for all types of performance than that achieved by Y Music. The difference is most marked when comparing **concerts in the home country**, with **Y Music's income per performance being over double that of X Music's**. This could be because audience sizes are smaller at X Music's performances or ticket prices may be lower, but on the basis of the data provided it is not possible to state definite causes. If you were able to provide me with attendance figures and information about ticket prices I could provide you with a more detailed analysis.

3.3 **X Music's other earned income** of $466,000 in 20X7 (16% of total earned income) is significantly **higher than that of Y Music** ($133,000, representing 4% of total earned income) and hence its catering and merchandising activities are probably considerably more effective than those of Y Music. X Music's figure also compares well with the $56,000 earned ten years previously.

3.4 On the other hand, **business sponsorship** appears to have been extremely **lucrative for Y Music** in 20X7, bringing in $607,000, almost the same income as that earned from concerts in other parts of the country. X Music's business sponsorship at $397,000 was only 65% of Y Music's, although both societies have shown significant increases from the levels in 20W7 (X Music $56,000; Y Music $44,000) and 20X2 (X Music $141,000; Y Music $135,000).

3.5 The **grants** from both central government and the local authority **awarded to Y Music** in 20W7, 20X2 and 20X7 were **higher than those awarded to X Music**. In 20X7, grants represented 44% of Y Music's total income, compared with 41% of X Music's, with Y Music receiving $2,450,000 in grants compared with $1,955,000 by X Music. **Y Music's committee** appear to be **far more effective** in **applying for grants** and X Music's committee should be encouraged to actively pursue this source of income.

4 COSTS

4.1 Despite the fact that X Music put on more performances than Y Music in 20W7, 20X2 and 20X7, X Music's costs have always been lower. In 20X7, X Music's costs per performance were $32,480 ($4,872,000/150) whereas Y Music's were $41,519 ($5,356,000/129). Given that one would expect overseas concerts to be the most expensive to put on, and both societies gave eight overseas concerts, this cost difference may highlight particular cost control skills at X Music (or alternatively, of course, particularly poor cost control at Y Music). On the other hand, because 75% of the costs are related to the orchestra, it could point to lower quality performances by X Music (which might explain X Music's lower income per performance) or to different forms of performance by the two societies, the two forms requiring different numbers of musicians.

5 RECOMMENDATION

5.1 Given that X Music's total costs were not covered by total income in 20X7, and that there is no guaranteed level of grant income, X Music should carry out a detailed review of expenditure.

Signed: Financial Manager

Comment on answer

This answer is a very thorough examination of the issues. In terms of format, some of the comparative data could have been put into tables, rather than being incorporated in the narrative.

Notice the structure of the answer. It starts with an executive summary, then sets out numbered points and then finishes with a recommendation. We shall discuss report writing in detail in Chapter 5, but this provides a good example.

Step 2.2 **Consider the overall position of the business**

Give some thought to the general and competitive environment of the business. These are factors that you will not specifically have covered in the four subject areas for the DipFM qualification, but common sense and some basic research should help.

Consider for example:

- Environmental issues, such as new anti-pollution legislation

- Technological issues, such as the development of more sophisticated means of communications (eg 3G phones, broadband internet access)

- Economic issues, such as the state of the economy as a whole, or factors relating to a specific sector. An example could be the downturn in the aviation industry in the aftermath of the US terrorist attacks in September 2001, or the impact of the introduction of the Euro.

Comments you make related to these issues will add to the overall impression given by your answer.

Step 2.3 How does the business add value?

Here, you can apply your knowledge of **value chain analysis**, say, and other techniques such as **functional cost analysis** to identify what is special about the business.

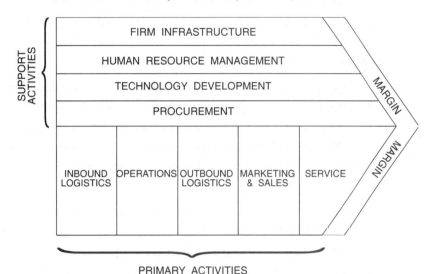

You can then comment on each areas of the value chain.

Exercise

EF is a long-established company which manufactures a large range of computers, from mainframe to portable, on a single site. Its sales revenue is about $500 million per annum. The company has recently undergone a major information systems change involving the following.

(a) Capital expenditure of $50 million over three years (the NPV will be $7 million)

(b) Workforce change from 10,000 to 7,000 employees

(c) Radical changes to work practices, both in the manufacturing systems (use of CAD/CAM) and reorganisation of managerial and administrative functions

The new Managing Director needs to identify and understand some indicators which can be used to evaluate the success or otherwise of this change.

Required

Recommend to the Managing Director up to five key indicators that he can use and explain why each is relevant to his requirements.

Answer

REPORT

To: The Managing Director, EF
From: Accountant
Date: 23 November 20X6
Subject: Recommendations for key indicators

In evaluating the effect of the recent changes within EF the following indicators can be recommended.

(a)   **Added value per employee** is useful as a possible measure of **productivity.** This could, for example, be defined as sales income less bought in services (including finance charges) and material, divided by the number of employees.

The company has proceeded down the route of replacing personnel with capital equipment. The productivity of the remaining workforce should therefore be significantly greater than before.

The **information** for this indicator is readily available from the **usual management accounting sources**. Knowing the cost of capital, the savings in payroll costs, and the budgeted throughput, a target added value per employee can be calculated that represents breakeven on the financial effect of the changes.

A **weakness** with this indicator is that certain elements are susceptible to **changes in economic conditions** as well as to internal changes.

Any business process re-engineering of this nature should bring about significant gains in productivity by **eliminating inefficient and outdated processes** altogether. New procedures should reflect **best practice** in the industry, and, for this reason, some use of **benchmarking against competitors** in the industry is also recommended.

(b)   **Responsiveness** to customers and the marketplace is vital.

The purpose of the changes is not simply to save money, but to enable the company to **react speedily to consumer needs**. The information technology industry is becoming a prime example of 'relationship marketing', wherein the supplier is attempting to become closer to each customer. This is a means of seeking competitive advantage. Thus the organisation will be trying to behave as if it were 'lean and mean' and provide fast response to each customer, not simply manufacturing 'boxes'. Hence the introduction of CAD/CAM.

An **important indicator** therefore, as an example of speed of reaction, is the **speed at which bespoke customer needs are met**. To make this indicator consistent, project times from agreement of customer specification to delivery need to be measured.

A **problem** with this is that the size of the project will affect the speed of delivery. Perhaps project times could be divided by the sales margin for comparability and consistency. The lower the ratio the better. A company target figure should be established as a yardstick.

(c)   **Financial** indicators, such as **management accounting ratios** (credit risk, receivables days, WIP turnround etc) should also be used. Although **care** is needed in **interpretation**, because of distortions caused by accounting policies and the need for consistency from period to period, the **traditional measures** of working capital efficiency (summarised perhaps as 'working capital days', namely receivable days plus inventory days less payables days) are **as relevant as ever** to modern industry.

The improvement in the **manufacturing systems** will have included measures designed to improve **inventory management** and **financial control**, probably one of the variants of JIT (just-in-time) and

BPP
LEARNING MEDIA

perhaps ABM (activity based management) or other relevant costing/management systems. The effect on cash flow should be dramatic once the new systems are in place.

These cost savings can be set against the capital costs incurred in developing new systems. Standard **investment appraisal** techniques can be used here: current thinking suggests that a balanced measure, incorporating NPV, payback and IRR gives the most rounded view. In addition **project management measures** relating to budget, timetables and quality (availability, response etc) can be used.

(d) **Strategic direction** is extremely difficult to assess as it involves such long-term factors. Major systems change of the type undertaken is certainly part of a strategic process and its success can only be seen by reference to the **overall market position** of the company and its **reputation**. The value of the **brand name** may be measured, but such measures are **subjective**. Better is a **long-term tracking of share price** and **market share**.

Although **strategic planning is long-term**, IT can sit awkwardly with this, as so much **technology is short-term** in nature, with manufacturers reducing product life cycles in their quest for competitive advantage. This means that IT-based decisions may need to be changed within the life of a particular strategy. This problem can to some extent be addressed by a formal **Information Systems Planning** exercise, which creates a framework for development, providing guidelines over a period of time to ensure that activities fit into strategic criteria.

(e) **Critical success factors** can be used. Each CSF will already have been ascribed one or more performance indicators. CSFs are fundamental to the strategic direction of the company. Here, the changes to be evaluated are more than just small improvements to individual parts of the company, they are a fundamental change to the very nature and shape of the organisation.

The ultimate measure of their effectiveness could be said to be in the **bottom line results** of EF; however, other factors will also be relevant, for example, **reliability indicators**. This might take the form of warranty claims/sales, or claims/number of products supplied, or may be based on customer surveys measuring the elusive characteristic of 'customer satisfaction'. The reputation of the company, and thus its potential to generate future cash flows – the definition of the value of the enterprise – depends on the quality of its service. It is important to know that the reduction in personnel numbers, and the introduction of automation have not compromised quality.

The above should be read in the light of the assumption that **systems development** is undertaken in general to **meet business needs** and **fulfil organisational objectives**. These might be categorised as:

- Reductions in cost base
- Investment in IT infrastructure
- Responding to, or anticipating, changing market conditions
- Ensuring that IT supports strategic plans

It is only by setting **appropriate performance indicators**, such as the above, that the success of systems development can be **measured**.

In conclusion, the measurement of the key components of the strategy of the company are vital to the **control and updating** of that strategy as it links **'hard'** cost/benefit analysis with **'softer'** areas which are difficult to quantify and often subjective.

Signed: Accountant

Step 2.4   Identify investor objectives, capital structure and other stakeholder objectives

		Investors	Comment
	Step 1.	Identify share owning structure: • Privately owned? • Publicly traded?	
	Step 2.	Note information as to the return shareholders and investors are expecting from the company – use comparative information.	
	Step 3.	Note trends in the share price, if this information is given.	
	Step 4.	If you have a P/E ratio and an earnings figure, calculate a **possible value for the business.**	
	Step 5.	Do you have information to calculate the WACC? If yes, do so.	
	Step 6.	Note comparative information about other companies for a benchmark as to shareholder expectations.	
	Step 7.	Note data as to the risk of the company (eg the beta).	
	Step 8.	Review gearing ratios.	
	Step 9.	Would you invest in this company?	
		Managers	Comment
	Step 10.	Objectives Remuneration Performance	
		Employees	Comment
	Step 11.	Objectives	
		Lenders	Comment
	Step 12.	Exposure Relationship	
		Government (central and local)	Comment
	Step 13.	Relationship Power to influence	
		Customers and suppliers	Comment
		See '5 forces' analysis	
	Step 14.	Community	Comment
		Pressure groups etc	

The purpose of this is to indicate to you the possible objectives of the parties involved in the assignment.

Step 2.5   Carry out a company valuation
You should have encountered aspects of this throughout your DipFM studies as it features to one degree or another in all four subject areas.

Exercise

PMS is a private limited company with intentions of obtaining a stock market listing in the near future. The company is wholly equity financed at present, but the directors are considering a new capital structure prior to it becoming a listed company.

PMS operates in an industry where the average asset beta is 1.2. The company's business risk is estimated to be similar to that of the industry as a whole. The current level of earnings before interest and taxes is $400,000. This earnings level is expected to be maintained for the foreseeable future.

The rate of return on riskless assets is at present 10% and the return on the market portfolio is 15%. These rates are post-tax and are expected to remain constant for the foreseeable future.

PMS is considering introducing debt into its capital structure by one of the following methods.

(a) $500,000   10% Debentures at par, secured on land and buildings of the company
(b) $1,000,000   12% Unsecured loan stock at par

The rate of tax is expected to remain at 33% and interest on debt is tax deductible.

Required

Calculate, for *each* of the *two* options:

(a)   Values of equity *and* total market values
(b)   Debt/equity ratios
(c)   Cost of equity

Answer

The first step is to calculate the present cost of equity using the **capital asset pricing model** (CAPM):

$$E(r_j) = r_f + [E(r_m) - r_f]\ \beta$$

where $E(r_j)$ = cost of equity (expected % return)

r_f = risk free rate of return (10%)

β = beta value (1.2)

$E(r_m)$ = market rate of return (15%)

In this case:

$E(r_j)$ = $10\% + (15 - 10)\% \times 1.2$

= 16%

This cost of equity can now be applied in the **dividend valuation model** to find the **total market value of the firm**. It is assumed that all earnings are distributed as dividend; earnings and therefore dividends do not grow.

p_0 = d_0/r

where p_0 = market value

d_0 = current level of dividends (post tax)

r = cost of equity

p_0 = $\$0.4m \times 0.67/0.16$

= $1.675m

(a) The situation under the different scenarios can be summarised as follows.

	Current $'000	Scen 1 $'000	Scen 2 $'000
Profit before interest and tax	400.0	400.0	400.0
Less interest	(0.0)	(50.0)	(120.0)
	400.0	350.0	280.0
Less tax at 33%	(132.0)	(115.5)	(92.4)
Distributable profits	268.0	234.5	187.6

According to the basic theory of capital structure developed by **Modigliani and Miller**, the market value of a firm is independent of capital structure. When tax is introduced into the calculations, the market value of the firm will increase as debt is added to the capital mix because of the present value of the **tax shield** on interest payments. This can be expressed as:

$$V_g = V_u + DT_c$$

where
V_g = market value of the geared company
V_u = market value of the ungeared company
D = market value of debt
T_c = rate of tax

In this case:

	Current $'000	Scen 1 $'000	Scen 2 $'000
V_u	1,675	1,675	1,675
D	0	500	1,000
T_c	33%	33%	33%
$D \times T_c$	0	165	330
Total market value (V_g)	1,675	1,840	2,005

The value of the equity can now be found:

$E = V_g - D$
Scenario 1: $1.84m – $0.5m   = $1.34m
Scenario 2: $2.005m – $1.0m   = $1.005m

(b) The ratio of **debt to equity** is given by D/E:

Scenario 1: 500/1,340   = 37.3%
Scenario 2: 1,000/1,005   = 99.5%

(c) Assuming that all distributable profits are paid as dividends, the **cost of equity** can be found using:

$$r = d_0/p_0$$

where:
r = cost of equity
d_0 = dividend (distributable profit above)
p_0 = market value of equity

Scenario 1: 234.5/1,340   = 17.5%
Scenario 2: 187.6/1,005   = 18.7%

Step 2.6 Identify and analyse possible business projects

The assignment data may provide you with information about business projects.

(a) By this, we mean, for example, **new product development**, a proposed **acquisition**, new **information systems**. There could be projects currently in progress or being proposed. You may be given numerical data to evaluate the project. **Remember decision-making (eg theory about sunk costs, money already spent)**. Your **numerical skills** could be beneficial here.

(b)   A project could on the other hand be an **opportunity** in the market, or something **crying out** from the data. (It could be a project suggested by a deficiency in current operations, for example, which could be dealt with by improving the information system.) This is an examination of your ability to think critically and your **business and financial management awareness.**

(c)   We suggest you note down possible business projects in a schedule, with a rationale.

No	Project – rationale	Main para refs in assignment
1		
2		

Exercise   **Marks and Spencer**

Over the last few years, newspaper reports have suggested that Marks & Spencer (a UK clothing retailer) has encountered difficulties, for a variety of reasons, and a programme of change has been put in place. One reason is that M&S is alleged to have failed to respond appropriately to customer needs. At one time the inventory for each store was determined centrally. Every store was supposed to stock goods in pre-determined quantities, on the basis of **store size alone** (not patterns of actual consumer purchases). If a particular store ran out, in the past people would have driven to the next nearest Marks & Spencer store, perhaps in another town. In recent years, however, they have just gone to another retailer, such as Gap or even Matalan.

Can you identify any 'business projects' from the data above?

Answer

This is based on a real life example, the key issues being inventory and purchase information. From the data, the information system is at fault in that inventory decisions are taken **centrally** and not related to the individual buying patterns of each store. With data mining software, M&S has been able to identify store buying patterns and has been able to respond more quickly – leading to a 30% increase in revenue at selected sites, revenue which would have gone to competitors.

In the schedule proposed, you could have analysed this as follows. If you had been provided with financial data, then you could have identified some of the cashflows.

No.	Project – rationale	Main para refs in assignment
1	Data mining • Protect/increase revenue by retaining customers • Provide information to ensure no stock-outs	x.1

It is quite possible that the assignment will provide you with details of current projects. You may be able to do a DCF analysis on these.

4 Reviewing the data

In some cases the project may present you with a large volume of data. As we have already said, the Module B examiner has said that the Financial Strategy assignment within the Module B project could contain up to 6 to 7 pages of information.

You may therefore need to apply organisation skills to the data in the assignment, to ensure that you extract the maximum from it.

4.1 Data health check

It is worth your while carrying out a health check on some of the data obtained, particularly secondary data. The project may well contain data such as newspaper articles, extracts from accounts and company press releases, and you should consider the extent to which you can rely on this.

Is the data up to date?	
Who is the data intended for?	
Why has the data been produced and what are the interests of the producer of the data?	
What does the data leave out?	

If this is **too** specific, use the following guidelines

Guideline	Comment
Common sense	Clearly data which is 'dated', which emanates from dubious sources or which is based on unrepresentative samples should be treated with caution.
Statistical approaches	There are a variety of sampling methods for survey data, which are appropriate to different situations. All of them involve some degree of risk (some probability of error). The degree of risk of statistical error can, however, be computed.
Expert judgement	The same data can be interpreted differently by different people The following array – 98.7, 98.6, 98.6, 98.4, 98.1, 98.1– might be regarded by a statistician as a declining trend but to a business manager the figures may represent a very steady state.
The intuitive approach	Some people have a better feel for figures than others and seem able to judge the value and validity of data intuitively. However, this requires specific knowledge and experience.
The questioning approach	Always question the origin and the basis of the data. Recognise that human errors occur when manipulating data, that bias can occur in questionnaire design: ask to see the questionnaire, check the figures.

5 Organising the data

Once you have reviewed your data, you should now be in a position to extract information from it. This process can take a variety of forms, depending on the volume and variety of the data collected. The starting point is going to be **organisation**. Key tools are:

- Your **project file** organised in the most suitable way to structure the data to meet the project objective

- A **spreadsheet** perhaps to collect and arrange data you may have collected

- A **photocopier** so that data relevant to different areas of your report can be duplicated, so that you do not have to go back and forth in your files for key results

- **Highlighter pens** to mark up key words and key points

You will need to organise your data and your analytical work in the light of the objective of the project.

(a)   We have drawn on the distinction between structured and unstructured data in Chapter 2.

(b)   Structured data may be primary (collected by you for your specific purpose) or secondary (collected by someone else, for the specific purpose of their work), but you need to incorporate it into a model for further analysis.

(c)   Unstructured data needs to be organised in your mind so that you can draw lessons from it and relate it to other areas of data.

5.1 Example

The data below is taken from an unpublished undergraduate dissertation.

'My approach was successful, indicated by the 73% response rate of which 18% were unwilling to take part (see note below). This left me with 18 completed questionnaires, spilt equally over service and manufacturing industries.

I analysed the data by dividing it into three groups.

- Company's internal environmental background
- Company's environmental information available for external parties
- Environmental information used for internal management decisions

The questions asked were designed to fit these categories enabling linkages and hypotheses between them to be made in answering the original objective of the chapter.

Obviously there are certain limitations such as a lack of knowledge by the respondent or differing interpretations of the questions. This may be improved by using a telephone survey, however, this would be a lengthy process, meaning that I would have to reduce the questionnaire and so may harm data in this way.'

Note

A 73% response rate is truly amazing, but may have been achieved by detailed preparation, choice of sample, or pre-arrangement. Response rates are more commonly between 15 – 20%.

A good place to start is an **example**. Here, the author has written to a number of companies and has obtained data in a **variety of formats**, but wants to extract relevant information for purposes of comparability. This is the start of a thorough review to see how companies report environmental data.

5.2 Example

Analysis of a company environmental data

COMPANIES	QUESTION							
	1	2	3	4	5	6	7	8
A plc	Y	Y	Y	Y	Y	?	N	Y
B plc	N	N	Y	-	-	-	-	-
C plc	Y	N	Y	Y	Y	Y	Y	?
D plc	Y	N	Y	Y	Y	N	N	Y
E plc	N	N	Y	-	-	-	-	-
F plc	Y	Y	N	Y	Y	Y	Y	Y
G plc	Y	Y	Y	Y	Y	Y	Y	Y

Key:

About the Environmental Information Available

Question 1: Is separate environmental information published other than that included within the financial annual report and accounts?

About the Financial Annual Report and Accounts

Question 2: Is any environmental financial[1] information given?

Question 3: Is any narrative environmental information given?

About the Separately Published Environmental Information

Question 4: Is any narrative environmental information given?

Question 5: Are visual environmental performance charts given?

Question 6: Are environmental targets detailed?

Question 7: Do they give an environmental policy?

Question 8: Is the environmental data externally verified?

  Y = yes

  N = No

  ? = To some extent

  − = Not applicable

  [1] Includes both figures and financial policies regarding environmental issues.

By 'organising' your data you are beginning to identify connections and relationships.

You could prepare a spreadsheet in order to capture the data of a spreadsheet application. Spreadsheets offer a variety of tools from simple arithmetic – still very useful – to more complicated statistical analysis as revealed by the formula keys.

5.3 A very simple application of Excel to collect data

If you use Microsoft Excel, look at the manual or try the help keys. Even with quite simple spreadsheet operations, you can generate a lot of information. Here is an example.

(a) **Head up the columns of the spreadsheet** with the names of the five companies. Indicate the date you received the responses, if at all. Alternatively, you might set up a separate spreadsheet schedule for this planning aspect.

(b)   Head up further columns: total, percentage and so on, for some work to do on the data.

(c)   The questions are on the rows. Each response has a row to itself.

(d)   Now, you want to turn these responses into data. Not all will be susceptible to manipulation, but for some responses you could give a YES the value of 1. By adding across you can get the total number of companies answering YES to a question and you can carry out a percentage calculation.

	A	B	C	D	E	F	G	H	I	J	K	L	M	N
1	**Version 1**													
2				**A**	**B**	**C**	**D**	**E**					**Total**	**%**
3	**Is your company**													
4	**predominantly in**													
5														
6	Services		Yes = 1	1			1						2	40%
7	Manufacturing		Yes = 1		1	1		1					3	60%
8														
9	**Does your company**													
10	**utilise**													
11	Energy conservation		Yes = 1	0	0	1	0	0					1	20%
12	Emission control		Yes = 1	0	0	1	0	0					1	20%
13	Recycling		Yes = 1	0	1	1	1	0					3	60%
14	Reuse		Yes = 1	0	1	1	0	0					2	40%
15	Eco-friendly suppliers		Yes = 1	1	1	0	0	0					2	40%
16	Waste monitoring		Yes = 1	0	1	0	0	0					1	20%
17	Recycled stationery		Yes – 1	1	1	0	1	0					3	60%
18	Tree planting		Yes = 1	0	0	0	0	0					0	0%
19	Other		Yes = 1	0	0	1	0	0					1	20%

You could organise your data further. Before you input it, you could identify which companies are in **services** and which are in **manufacturing**, thereby enabling you to calculate percentages for each. Of course, **you can use formulae and modelling tools** to do this – but if you think a key difference will be between services and manufacturing companies, simply organising your data into these columns can provide you with more information. You can see for example that whereas 60% of all the sample use recycled stationery, 100% of service companies do so.

	A	B	C	D	E	F	G	H	I	J	K	L	M	N
23						**Services**			**Manufacturers**				**ALL**	
24	**Version 2**			**A**	**D**	**Total**	**%**	**C**	**B**	**E**	**Total**	**%**	**Total**	**%**
25														
26	**Is your company**													
27	**predominantly in**													
28														
29	Services		Yes = 1	1	1								2	40%
30	Manufacturing		Yes = 1					1	1	1			3	60%
31														
32	**Does your company**													
33	**utilise**													
34	Energy conservation		Yes = 1	0	0	0	0%	1	0	0	1	33%	1	20%
35	Emission control		Yes = 1	0	0	0	0%	1	0	0	1	33%	1	20%
36	Recycling		Yes = 1	0	1	1	50%	1	1	0	2	67%	3	60%
37	Reuse		Yes = 1	0	0	0	0%	1	1	0	2	67%	2	40%
38	Eco-friendly suppliers		Yes = 1	1	0	1	50%	0	1	0	1	33%	2	40%
39	Waste monitoring		Yes = 1	0	0	0	0%	0	1	0	1	33%	1	20%
40	Recycled stationery		Yes = 1	1	1	2	100%	0	1	0	1	33%	3	60%
41	Tree planting		Yes = 1	0	0	0	0%	0	0	0	0	0%	0	0%
42	Other		Yes = 1	0	0	0	0%	1	0	0	1	33%	1	20%

5.4 Organising other data in your file

The other data you have obtained may appear in a variety of formats: newspaper articles, extracts from textbooks, website download, notes you have taken of interviews. Doubtless you have read them in some detail, but you want to start thinking of the story that you are going to tell about them.

We have already suggested various different tasks in setting up your filing system.

5.5 Dealing with organising qualitative data

The key in any project file is to be practical – so that you know where the data is when you want to find it.

(a)   If you have taken notes of interviews, say, you should summarise them on a front sheet.

(b)   If an item of data such as an article is relevant to more than one area, make copies.

(c)   By **organising your data**, you are, in a way, **taking a decision** about how to use it.

(d)   If data is unstructured and awaiting further analysis you might leave it in a separate 'unprocessed' section.

6 Modelling the data

In a **model**, you are, effectively, seeking to set up relationships to allow further analysis. You can do this in a number of ways.

(a)   Spreadsheet modelling. As well as using a spreadsheet as a glorified calculator, it does offer a variety of statistical tools.

(b)   There are various techniques of modelling and analysing **qualitative** data.

6.1 Spreadsheet models – an example

A spreadsheet is a means of capturing and organising data in a very simple way.

Constructing a spreadsheet model is something you might do as a matter of course in your work, in preparing budgets or analysing performance. We do not intend to provide a guide to working with spreadsheets but here is a possible application.

Any spreadsheet model is constructed using formulae. You will find a simple guide in the **help facility** of your spreadsheet package – print this out, if you want a manual record. Here are examples.

(a)   =C4*5. This formula **multiplies** the value in C4 by 5. The result will appear in the cell holding the formula.

(b)   =C4*B10. This **multiplies** the value in C4 by the value in B10. In general this is better than option (a). Why? Because the result is in a separate cell and if '5' is a variable that can change, you can first enter the new number to the cell.

(c)   =C4/E5. This **divides** the value in C4 by the value in E5. (Note that * means multiply and / means divide by.)

(d)   =(C4*B10)–D1. This **multiplies** the value in C4 by that in B10 and then subtracts the value in D1 from the result. Note that generally the computer will perform multiplication and division before addition or subtraction.

(e)   =C4*117.5%. This **adds** 17.5% to the value in C4. It could be used to calculate a price including 17.5% VAT. When you enter 17.5%, it may be displayed on screen as 0.175, depending on how the spreadsheet is set up.

(f)   =(C4+C5+C6)/3. This, in effect, calculates the **average** of the values in C4, C5 and C6. Note that the brackets tell the computer to perform the addition first. Without the brackets the computer would first divide the value in C6 by 3 and then add the result to the total of the values in C4 and C5.

(g)   = 2^2 gives you 2 **to the power** of 2, in other words 2^2. Likewise = 2^3 gives you 2 cubed and so on.

(h)   = 4^ (1/2) gives you the **square root** of 4. Likewise 27^(1/3) gives you the cube root of 27 and so on. Do not forget the brackets.

To **display all the underlying formulae** in your spreadsheet, instead of the numbers, click on Tools, then on Options, then on View and put an X in the box next to Formulas to display them or remove it to display numbers.

6.2 Example

The following four insurance salesmen each earn a basic salary of $14,000 pa. They also earn a commission of 2% of sales. The following spreadsheet has been created to process their commission and total earnings.

	A	B	C	D	E
1	Sales team salaries and commissions				
2	Name	Sales	Salary	Commission	Total earnings
3		$	$	$	$
4	Northington	284,000	14,000	5,680	19,680
5	Souther	193,000	14,000	3,860	17,860
6	Weston	12,000	14,000	240	14,240
7	Easterman	152,000	14,000	3,040	17,040
8					
9	Total	641,000	56,000	12,820	68,820
10					
11					
12	Variables				
13	Basic Salary	14,000			
14	Commission rate	0.02			
15					
16					
17					
18					
19					
20					

Possible formulae are as follows.

(a)   = B4*B14, for cell D4.

(b)   = C6+D6, for cell E6.

(c)   = SUM(D4:D7), for cell D9.

(d)   For cell E9, there is a **variety of possibilities** here, depending on whether you set the cell as the total of the earnings of each salesman (cells E4 to E7) or as the total of the different elements of remuneration (cells C9 and D9). Of course, it would be nice to **know that the calculation works in both directions.** This would give added assurance that there are no errors.

You may want to compare actual results with budgets or targets to see how far it has exceeded, or fallen short of, its expectations. It is useful to express **variations as a percentage of the original budget**, for example sales may be 10% higher than predicted.

6.3 Conditions in formulae

Suppose the company employing the salesmen in the above example awards a bonus (in addition to the commission) to those salesmen who exceed their target by more than $1,000. It is possible to **get the spreadsheet to work out who is entitled to the bonus**. (In our example you can see this for yourself easily enough, but if there were 100 salesmen it would be tedious to have to look down a long list.)

Look at the first section of the spreadsheet. We are trying to determine whether Northington would be shown as entitled to a bonus. The formula used may vary slightly from one spreadsheet program to the next. We will enter the following:

=IF(B4>1000,'BONUS',' ').

The formula could be entered in column F.

This formula has three parts inside the brackets.

IF (**condition**, result if **true**, result if **false**).

The **inverted commas** (') mean that **text** is to appear in the cell. Here the text will either be the word 'bonus' or, if the target was not exceeded, a **blank space**. The contents of the cell could equally well be a number.

Note the following symbols which can be used in formulae with conditions:

<	less than
<=	less than or equal to
=	equal to
>=	greater than or equal to
>	greater than
<>	not equal to

There is nothing very difficult about conditions in formulae, but great care must be taken to put **brackets** and **commas** in the right places.

6.4 Examples of formulae with conditions

6.4.1 Discounts

A company offers a discount of 5% to customers who order more than £1,000 worth of goods. A spreadsheet showing what customers will pay might look like this.

	A	B	C	D	E
1	**Discount Traders**				
2	*Sales analysis*				
3	Customer	Sales	5% discount	Sales (net)	
4		$	$	$	
5	Arthur	956.00	0.00	956.00	
6	Dent	1423.00	71.15	1351.85	
7	Ford	2894.00	144.70	2749.30	
8	Prefect	842.00	0.00	842.00	
9					
10					

The formula in cell C5 is: =IF(B5>1,000,(0.05*B5),0). This means, if the value in B5 is greater than $1,000 multiply it by 0.05, otherwise the discount will be zero. Cell D5 will calculate the amount net of discount, using the formula: =B5-C5. The same conditional formula with the cell references changed will be found in cells C6, C7 and C8. **Strictly**, the variables £1,000 and 5% should be entered in a **different part** of the spreadsheet.

6.4.2 Examination results

Suppose the pass mark for an examination is 50% and you want to see easily from a long list who has passed and who has failed. If a candidate's score is in cell B2, an appropriate formula for cell C2 would be: =IF(B2<50,'FAILED','PASSED').

As you may have noticed from an earlier example, the placing of text in inverted commas in a conditional function will cause the text to be printed out or displayed as appropriate.

6.5 Graphics

It is usually possible to convert tabulated data in a spreadsheet into a variety of bar chart or graphical formats.

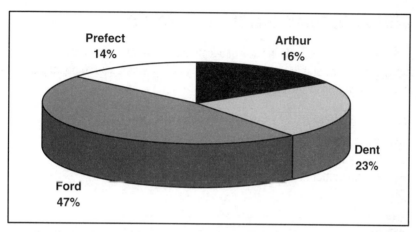

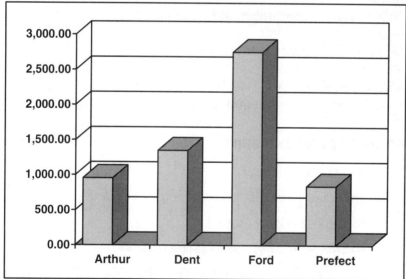

6.5.1 Other spreadsheet features

Excel offers many more facilities for analysing data.

(a)   If you go to the **formula bar** in Excel, and click on the = sign you will get a list of options such as SUM, AND so on, including Averages and NPV analysis, correlation and regression and so on.

(b)   The help facility also lists everything you can do.

6.6 Avoiding over-complex models

When building a spreadsheet model to analyse your data, be sure to remember the following key points.

(a)   **Do not make your spreadsheet more complex** than it has to be – for some calculations, a pocket calculator will be just as good.

(b)   Use **the auditing tool to check your formulae are correct.**

(c)   Check your formulae are correct by doing some manual calculations

(d)   Do a trial run. If you are not quite sure what you want to do, experiment with a small number of data items before applying them wholesale.

7 What the examiner wants you to do

The Pilot Projects and first live projects include between them several different examiner requirements. It is important that you notice what it is precisely that the examiner wants you to do, and this involves analysing carefully the wording of the project.

They include:

- Critically evaluate
- Examine in detail
- Explain and demonstrate or illustrate
- Discuss
- Suggest
- Assess
- Write a report ...... summarising and explaining
- Analyse
- Set out a recommended course of action ....
- Highlight the difficulties
- Identify and discuss
- Provide a preliminary evaluation of ....

7.1 What do these phrases mean?

Describe	State the key features of
Explain	Make clear, or state the meaning of or rationale behind
Identify	Recognise, choose or establish
Illustrate	Describe or explain something using an example
Demonstrate	Prove the accuracy or certainty of something; show that something happens
Reconcile	Make something consistent or compatible with something else
Solve	Find an answer
Analyse	Examine a structure in detail
Compare	Show the similarities
Contrast	State the differences
Discuss	Conduct an argument about; state the pros and cons
Evaluate	Appraise or assess the value (or lack of value) of something

Recommend	Advise and state a course of action
Suggest	Make a suggestion as to a course of action: it is not necessarily the only course of action
Assess	Evaluate a situation

You should also look out for any format that the examiner specifies. Quite often you are required to produce a report or a memo, but the requirement may be a little more unusual. For example, in recent projects students have been asked to:

- write an article for a magazine, addressing various issues
- prepare a presentation, including visual aids such as PowerPoint slides (the ability to present being regarded as a key management skill)

The Module A examiner has made it clear that if visual aids are part of the requirements of the question, then marks will be allocated to them, and therefore they are marks lost if no visual aids are produced or if they are of poor quality.

Chapter Roundup

- You should start by reading the project through a couple of times, in order to get the gist of it.

- Try to summarise the data by précising it for your own understanding and carrying out an information audit.

- Then explore the project in detail by analysing the numbers and considering the position of the business involved.

- Review and then organise your data, possibly using a spreadsheet package such as Microsoft Excel.

- If the data lends itself to this, you can then model the data.

- Make sure you understand what the examiner requires from you.

Further research

4

Introduction

You will probably have to research the topics covered in your project questions to some extent, even if the research only extends to consulting the relevant BPP Learning Media study text. The ACCA have said that any additional research required will not be extensive, however an understanding of the context in which the subject company operates is essential.

This chapter explains the difference between primary and secondary research, the two main types, and also suggests various avenues of research, depending on the project topic you are dealing with.

Since all projects will be different (and some may require no additional research at all), we can only approach the issues in fairly general terms here.

1 Research in the DipFM projects

It is possible, but not necessarily inevitable, that you will need to do some research of your own into the topics in your projects.

1.1 Example 1

The Pilot Assignment for Subject Area 1, Interpretation of Financial Statements, provides you with a supplement containing extracts from the accounts of Dorling Kindersley, the educational publishing company.

In part (a) of the assignment you are required to use the information in the supplement to critically evaluate a given quotation from the Chairman's Statement. Although the assignment wants you to focus on the position of Dorling Kindersley, it could be helpful to research the position of similar companies in order to obtain a better perspective on DK's financial position.

In part (b) of the assignment, you are required to engage in a more general discussion of revenue recognition and expenditure recognition in financial reporting. Additional research could be useful here, to enable you to analyse the policies of different companies in contrast to Dorling Kindersley.

1.2 Example 2

The Pilot Assignment for Subject Area 2, Performance Management, asks you to produce a report for the directors of a company on just-in-time and MRP II systems. Although your basic research for this part of the assignment would probably start with the BPP Performance Management study text, some further reading around these management techniques would be of value in producing your answer.

This chapter therefore will discuss various research techniques which you may find of help when carrying out the further research needed to answer the assignments for each Module.

2 Types of research methods: a short practical guide

Before launching into the practical detail, you might be as well to consider the **assumptions** upon which your choice of research methods is based. If you have certain prejudices as to what matters, then this might affect your review of the data or indeed the type of research you do.

There are many different approaches to research, but we will illustrate some contrasting approaches as used in business to draw out some of the key issues.

Exercise   **Research methods**

What would you say are the key differences between the research methods below?

Situation 1

You have just been into a new fast food outlet. After your meal, a uniformed member of staff approaches you and says 'I am carrying out a survey into how customers view the quality and service we supply. By collecting a representative view of our customers' needs, we will be able to improve our service. The results will be fed into a database and anonymity is guaranteed'. You are then asked a series of pre-scripted questions, to which you must choose an option for an answer. (For example, 'would you rate our food as poor, fair, good or excellent?') After answering the questions, the interviewer takes some of your personal details, thanks you and then proceeds to another table asking the same questions.

Situation 2

A pharmaceutical company is researching a new type of vaccine for influenza. Its scientists believe there could be a relationship between certain aspects of the virus's chemistry and the immune system.

It has given small doses of the vaccine to ten paid volunteers, who for the duration of the test are living in a special research facility. These volunteers are being monitored to see how the vaccine affects them when they are exposed to flu. At another research facility, the same number of volunteers is being given a 'placebo' and are also exposed to the virus.

Blood tests will be taken, so that scientists can see how the vaccine affects the body's response to the flu virus.

Situation 3

You have been asked to join a small group of five people for an evening to do some 'focus group research' on makes of car. The researcher introduces topics of conversation and asks people what they feel about motoring, what they feel about different brands of car, what their motoring habits are, and what frustrates them most about motoring and motor cars.

The researcher intervenes from time to time to steer the conversation to topics of interest or to clarify what people have said.

Situation 4

A researcher for an investment banking firm is reviewing companies engaged in e-commerce. She has obtained financial statements of twenty firms, and also details of movements in their respective share prices over the past four years. From this she compares data and compiles a report.

Answer

Situation 1

Seeks to find out **objective** facts that have some statistical relevance, from which inferences can be drawn. This sort of research is **quantitative** in that it aims to obtain a sample of data and generalise responses from it. It is **descriptive in that it describes the current state of affairs.** It might also seek to examine the relationships between two variables: rating of food and age of customer. Does a person's age correlate with their appreciation of the food?

Situation 2

Seeks to draw out **objective** facts, and is **testing a hypothesis** against empirical data. Of course, a small sample of ten may not be enough to get a general view, but it is strong evidence that further research could be useful.

Situation 3

Features quite often in the early stage of market research and, indeed, in other areas of research. It is called qualitative research.

Clearly the researcher is not trying to prove anything, nor is the researcher trying to find out objective facts from which statistical inferences can be made – the sample is obviously not meaningful and the questioning is not controlled. The researcher is trying to tease out ideas from what people say they feel about the situation.

What the researcher is probably doing is trying to come up with **ideas** for further research, no more. If, say, one of the people in the group was to say that 'car designers have no appreciation of the needs of parents carrying heavy shopping and looking after children', this would give them a lot to think about.

Situation 4

The data is easily obtained, and it is not new knowledge. The main purpose of the research is, however, to analyse and draw relationships between different areas of the data, to see if there might be common features which all the sample of companies share.

To summarise, here are some key words describing the type of research encountered in the situations.

Situation	Key words	Summary
1 Market research	Statistical Objective Descriptive Quantitative	Describing facts and relationships
2 Research into a vaccine	Objective Experimental Testing hypotheses Scientific	Testing hypotheses
3 Focus group	Qualitative Non-statistical Relationships Generate ideas	Exploring ideas
4 Investment banker	Relationships Analysis Factual	Analysis

Each of these types of research approach is legitimate in its own right, and you may use a combination of them in working on your project.

3 Primary and secondary research

3.1 What sort of research do I have to do?

There are two principal types of research, which we touched upon briefly in the last chapter; primary research, collecting primary data, and secondary research, collecting secondary data.

As you read through the notes below, it will help if you keep the following in mind.

	Secondary data	Primary data
What it is	Data neither collected directly by the user nor specifically for the user, often under conditions unknown to the user – in other words, data collected not by YOU but by someone else for their own purposes or for general use	Data that is collected specifically by or for the user, at source, in other words by YOU in the course of carrying out the project.
Quantitative, 'factual' or 'objective' example	**Government reports** – in the UK a good example is Social Trends, which contains government statistics about British society, employment in different industries, attitudes and so on. A company's published **financial statements summarise** and interpret company transactions data for the benefit of **shareholders**, not the needs of a student carrying out a DipFM project.	A survey you conduct with a questionnaire you have designed, with regard to a sample. You aim to get a statistically significant result. An experiment
Qualitative example	An article in *Finance Matters* or in a book about performance management techniques	A focus group you have conducted (in the manner of Situation 3 above) to talk about motivation

Below is an example from an unpublished undergraduate dissertation. Identify areas of primary and secondary research.

3.2 Example

1 Initially the work I carried out on the project was extremely informal in that whenever I met a salesman or spoke to a manager I would ask them about their feelings towards the present pay scheme or the method by which targets were allocated. When salesmen complained about errors in their commission payment due to faults in the payment scheme I was in an ideal position to suggest to managers changes and refinements in the pay scheme.

2 Following this initial exploration I decided to familiarise myself with the theory behind targeting specifically and, more generally, how information and control systems influence behaviour. At the same time as this I spoke to people outside Q both from academic backgrounds, so as to develop ideas, and in other selling companies, so as to compare Q with other selling firms.

3 Once I felt well briefed about the problem I sought permission from the Southern Sales Director (Mr X) to interview his sales managers. He requested a questionnaire which I forwarded to him. Mr X made minor adjustments to this in form rather than content. For example, one question I asked was, 'Why do you think Q has higher turnover of salesmen than other similar companies?', this was changed to: 'Do you think Q has a higher turnover of salesmen than other similar companies? If so, why?

4 I developed the questionnaire with the background knowledge I had acquired and discussed some of the questions with Mr A, the Statistics and Finance Manager, my immediate superior.

5 Over a period of about a month I interviewed five sales managers, each interview lasting about one hour. I felt the questionnaire was a little restrictive, therefore I chose to approach the interviews informally using the questionnaire as a check that I had covered most of the points. This was specifically important as I felt that the psychological atmosphere of the interview would be at least

as important as the mechanics of the interview. I realised that this would require me to be flexible, however, I didn't realise how flexible I would have to be. I organised one interview and found that this manager shared his room with another manager so I spent much of the interview making notes on discussion between the two of them, myself acting as a catalyst when discussion wained. This particular interview was especially useful since it uncovered issues such as the education and training of management that would otherwise have been overlooked. I decided to make written notes rather than a tape-recording because I thought this might be offputting to the managers.

6   During the interviewing and recording process I tried to avoid personal bias and judgement and when incorporating findings into this text I tried to avoid jumping to simplistic conclusions without considering their implications.

3.2.1 Comment

The vast majority of this is primary research both quantitative and exploratory. Secondary research is only referred to in paragraph 2.

3.3 How much research do I have to do?

This is the crux of the matter. For some projects, perhaps virtually no research, apart from referring to DipFM textbooks; for other projects, perhaps a great deal. Since the projects change every six months, it is difficult to predict.

Here are some examples of the types of additional research that would have been useful in projects set to date.

- Comparison of the accounting ratios of Dorling Kindersley with those of another educational publisher
- Research into revenue recognition
- Research into the use of JIT, MRPII and OPT
- Supply chain management
- Difficulties of applying the principles of corporate governance to a smaller quoted company
- Best accounting practice in the valuation of inventory for a chain of stores
- The attributes that a venture capitalist would find attractive in a management team
- Further uses for activity based techniques
- Telecoms: mobile phone operators in developing countries
- Use and value of the balanced scorecard
- Choice of accounting policy and use of operating leases by low cost airlines

3.4 Relevance to the projects

The main way in which you are likely to use primary research in producing an answer to a project assignment is by obtaining documents (most likely examples: sets of accounts) which you then analyse and compare with the data given in the project itself.

It is far more likely that your additional research will centre around secondary data.

4 Secondary data, including the internet

You are far more likely to use secondary data for the DipFM project assignments. Remember, that is information gathered by someone else, not for the specific purpose of producing an answer to an assignment.

The following is a guide to the use of secondary data. It can only be couched in the most general terms, as each project assignment is unique and has its own data requirements.

4.1 Where should you look?

The starting point could be the BPP Learning Media DipFM study text for the relevant subject area.

4.2 Example

The Pilot Assignment for Subject Area 4, Risk Management, starts with a quotation from a document published by the Organisation for Economic Co-operation and Development (the OECD). The assignment then asks you to discuss the implementation of good corporate governance, and to consider the difficulties that might face smaller quoted companies.

The starting point for your research would be the BPP Risk Management Study Text, to establish some basic principles, but you would then need to carry out some wider research, specifically perhaps into the issue of smaller companies.

4.3 External secondary data

It is hard to give detailed rules about where you should look, except that you should search for **relevant** data, and will probably make use of the Internet. Clearly, the use of **secondary** data is going to be more crucial for some topics than others.

Books

For the technical knowledge covered by the other syllabuses in the DipFM qualification, you might consult (in addition to the BPP Learning Media Study Text) the other books on the **ACCA's reading list** if they are relevant to your project. You will find the reading list at the front of each BPP textbook and also on the DipFM section of the ACCA's website.

Articles in the ACCA's *Finance Matters* magazine often refer to books that have been published recently – if there is an article relevant to your project then it might have **references**. (This is also true of other journals.)

Your college or public library. Even if you do not know what you are looking for, you may find some time spent browsing is quite useful. Many libraries use the Dewey Decimal System – there is no need to go into this here, but this is a well-established means of classifying books.

Bookshops which sell over the internet sometimes enable you to type in a Key Word, which might generate some titles about a topic – even if you do not buy them, you may find them in your local library.

4.3.1 Journals and articles

Your obvious first choice should be the ACCA's *Finance Matters*. This contains a wealth of articles relevant to the DipFM qualification, some by the examiners themselves. Otherwise, no list can be prescriptive.

A college library is likely to have other **academic journals**, such as the **Harvard Business Review**. Again, rather than list them here, you may be able to find a list from your own college library of what is published – perhaps an article may be obtained or copied for you.

Other business or current affairs journals and newspapers, such as the **Economist**, Financial Times, **Wall Street Journal** etc, may have surveys relevant to different business areas. These are all available on-line.

Trade journals are also useful – most countries have journals produced by relevant trade bodies, detailing developments in the industry. You can use the Internet to access the websites of **trade associations**. Increasingly, businesses in an industry are setting up electronic markets.

4.4 Example

The UK has a large and developed printing and publishing industry. The trade body, PIRA, aims to promote best practice and has an extensive publication programme. Two examples – of many industry publications – are:

- The Bookseller – for the retail book trade
- Paper focus – for paper buyers

The **Internet** is an excellent source of secondary data if used with care.

(a) For example, you can use a **search engine** which will bring up websites of interest. Some websites will allow you to download articles. Some of these websites – the **Economist Intelligence Unit** is one – offer articles for download. Another is www.ft.com. Many of these will be in PDF (portable document file) format. You will need to download **Adobe Acrobat Reader** for this – fortunately Acrobat Reader is **free** and it is possible that the site will have a link to Adobe to enable you to download the software yourself.

(b) Your internet service provider may also refer you to magazines and on-line newspapers.

Here are some general business websites which you may find helpful as a starting point when reading round issues covered in the assignments.

- www.ft.com

This website (the site of the Financial Times) provides information about current international business. You can search for information and articles on specific industry groups as well as individual companies.

- www.economist.com

Here you can search for business information on a week-by-week basis, search articles by business subject and use the resources of the Economist Intelligence Unit to research sectors, companies or countries.

- www.bpp.com

Our website provides information about BPP products and services, with a link to the ACCA website.

- www.strategy-business.com

This website includes articles from *Strategy & Business.*

- www.invweek.co.uk

This site carries business news and articles on markets from Investment Week and International Investment.

- www.pwcglobal.com/uk

The PricewaterhouseCoopers website includes UK Economic Outlook.

- www.bbc.co.uk

The website of the BBC carries general business information as well as programme-related content.

- www.accaglobal.com
- www.accountingweb.com

A US site with articles on current accounting related issues. The site is searchable by accounting topic.

- www.pwebopaedia.com

An online dictionary and search engine for computer and Internet terminology

Government ministries and agencies

Government agencies are good sources of economic and other statistical information. Most countries have an agency that provides national statistics. This varies significantly from country to country in terms of what is produced and the format, but you should be able to find:

(a) Economic data (eg UK Annual Abstract of Statistics)
(b) Social data (eg on population size and structure)
(c) Market data (eg export promotion)

4.4.1 Regulatory bodies and industry associations

There are many quasi-government and other public sector bodies which can provide data on particular industry sectors.

4.4.2 Other sources

There are some sources of data which you may not be able to access in a personal capacity, but which your employer might have access to, by virtue of being in a particular industry or dealing with clients from a particular industry. These include:

- A business directory (eg Kompass)
- Market research data (eg Nielsen consumer surveys)

5 Using secondary data

5.1 Introduction

Secondary data is used in many business situations, not just in academic research. Secondary data can:

- Provide a backdrop to primary research
- Act as a substitute for field research
- Be used as a technique in itself

5.1.1 Backdrop to primary research

Secondary data may also be used to set the **parameters** for primary research. In an **unfamiliar field**, it is natural that the researcher will carry out some **basic research** in the area, using journals, existing reports, the press and any contacts with relevant knowledge. Such investigations will provide guidance on a number of areas.

- Possible data sources
- Data collection
- Methods of collection (relevant populations, sampling methods and so on)

5.1.2 Substitute for primary research

The (often substantial) **cost** of primary research **might be avoided** should existing secondary data be sufficient. Given the low response rate available for questionnaires, secondary research might do the job just as well. There are some situations however, in which secondary data is bound to be **insufficient**.

5.1.3 A technique in itself

Some types of information can **only be acquired through secondary data**, in particular **trends** over time. The **historical data** published on, say, trends in the behaviour of an industry over time, cannot realistically be replaced by a one-off study.

5.2 How reliable is secondary data?

The quality of the secondary data

(a) Why was **the data** being collected in the first place? Preparers may have an axe to grind; trade associations may not include data which runs counter to the interest of its members.

(b) Random samples with a poor response rate are particularly questionable.

(c) The secondary data may be old and out of date. Government statistics and information based on them are often relatively dated, though information technology has speeded up the process.

Advantages arising from the use of secondary data.

(a) Secondary data may solve the problem **without** the need for any primary research: **time and money is thereby saved**.

(b) Secondary data sources are a great deal **cheaper** than those for primary research.

(c) Secondary data, while not necessarily fulfilling your information needs, can be of great use by:

(i) **Setting the parameters**, defining a hypothesis, highlighting variables, in other words, helping to focus on the central problem

(ii) **Providing guidance**, by showing past methods of research and so on, for primary data collection

(iii) **Helping to assimilate the primary research** with past research, highlighting trends and the like

5.2.1 Issues to bear in mind in secondary data

Topic	Comment
Relevance	The data may not be relevant to the research objectives in terms of the data content itself, classifications used or units of measurement.
Cost	Although secondary data is usually cheaper than primary data, some specialist reports can cost large amounts of money.
Availability	Secondary data may not exist in the specific product or market area.
Bias	The secondary data may be biased, depending on who originally carried it out and for what purpose. Attempts should be made to obtain the most original source of the data, to assess it for such bias.

Topic	Comment
Statistical accuracy	Was the sample representative?
	Was the questionnaire or other measurement instrument(s) properly constructed?
	Were possible biases in response or in non-response dealt with and accounted for?
	Was the data properly analysed using appropriate statistical techniques?
	Was a sufficiently large sample used?
	Does the report include the raw data?
	In addition, was any raw data omitted from the final report, and why?
Sufficiency	Even after fulfilling all the above criteria, the secondary data may be insufficient and primary research would therefore be necessary.

The golden rule when using secondary data is **use only meaningful data**.

(a)   **Begin with internal sources** and a firm with a good management information system should be able to provide a great deal of data.

(b)   External information should be consulted in order of ease and speed of access: directories, catalogues and indexes before books, abstracts and periodicals

(c)   **Do not accept it at face value.** The **internet, for example, is a mine of misinformation**.

For the DipFM projects, follow the **key rules** below to keep control of your use of secondary data.

```
KEY RULES

Reference

Record

Review

Relate
```

We suggest that whenever you use an item of secondary data, you prepare a **sheet** as follows.

Data item	Fill in
Reference	
• Source	
• Author	
• When and how obtained	
Record	
Attach photocopy/print out or take notes – see Reference above if you want to rely on them	

Data item	Fill in
Review	
• What is the data saying?	
Relate	
• How does this tie in with the assignment objectives?	
• How does it relate to other areas of the project, eg primary research?	
• Do I intend to use it – if so, how?	

6 Primary research

Primary research obtains the data particularly relevant to the project you have. Read the following extract from an unpublished undergraduate dissertation.

6.1 Example

The **aim** was to find out what environmental information companies make available to external parties and how useful this is. I decided that the best **method** to gather this information was to become an external party myself and write to them asking for their annual reports and any published environmental information. This way, my research would **not be subject to individual company bias** concerning what they publish, as a survey or interview may be.

Comparisons were only made on the information that I received. This may have had its limitations in that more information could exist, but this was **a representative sample of what an average external reader** would receive – the objective in question.

I **selected** seven companies to request such information from, this small number would allow a more detailed focus on issues. Companies were selected from those mentioned in past ACCA environmental reports together with two randomly selected companies of my own (Dixons and Allied Domeqc).

The dimensions of performance that I concentrated my analysis on were based upon the main points that the first chapter of the literature review discovered. This would enable me to discover if what writers believed was actually being communicated and if what I found was disclosed in reality, matched.

The **annual reports** were requested, to see what **environmental disclosure** they contained and also to discover if any financial environmental information was present in anticipation of the future environmental accounting chapter.

I feel this chapter was a very effective use of primary research. However, one **weakness** was the narrow range of companies considered. A study of companies not recommended by ACCA and operating in several differing industries, may provide more issues. Although this may prove difficult if not enough environmental data is disclosed to make comparisons. To question the companies via telephone rather than an 'official' letter may result in a more relaxed attitude reaping more open responses.

6.1.1 Environmental questionnaire

Next, I wanted to discover how the **internal background of the firms can affect the external environmental communication** they may or may not produce.

I thought a **questionnaire** was appropriate to reach the large amount of companies that I wanted to involve. I chose thirty companies from the catalogue of annual reports at Wheatley library (see appendix twelve), consciously trying to include a range of industries. Measures were implemented to increase the chances of companies replying.

- I obtained contact names by telephoning the companies beforehand.
- A stamped addressed envelope was enclosed for replies.
- Anonymity was ensured.
- The questions took a closed category format, meaning all respondents had to do was tick relevant boxes.
- Only fourteen questions were asked.

I also structured the questions to start general before getting more specific to ease respondents into the correct way of thinking. The questionnaire can be seen in appendix eleven.

My approach was successful, indicated by the 73% response rate of which 18% were unwilling to take part. This left me with 18 completed questionnaires, split equally over service and manufacturing industries.

To conduct my analysis I first **identified the main categories** of environmental disclosure methods and issues that the majority of the companies portrayed. I then **formed questions** from these categories, seen in table 6.1, which I used for testing. These were answered in a basic 'yes' or 'no' manner but supplemented with detailed information within the appendices. I only based observations upon the companies I was studying and so they became each others benchmarks for my comments.

6.2 Points to note

Some matters to note – from the words in the text highlighted in **bold**.

(a) The research had a purpose or aim.
(b) The method was developed from the aim.
(c) The author is concerned about the reliability of the data.
(d) The author described the analysis done.
(e) The questionnaire required quite a lot of work in designing and getting them completed.

We do not go into any further detail about primary research here, as it is extremely unlikely that you will use it in the context of completing your DipFM projects. If you engage in research it will almost certainly be secondary research.

7 How good is your data?

Once you have done the research you **intended** to do, you should draw your data together and take a hard look at it as a whole, the secondary data and possibly the primary data.

Remember that the DipFM Projects are only **deadline driven** to the extent of the twice-yearly dates for submission, nor is there a syllabus as such, apart from the broad parameters of the syllabus for each subject area. You will be marked on your ability to do some analysis and communication.

7.1 Ask yourself these questions

Question	Yes/No
1 Have I done all that I set out to do?	
2 Does the data I have obtained give me a chance to conduct an analysis on the lines of the assignment objective?	
3 If the answer to (1) or (2) is no, have I obtained data by another adequate route?	
4 Have I made sure I have referenced and recorded my data?	
5 ACID TEST Does the data I have collected put me on the right path for fulfilling the project objective?	

8 Plagiarism

As a committed professional, you should not have to read this section!

Your project is original work. Do not pretend that others' work is your own – always cite your sources, and give credit where it is due.

Sadly, some students seem to ignore the strictures against syndication and plagiarism. It is equivalent, perhaps, to cheating in a exam. Academic staff the world over are wise to all the ploys – you will get caught, so don't try.

Plagiarism can be defined as the borrowing, copying, stealing or unacknowledged use of work done by another person.

If you quote someone else's work, you must acknowledge that fact, by constructing a bibiography at the end of your assignment answer, and you must also acknowledge the fact that you are quoting someone else in the text of the answer itself.

The completion of the DipFM projects is intended to be the work of the student submitting the project, not that of anyone else. The ACCA has warned that it will take very seriously any accusations of cheating, or the suggestion that a student's work is not entirely their own.

To this end, the ACCA demands that all projects be submitted in typed format. This will enable the scanning of your project and the application of software that can, for example, detect a change in writing styles and other indications of more than one author. It is vital therefore that you ensure that the work is your own. The ACCA is also likely to monitor organisations offering DipFM tuition.

The ACCA published an article on plagiarism and its various forms in issue 53 of *Finance Matters*. We reproduce an extract from it here.

CHEATING AND PLAGIARISM

Cheating is a deliberate and intended action, using trickery, practising deceit, or violating rules dishonestly. For the Diploma in Financial Management, ACCA requires that projects are a reflection of the candidate's own work, own ideas and own words. Any of the following acts would lead to candidate failing a project and the likely removal of the candidate from the programme:

- Impersonation – this means to undertake a piece of assessed work on behalf of, or to pretend to be, another student, or allowing another person to undertake an assessment on your behalf, or pretend to be you.

- Substitution – this means submitting other people's work as though it were your own – either with, or without, their knowledge.

- Duplication – this means submitting work for assessment that is the same as, or broadly similar to, work submitted earlier for academic credit, without acknowledgement of the previous submission.

- Falsification – this includes the invention of data, their alteration, copying data from any other source, or otherwise obtaining them by unfair means, or inventing quotations and/or references.

- Collusion – this is a secret agreement or co-operation with others, especially for a deceitful purpose, and includes copying or sharing another candidate's work, with his/her secret agreement that you can do so, or lending your work to another candidate in the reasonable knowledge that some or all of it will be copied, or secretly working with others jointly to produce a piece of work that is supposed to be your own work.

- Plagiarism – this means taking or using another person's thoughts, writings or inventions and presenting them as though they were your own.

To acknowledge the work of others is more than a matter of good academic practice – it is the foundation stone of all academic practice. This is why so much attention is placed on correct referencing, and why candidates may find themselves unwittingly guilty of plagiarising because they have failed to follow the correct referencing procedures. Ignorance, however, is no excuse and plagiarism will be heavily penalised as it is viewed as a serious matter of cheating.

Plagiarism is not a complicated issue – if you quote/use the actual words of another author, or if you express the thoughts of an author in your own words, and you do not indicate (a) that you have done so, and (b) where those words or thoughts can be found in published form, then you have plagiarised.

You will find more information and advice about how to avoid plagiarism at the following website: http://cibs.tamu.edu/eden/plagiarism.html, which gives a list of other useful websites on plagiarism. In particular, the website http://sja.ucdavis.edu/avoid.html gives a very readable set of examples of what is plagiarism and what is not – with a few tips on how to deal correctly with attributing the work of others.

9 Referencing

9.1 How to Reference Your Work and Construct a Bibliography

9.1.1 Referencing

Whenever you are directly quoting or referring to one of your sources of information, you should acknowledge this in the text as you go along. References should be clearly set out using the Harvard System. It is important to double check that all references in your text appear in the bibliography.

9.1.2 Bibliography

Your bibliography comes at the end of your Report. It is a list of all the sources you have used in compiling your Report eg books, articles, company publications, newspaper articles etc. The bibliography should be set out alphabetically using the Harvard System.

9.1.3 How to reference your work and construct a bibliography

Correctly referencing your work is simple, and compulsory. You must reference all your sources of information. We do advise you to reference as you go along, rather than leaving it until the end of your assignment. There is nothing more time consuming than constructing a bibliography retrospectively.

9.1.4 References within your text

In the Harvard system references within the text are set out as follows:

9.1.5 EXAMPLE

In any organisation made up of different interest groups some conflict over goals is inevitable (Needle, 1994).

In the bibliography the reference shown above would appear in this way:

EXAMPLE OF A BOOK REFERENCE

Needle, D. (1994) <u>Business in Context</u>. 2nd Edition, London, Chapman & Hall

NB: You only cite the edition if it is not the first. Please note that the title of the book is either underlined or emboldened.

EXAMPLE OF A JOURNAL OR NEWSPAPER REFERENCE

Buxton, J. (1998) Management: The Growing Business: Co-operative's Wheels of Fortune. <u>The Financial Times</u>, February 24

NB: It's the title of the journal or newspaper that is either underlined or emboldened.

EXAMPLE OF A JOURNAL ARTICLE WHERE NO AUTHOR IS GIVEN

<u>The Economist</u> (1997) 'New technology is no snap', October 11, p125

Citing Electronic Sources

No standard, agreed method has yet evolved for citing electronic sources. Electronic sources may include eftp sites, telnet addresses, WWW and gopher pages, newsgroups and e-mail messages. The following book should help:

Li, Xia and Crane, Nancy B. (1996) Electronic styles, a handbook for citing electronic information 2nd Edition, Medford, N.J., Information Today

There are also several guides you can view on the Internet.

A recommended example of a guide to citing Internet sources is accessible via: http://cis.bournemouth.ac.uk/servicedepts/newlis/LIS_Gen/citation/harvardsystint.html

NB: This has a useful one-page summary as an appendix.

A simplified solution might be:

Author's last name, First name. Title of work. *Title of complete work if applicable in italics.* [protocol and address] [path] (date of message or visit).

9.1.6 EXAMPLE

Walker, Janice R. MLA-Style Citations of Electronic Sources.

http://www.cas.usf.edu/english/walker/mla.html 11 September 1996

If you have a variety of sources, you may want to split them into categories for your bibliography. A logical split might be:

(a) **References**: publications etc to which you have referred specifically in the text
(b) **Bibliography**: additional reading undertaken but not directly referred to in the text

Referencing correctly is also vital because it provides comfort that you have not plagiarised the work of anyone else. Whenever you mention thoughts or words of other people, you must attribute the source in the text and then give it in full in the bibliography. The external examiner has commented that in some cases students don't use enough external references, and in others they don't reference them properly. This can cause you to fail the project.

You may see in one book you are reading a reference to a source that the author has used and you may want to refer to that source yourself. In such a situation, you should make every effort to find a copy of the quoted source, so that you can quote it directly. If that is not possible (for example it is out of print or your library cannot locate a copy to borrow for you) you can refer to the book as follows:

Raimond, P. (1993) Management Projects. London, Chapman and Hall. Cited in Saunders, M., Lewis, P. and Thornhill, A. (2000) Research Methods for Business Students 2nd edition, Harlow, Financial Times Prentice Hall

This indicates clearly to the reader that you are citing something you have not read yourself, merely seen cited in another book.

Chapter Roundup

- This chapter has covered research.

- The type of research you adopt will vary according to the assignment objective.

- The research you do should be determined by the project objective. It may be the case that you will need to do none apart from refer to the relevant BPP study text, although it is likely that you will have to read around the topic to an extent.

- There are many sources of secondary data. You may need to do some primary research also.

- It is absolutely vital that your work is entirely your own. If you include the writings or thoughts of another person, you must acknowledge that fact. If you do not, you could be guilty of plagiarism.

Report writing skills

Topic list
1 The DipFM requirements
2 Writing your report
3 Style
4 Suggested structure
5 Format
6 Writing good English
7 Writing bad English
8 Common mistakes
9 Punctuation
10 Spelling problems
11 Language

Introduction

The various projects issued by the ACCA will have different requirements, but the feature that they are most likely to have in common is the production of a report. Even if you are not specifically asked for a report, you will inevitably be doing some lengthy piece of writing. In Module A in spring 2003 it was writing a speech.

This chapter covers the style and structure of a good report, and aims to make you aware of some of the problems habitually encountered by students.

Please do not feel insulted by the inclusion of some of the points mentioned here, if you feel that they are not relevant to you because your writing style is already well polished. Have a glance through them: you may find an explanation for an area of grammar you have never understood!

1 The DipFM requirements

Completing the questions that are included in the two projects will test different skills from those tested in the formal exams on Modules A and B. The projects themselves will be very different from those exams, and, in all likelihood, any exams that you have done before.

You have a maximum of up to 5,000 words for each entire project. Given the move towards greater integration of subject areas by the two examiners, the projects are tending to consist of a number of sections of one longer question, with marks allocated to each section. See the 2005 Module A project as an example of this. You should use the mark allocations to calculate roughly how much of your overall word count to devote to each section of the project. For example, if part (a) is worth 40 marks, it would be reasonable to allocate about 2,000 (40% × 5,000) words to that part. Don't waste your word allowance by using too many in proportion to the marks available for the earlier sections, so you cannot devote enough attention to the later sections.

This will be much longer, and much more detailed than the answers you are required to produce in the exams. The full written exam questions are each worth 20 marks, and should therefore take you 36 minutes to complete. At best, your answers to those questions will only be a few hundred words long.

You need to develop and practise your skills of report writing and writing in depth. You may even find that the 5,000 word suggestion for each of the projects is too restrictive for you, so that you write more than that. If that is the case, you will need to be capable of cutting the word count by the use of more succinct and precise language. Make sure also that you absorb the requirements. If an assignment tells you to discuss six issues, don't discuss more than that as it would use up some of your precious wordcount.

You must show the word count for your answer to each particular question within each assignment, and the total word count for the project as a whole. The individual word count must be shown clearly at the end of each individual answer. The total word count for the entire project must be shown on the submission form, which is supplied to you by the ACCA. Make sure that the sum of the individual work counts matches the total!

If you exceed 5,000 words, the marker will just stop marking at that point, no matter the quality of the work that may still be to come.

2 Writing your report

Your research turns up raw materials. Writing and rewriting turns them into finished, usable products.

For the writing to proceed efficiently, a logical structure for the report is needed. When you begin writing-up you might want to consider the following points:

(a) Is the purpose of the report clearly defined from the outset?

(b) Who or what is the target of your report? The intended target of the report can influence the way data is handled or the recommendations made.

The wording of the assignment itself should make this clear.

Examples

Write a report to the managing director ....

Write a report to the management accountant ....

Draft a memo to the members of your department .... (so are you in charge of the department, or are you one of its members, writing the memo to your colleagues?)

If the requirement of the assignment does not specify a recipient, assume that you are addressing the report, or other document, to the examiner and marker of the assignment.

(c) Is there a wider audience for the report? The likely audience could influence the style in which the report needs to be written (for example use of technical jargon, diagrammatic presentation of information). Again this will be made clear by the wording of the assignment's requirements. One project in the past has asked you to write a presentation for the Board of Directors.

(d) Are any recommendations made likely to be considered for action by the targeted audience?

The ACCA have offered the following guidance on presentation:

'Unless a question requires a particular format – for example, a report or a memo – projects may be presented in whichever format appears to be most suitable. The main concern should be to choose a format which is most helpful in supporting your analysis, arguments and conclusions. Projects must be written in English.'

2.1 Report plan

The advantage of having a clear structure is that your ideas and material are forced into some sort of order. If there is a great deal you want to say then order is essential, and a good way of achieving it is to produce a **report plan** at an early stage.

The best approach is to jot down all the things you want to say as a series of headings, with perhaps a little expansion of some points. Then look at them together and, by experiment if necessary, put them into a logical order by putting numbers against each. Only if you are very certain that your thoughts are logical and coherent should you omit putting them on paper as a plan - apart from any other reason, you are likely to forget vital material if you do not have a plan.

You might try writing 'network' notes to present your headings visually (see the diagram).

A network note

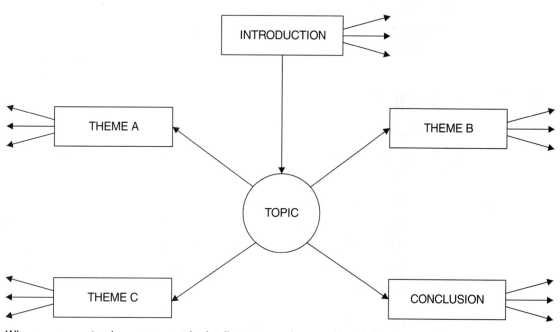

When you come to plan your report in detail, you can ask yourself the following questions.

(a) What is relevant to the user's requirements? Some of the information you have collected or produced by analysis will go in the main body of the report. Other information will be included as backing documentation.

(b) What is the information for: explanation? description? recommendation? instruction?

(c)   Do I need to follow a line of reasoning? If so, what is the most logical way in which data can be broken down, grouped, and organised, to make my reasoning clear?

(d)   Do I need to include my own personal views? If so, at what point: final recommendation, or throughout? What form should these take: recommendations or suggestions? interpretation? opinion? appraisal of options?

(e)   What can I do to make the report easier to read?

      (i)   Are there suitable section or sub-headings I can use to indicate effectively each stage of the information or argument?

      (ii)   Is the subject of the report too technical for the user? What vocabulary should I use to assist understanding? Will background or supporting information be helpful, perhaps in appendices to the report?

      (iii)   Do I have a clear introduction to ease the reader in to the subject, and a clear conclusion that will draw everything together?

      (iv)   Can I keep the main body of the report more concise by removing supporting information to **appendices**?

You could use the above questions as a **checklist** for planning your report. If you can then jot down a skeleton of the headings and sub-headings you have decided to use (with notes of any particular points that occur to you as you go along) you will be ready to write. The formal headings of standard business reports may be useful to help you to organise your thoughts - but may not be necessary or even advisable, if they simply act as a constraint on what you actually want to say, and how you want to shape your argument. You should not worry at this stage about having 'Terms of Reference', 'Procedures', 'Findings' and so on (discussed below), unless they provide a **relevant** framework for your report.

2.2 Draft version

Once you have assembled your material and established your plan, it is time to write the report itself along the lines of the plan. Many people suffer from writer's block at this point and simply cannot get started, writing paragraph after paragraph of introduction and throwing each away. If you have this problem, try starting on the main body first, then go back to the introduction and end with the conclusion.

3 Style

There are certain stylistic requirements in the writing of reports, formal or informal.

(a)   **Objectivity and impersonality**. Even in a report designed to persuade as well as inform, subjective value judgements and emotions should be kept out as far as possible: the bias, if recognised, can undermine the credibility of the report and its recommendations.

      (i)   Emotional or otherwise loaded words should be avoided.

      (ii)   In more formal reports, **impersonal constructions** should be used rather than 'I', 'we' and so on:

        It became clear that...
        Investigation revealed that...
        It can be argued that ...

      (iii)   Colloquialisms and abbreviated forms should be avoided in formal written English: colloquial 'I've', 'don't' should be replaced by 'I have' and 'do not'. You should not use slang expressions like 'got cheesed off': say 'was irritated'.

(b) **Ease of understanding**

(i) Avoid technical language and complex sentence structures for non-technical users. For example, the Spring 2002 project for Interpretation of Financial Statements required a report in response to a request from a shareholder. It therefore had to be written in relatively simple, non-technical language.

(ii) The material will have to be logically organised, especially if it is leading up to a conclusion or recommendation.

(iii) Relevant themes should be signalled by appropriate headings, or highlighted for easy scanning.

(iv) The layout of the report should display data clearly and attractively. Figures and diagrams should be used with discretion, and it might be helpful to highlight key figures which appear within large tables of numbers.

(c) **Precision**

(i) Be as precise as possible and avoid vague generalisations. Note the important differences between 'a few', 'some', 'many' and 'most'.

(ii) Recommendations should be specific and firm. 'I feel more could be done...' is too vague to be helpful. Say precisely what should be done: 'customers should receive a verbal explanation in layman's terms...'.

Various display techniques may be used to make the content of a report easy to identify and digest. For example, the relative importance of points should be signalled, each point may be referenced, and the body of text should be broken up to be easy on the eye. These aims may be achieved as follows:

(a) **Headings**

Spaced out or **emboldened.** CAPITALS may be used for the main title.
Important headings, like sections of the report, may be in CAPITALS.
Underlining, *italics* or **bold** may be used for subheadings.

(b) **References**

Each section or point in a formal report should have a code for easy identification and reference.

Use different labelling for each type of heading

Main section headings

I,II,III,IV,V and so on or A,B,C,D,E

Paragraphs

1,2,3,4,5

Points and subpoints

(a), (b), (c) and (i), (ii), (iii)

Alternatively a 'decimal' system may be used (like the one used in this book):

- 1   Section 1
- 1.1   Subsection 1
- 1.1.1 Point 1
- 1.1.2 Point 2
- 1.2   Subsection 2
- 1.2.1 Point 1
- 2   Section 2

(c) **Spacing**

Intelligent use of spacing separates headings from the body of the text for easy scanning, and also makes a large block more attractive and digestible.

(d) **Consistency**

When you have chosen your style of headings, references and so on, apply it consistently in your report.

4 Suggested structure

Any report should be arranged so that the basic message and the main topics of argument emerge progressively and so that the conclusions and recommendations follow logically from those arguments and analysis.

All documents to be presented in a report, including any appendices, need to state clearly their contents, the source of the information and the date.

No strict version of a DipFM report structure is, or could be, imposed. The topics of the assignment will, in part, determine the structure of the report. However, a **generalised** structure is suggested below, with appropriate guidelines as necessary.

(a) **Title**

A succinct but precise title is desirable. It should immediately identify the subject matter.

(b) **Contents**

Besides detailing the chapters/sections involved, the contents page should also include a list of tables, diagrams and so on. It is the last thing to be written! Even if it only lists an introduction and one or two sections, it still gives a professional 'look' to your report.

(c) **Introduction**

This will probably be where the following topics are addressed.

(i) **Objectives and terms of reference**. What is the report about and why has it been written?

(ii) **Background material**

(iii) **Data collection and methods**

(d) **Findings**

Presentation, analysis and discussion of data and other research information. There should be a logical flow, with ideas being presented in sequence. In some cases, a chronological sequence may be appropriate.

If there is any sort of **problem** in the question in the assignment, your structure should be on the following lines.

- Analysing the facts of the situation
- Stating the principles of the matter in hand and any exceptions to them
- Applying those principles to the facts of the case
- Identifying any ambiguities and problems thrown up by this process

(e) **Conclusions**

The conclusions are directly drawn from the analysis and discussion. In the conclusion you are asked to present your findings, and use your judgement as to what the data means. The conclusion should be supported by the arguments in your report. A conclusion should contain:

- A clear presentation of findings from the information gathered
- Appropriate conclusions from the analysis related to the objectives of the report

To force yourself to ensure your conclusions are backed up by evidence, refer to relevant paragraph numbers in the main body of the report.

Example

Report

1   Meldarks ROCE has fallen from 15% to 10% in the past five years.

2   Net cash flows have switched from a net inflow of $3m to a net outflow of $0.5m.

3   Meldarks has kept buildings in the accounts at historical cost even though they are worth a lot more on a market value basis.

Conclusion

Meldarks' deteriorating ROCE (para 1) is made to look less obvious by low non-current asset valuations (para 3). This and the deteriorating cash flow (para 2) suggest that the company is in difficulties.

(f) **Recommendations**

Strong, well-founded proposals for change will reflect a successful project and an impressive report. Avoid non-committal recommendations and try to present recommendations in a logical order, for example presenting recommendations for the short, medium and long term in sequence.

For each recommendation the following can be tabulated.

- **What** is recommended
- **Who** needs to act on the recommendation
- **Costs and benefits** of the recommendation, with figures if possible, indicating the time scale involved
- **Cross-references** to the points in the report leading to the recommendation

(g) **Appendices**

To be included here are a listing of any references, any other appropriate bibliography, glossaries of technical terms used, and copies of any important supporting documentation. It may be necessary to include in an appendix any body of material that is too large or detailed for the findings section (for example extracts from sets of accounts).

The contents of your appendices are included in the overall word count. You should make sure that you cross refer the appendices to the main body of the project, so that the reader can follow your facts and argument easily.

(h)   **Executive summary**

Some long reports contain an executive summary, and you may well have encountered these at work. An executive summary is effectively a brief summary of the conclusions reached, and it is placed almost at the front of the report, straight after the terms of reference. This enables the reader to read the information in the main body of the report while already being aware of the conclusions reached.

The reports to be produced in answer to the style of DipFM assignment seen in the Pilot Projects and 'live' projects issued to date are probably not sufficiently long to warrant the inclusion of an executive summary. However, you could include one if you feel that it would be of benefit to the reader.

4.1 Presentation

The key is organisation: into sentences, into paragraphs, into chapters, into parts. A poorly organised report will be hard to read and it will be difficult for the reader to extract the value of the research you have done.

The ACCA specify that your projects must be word-processed on A4 paper in black ink, double line spaced and single sided. There must be a one inch margin, and you must use a minimum 12 point font size.

Your college may be able to devise a standard template for things like cover pages, contents pages, page layout and so on: this could be used by all your fellow students and would save a lot of time.

On the front page you should include the following information:

- student number
- date
- project title (eg Module A project)

The ACCA also request that you include all this information at the top of each page of the project, for example in the form:

0123456, Module A Project, May 2005, Page 1

The project submission form will require you to state the total number of pages being submitted. This will act as a cross check that all pages have been received when the project arrives at the ACCA.

The project document should be held together by a single staple in the top left hand corner, and the submission form should be placed separately on the top.

Make sure that the final version is spell checked by the computer. Some packages also have a grammar check, which you may find useful.

A word of warning about spell checkers: they will only detect wrongly spelt words, not situations where you have used the wrong word, albeit correctly spelt.

4.2 Example

'From' can be written as 'form'.

A spellchecker will not detect when you have omitted a word completely, especially a critically important word like 'not'.

4.3 Example

Consider the degree of difference between these two sentences.

'Therefore it is recommended that the company does go ahead with the project'.

'Therefore it is recommended that the company does not go ahead with the project'.

Your whole answer could hinge on one three letter word!

It is vital, therefore, that you **read through your report** in order to spot any errors like that. Even better, ask someone else, such as a friend or colleague, to read through it, as a fresh pair of eyes can often immediately see something which you have missed on half a dozen separate read throughs.

You may need to include graphs, charts or other diagrams where relevant. You should try to produce these using your PC, but if that is impossible, be very neat when drawing them (they should be clearly labelled) and make sure you include all the visual material to which you refer. Spreadsheet software might be used for presenting tabular information, and most modern packages also have fairly sophisticated graphic capabilities.

4.4 Accuracy and unity

Accuracy is probably the most important requirement of any research project - not just in terms of the honest presentation of data, but also in giving the correct emphasis to the main themes - in order that an objective and useful report results.

Keeping within the terms of reference and only addressing the central issue at hand will **enhance the unity** of the report. Leave out material that is not really relevant and avoid discussions of marginal issues.

4.5 Final version

Work on your draft so as to produce a finished report. The draft will have given you confidence and shown you, perhaps, any flaws in your argument. The break will have allowed your brain to sort things out into a better order and more fluent style. All new ideas should be noted on the draft copy before you start afresh to write the final version.

Suppose you prepare an early draft of your report and find that you have already written far too much?

4.6 Completing your project

A well-presented, professionally produced report attracts more positive attention than a scruffy set of papers.

Also remember that the finishing touches - typing, proofing, copying - nearly always take longer than you would expect.

4.7 Example: short reports

Just to give you a better feel for what a report is, here is a short report in skeleton form and then a written up report.

The short formal report is used in contexts such as middle management reporting to senior management. It is traditionally laid out according to certain basic guidelines. It will be split into logical sections, each referenced and headed appropriately.

TITLE   Ask yourself
I   TERMS OF REFERENCE
        (or INTRODUCTION) *What have I been asked to do?*
II   PROCEDURE (or METHOD) *How do I go about it?*
III   FINDINGS   *What do I discover?*
1   Section heading
2   Section heading
(a)   sub heading
(i)   sub point
IV   CONCLUSIONS   *What is the* general thrust *of the result?*
V   RECOMMENDATIONS   *What* particular recommendations *do I wish to make?*

SHORT FORMAL REPORT

TITLE   At the top of every report (or on a title page, for lengthy ones) should be the *title* of the report (its subject), **who** has prepared it, for **whom** it is intended, the **date** of completion, and the **status** of the report ('Confidential', 'Urgent' or whatever).

I   TERMS OF REFERENCE

Here is laid out the scope and purpose of the report: what is to be investigated, what kind of information is required, whether recommendations are to be made. This section may more simply be called '**Introduction**', and may include the details given above under '**Title**'. The title itself would then give only the subject of the report.

II   PROCEDURE or METHOD

This outlines the steps taken to make an investigation, collect data, put events in motion. Internet or library research carried out, documents or computer files consulted, computations or analyses made and so on should be briefly described.

III   FINDINGS

In this section the information itself is set out, with appropriate headings and sub-headings, if the report covers more than one topic. The content should be complete, but concise, and clearly structured in chronological order, order of importance, or any other *logical* relationship.

IV   CONCLUSIONS

This section allows for a summary of main findings (if the report is complex and lengthy). For a simpler report it may include **action taken** or decisions reached (if any) as a result of the investigation, or an expression of the overall 'message' of the report.

V   RECOMMENDATIONS

Here, if asked to do so in the terms of the assignment, the writer of the report may suggest the solution to the problem investigated so that the recipient will be able to make a decision if necessary.

4.8 Example: a short formal report

You are the management accountant of a company which specialises in producing dairy products for the slimming market. The results of your latest research have just been published (see below) and you have been asked to do the following.

(a)   Write a short formal report to the Marketing Director, Mr David Forsythe, highlighting the conclusions drawn from this research. Your recommendations will be used to help identify new products for possible development in this market

(b)   Choose an appropriate method for graphical presentation of each of the categories of research information provided and use it to present this data more effectively.

4.9 Market Research Results

This research was carried out from January to June 2006, using in-depth interviews in the respondents' homes, recorded on tape and interpreted by ourselves, 'The XYZ Research Agency', specialists in market research for the food industry.

Sample size: 500
Age range: 15-55
Socio-economic groups: ABC1*
Locations: Bristol, Manchester and Greater London
Sex: Males and Females

Three broad categories were tested and the results are as follows:

Motives for wanting to lose weight	% of respondents with weight problems mentioning
To feel good physically	68
For health reasons	67
To stay fit	43
Because I want to live longer	25
To stay mentally alert	23
To be more attractive	21
To be more popular	15

Methods for weight control	
Avoid certain foods, eat 'slimming items'	32
Eat and drink less	23
Play sports, keep 'fit'	22
'Have certain diet days'	7
Take medicines, stimulants	3

Food which people dislike giving up	% of respondents with weight problems mentioning
Cakes, pies, bakery products	31
Sweets, sugar	23
Beer, alcoholic beverages	17
Meat, sausages etc	15
Chocolate	13
Cream	9
Fruit juices	9
Potatoes	9
Pasta	9

In general, the comments also revealed that dieting means a loss of pleasure at mealtimes, causes problems when one can't eat the same as the family and also one is regarded as being 'ill' when dieting.

* Socio-economic groupings:

A   Higher managerial, Chief Executives etc.
B   Managerial, Executives etc
C1   Higher clerical, Supervisory etc

4.10 Solution

REPORT ON NEW PRODUCT DEVELOPMENT

(a)

Confidential

I   INTRODUCTION

This report highlights the conclusions drawn from market research into the slimming market conducted by The XYZ Research Agency between January and June 2006. The report, to include recommendations for possible new product development, was requested by Mr David Forsythe, Marketing Director. It was prepared by [Your Name] and submitted on [today's date].

II   METHODS

This report has been compiled from research findings designed to show:

(a)   respondents' motives for losing weight
(b)   respondents' methods of weight control
(c)   foods which respondents were reluctant to give up

Respondents were a sample group of 500 ABC1s aged 15-55 of both sexes in the Bristol, Manchester and Greater London areas. In-depth interviews were recorded in the respondents' homes, and analysed by XYZ Research: see part (b).

III   FINDINGS

1   *Motives for losing weight*

Most respondents expressed their motives for losing weight as the desire for physical well-being (68%), health (67%) and fitness (43%), with related concerns, such as longevity and mental alertness, also scoring over 20%.

Perhaps unexpectedly, the motives most commonly associated with 'slimming' - increased attractiveness and popularity - scored comparatively low, with 21% and 15% respectively.

2   *Methods of weight control*

The most frequently-stated method of weight control (32%) was based on food selection: consuming slimming items and avoiding certain foods. Reduced consumption in general (23%) and increased physical activity (22%) featured strongly, however, compared to the use of medicines and stimulants, mentioned by only 3% of respondents.

3   *Foods respondents disliked giving up*

A significant proportion of respondents were reluctant to give up foods in the high-calorie snack categories: cakes, pies and bakery products (31%), sweets and sugar (23%). Alcohol (17%), meat (15%) and chocolate (13%) also featured significantly, compared to the more 'healthy' food groups such as fruit juice, potatoes and pasta (9% each). Cream was the only dairy product mentioned, (9%)

4   *General comments*

Respondents experienced dieting as a loss of pleasure, an inconvenience when it comes to family meals, and a social stigma.

IV   CONCLUSIONS

The prime reason for losing weight was health and fitness, mainly achieved through regulated food intake and increased activity. However, respondents felt deprived in general by the dieting process, and particularly disliked giving up snack foods and food generally regarded as unhealthy: processed foods, high in fats and sugars, low in fibre.

V   RECOMMENDATIONS

These findings present opportunities in several areas.

1   In order to maximise sales of our existing products, we should reappraise our promotional strategy in the light of these findings, to ensure that:

(a)   we are emphasising the health rather than the cosmetic benefits of our products

(b)   we are emphasising that our products are tasty, convenient and normal: not like dieting

2   We may also be able to widen the market for our existing products. Since health and well-being was the most common reason for losing weight, we might extend our marketing message to include non-dieters: emphasising the healthy image of dairy products in general and low-fat alternatives in particular.

3   Respondents' desire to eat normally while dieting suggests a continuing market for low-fat, low-calorie adaptations, especially of those foods which people dislike giving up. Since dairy products currently feature quite low on this list, however, we should consider diversifying into the most significant areas highlighted by the research. Chocolate products may be an initial avenue, being closest to our existing product portfolio, but we may need to look at bakery and confectionery products. This would offer the potential to develop a more extensive brand, and to capture a larger share of the wider slimming market.

(b)   *Motives for wanting to lose weight*

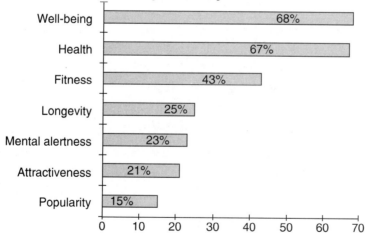

% of respondents with weight problems who mentioned each motive

Methods of weight control

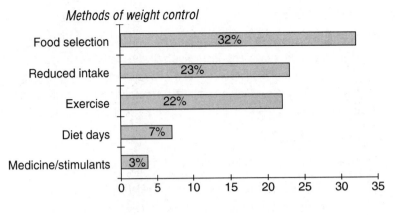

% of respondents with weight problems who mentioned each method

Foods which people dislike giving up

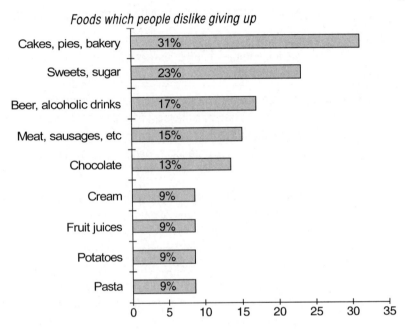

% of respondents with weight problems who mentioned each food

5 Format

The assignments will be assessed and awarded a percentage mark. 50% and above for the project for that Module (ie both assignments) is classified as a pass. Here is a table which shows the criteria on which presentation will be judged for a clear pass (which you will be intending to achieve), a marginal pass (which might therefore have to be the subject of some discussion) and a fail (which you are trying to avoid).

Clear pass	Precise, professional format and structure	Format = look at any formal business report that you can find. Try your workplace.
Marginal pass	Recognisable format and structure, although occasionally unclear Limited irrelevant use of appendices	Overlap of topics Poor use of appendices – information which is not strictly necessary.
Marginal fail	Recognisable format, but ...poor use of structure Difficult to navigate	OK, it **looks** like a business report but this is not good enough. You have not **organised** your material in a logical way. The marker finds it hard to find the way around your report; he/she has to jump to and fro to find relevant data.

Exercise

Carnelian

Here is a paragraph containing some facts about Carnelian, in no particular order. This paragraph illustrates two things.

- It will show you quite how irritating unstructured and unformatted data is to read and make sense of. The marker may be under time pressure, so don't annoy him or her.

- It introduces you to the concept of format and structure.

Carnelian was founded in 1872. 50% of its sales are exports to Germany. It has two principal shareholders, Ms Underwood and Mr Mongrove, who each own 50% of the issued share capital. Net assets are $150,000. The company specialises in making artificial flowers for sale. The Finance Director is Mr Mace. There are 20 employees, of whom five are employed in marketing (reporting to Ms Underwood). The production department report to Mr Mongrove. Sales revenue per annum is $1m. Issued share capital is 1,000 ordinary shares of $1 each. The company used to market by mail order, but now mainly promotes itself through its website. The two people who work in accounts and the IT expert report to Mr Mace. The best selling flower is the silk orchid accounting for 30% of revenue. Profit before tax was $50,000 in 20X1. No one customer accounts for more than 1% of revenue.

Required

Produce a report about Carnelian incorporating all the data above.

Answer

You could have chosen a number of different formats. At the very least, you could have organised the data in logical order.

Report

To: The marker
From: A Candidate
Date:

Re Carnelian

Contents

1   Executive summary
2   Products and markets
3   Organisation and management
4   Financial position

Appendix A: customers
Appendix B: financial position

1   Executive summary

1.1   Carnelian is a long established, privately owned company specialising in the manufacture of artificial flowers for sale worldwide, employing a functional departmentation structure.

2   Customers and markets

2.1   Revenue from artificial flowers is $1m per annum.
2.2 $300,000 derives from one product, the silk orchid.
2.3   Exports to Germany account for 50% of revenue.
2.4   No one customer accounts for 1% of revenue. See Appendix A for a list of customers.
2.5   The main marketing activity is the website, which has replaced mail order.

3   Organisation and management

3.1   The company employs 23 people, including the directors.

3.2   The company is divided into three departments.

- Marketing – 5 personnel reporting to Ms Underwood.
- Production – 12 personnel reporting to Mr Mongrove.
- Finance and IT – three personnel reporting to Mr Mace.

4   Financial position and capital structure

4.1   The company makes a profit margin of 5% and a return of assets of 33%. See Appendix B for workings.

4.2   The sole shareholders are Ms Underwood and Mr Mongrove, each of whom own 500 of the issued share capital of 1,000 ordinary shares of $1 each.

Appendix A

List of customers

> **Appendix B: financial position**
>
> B.1   Profit margin
>
> Profit $50,000/sales $1m = 5%
>
> B.2   ROCE
>
> Profit $50,000 / net assets $150,000 = 33%

5.1 Comment on the answer

You will note that the very requirement to produce a report structuring the data suggested some useful analysis such as calculating ROCE and profit margins. We are not saying that this is perfect by any means, but you can tell that the data about Carnelian is much easier to grasp than it was before. You may have chosen a different structure of course.

6 Writing good English

Lecturers tell BPP that one of the commonest failings of students at this stage of their studies is poor English, so if you are a bit uncertain of your skills in this area, or English is not your first language, you are probably in the majority.

To be brutally frank, if your written English is poor the people who read it will think you are unintelligent. People judge by appearances. Rightly or wrongly this is a fact of life. If you do not try to do something about it you may well hinder your career progression.

If you think you need help in this area, read on. You will not be able to take in all the hints and rules that we give in one reading. You should keep these pages with you and use them as a source of reference whenever you are drafting a passage of your report.

If your written English has never caused you any problems, and a fluent style is second nature to you, you need only skim through these sections. Please do not be offended at their inclusion: some students will find them invaluable!

7 Writing bad English

There are four common faults in bad formal written English.

    (a)   **Being too colloquial**, just writing down what you would **say** if you were speaking to the person you are writing to

    (b)   **Writing in note form**, leaving out words that you would not leave out in normal speech, let alone in formal writing

    (c)   **Bad spelling**

    (d)   **Bad punctuation**

In the remainder of this chapter we are going to go through some basic rules and some very common mistakes that people make. Some of this may take you back to primary school days, but we have tried to make the examples a little more relevant to your current studies.

7.1 Sentences

Always write in full sentences. A sentence has the following characteristics.

(a)   It starts with a capital letter and ends with a full stop.

(b)   It must always have a minimum of one thing/person and one action (or one noun and one verb, to use the technical terms).

Clocks tick.

I am writing.

Most of the sentences you write will have an additional thing/person, with one of the things performing the action on the other one.

I am writing a book.

I am writing to you.

(c)   Things or persons can be collections of words as well as single words. Though it might look more complicated the following sentence is in the standard form *person does thing.*

The senior manager of ABC has written a report on the future of the industry.

(d)   There are two ways of looking at anything that happens. Either:

(i)   things *perform* actions; or
(ii)   actions *are performed by* things.

As you can see, the action word may also be either a single word or a collection of words.

Method (i) is generally preferable in business writing.

(e)   Sentences can, and usually will, be longer than the examples given so far. They can be joined up by words like *and* or *but* or *although,* or you can give extra information about something in the main part of your sentence using words like *who, which* or *that.*

As a general rule, in business communications, the simpler your sentences are the better. This means that you should keep them fairly short.

Try not to write sentences that are all the same length, however, because this is very monotonous to read.

7.2 Paragraphs

If you just write sentence after sentence with no breaks your writing will be very tiring to read and difficult to follow. For this reason groups of sentences are split into paragraphs and there is a space between each paragraph.

A paragraph should have **only one main idea**. This may mean that it only has one sentence, or there may be additional sentences exploring the implications of the main idea, or leading up to the main idea. This paragraph that you are reading now has one main sentence (the first) and two additional sentences exploring the main idea.

In practice it is often difficult to decide where one main idea finishes and the next one starts. The rule again is to keep things **short and simple** but not to the extent that your writing gets monotonous.

In day to day business communications, which tend to be fairly short anyway, it will quite often be appropriate to have a new paragraph for each sentence. Most newspapers tend to be written in this style, too. In a 2,500 word report, however, this is liable to get very monotonous.

7.3 Brevity

Brevity is said to be the soul of wit. It is certainly essential in business writing. You must make your meaning clear, but you should use as few words as possible to do so. Superfluous words obscure the meaning and waste the reader's time.

Consider these sentences from a management text book and compare them with the edited versions.

7.4 Original sentences

- *A high staff turnover may be indicative of a wider problem such as poor morale.*

- *Identify the development areas that need to be addressed.*

- *Check to ensure that the activity has been carried out and successfully completed.*

- *The job description details the characteristics that a successful candidate would need to demonstrate.*

7.5 Edited sentences

- *A high staff turnover may indicate a wider problem such as poor morale.*
- *Identify the development areas to be addressed.*
- *Check that the activity has been carried out.*
- *The job description details the characteristics of a successful candidate.*

Overall, the word count has been reduced from 51 to 38: a 25% reduction.

It is actually quite difficult to write briefly and clearly. The secret is to **read what you have written** and ask yourself if it could be improved.

8 Common mistakes

8.1 A, an, the

These little words are the simplest in the language. They are so simple that you often leave them out in informal writing and in notes.

Do **not** leave them out in formal writing.

8.2 Etc, etc

Avoid *ie* (in other words) and *eg* (for example), and never use *etc* (and so on).

If you are tempted to use these abbreviations take note of the following points.

(a)   To people who know better you will look very silly if you use *ie* when you mean *eg* or *eg* when you mean *ie*. This is a very common mistake.

   (i)   You use *ie* when you are *clarifying* what you have just said.

      ... any of the standard colours available, ie green, red or blue.

      This fell off the back of a lorry, ie it is stolen.

   (ii)   You use *eg* if you are only giving selected *examples* (or a single example) of what you have just said rather than a complete list.

      ... any colour you like, eg sea-green, pillar-box red, tartan, pink ... .

      ... retailers, eg Sainsbury's ...

   To avoid mistakes do as we suggest initially: don't use these abbreviations at all!

(b)   Either punctuate properly or don't punctuate at all. Do one or the other consistently.

i.e.   e.g.   etc.   OR   ie   eg   etc

BUT NOT   ie.   eg.   e.t.c.

(c)   When you write **etc** at the end of a list, you are saying that both you and the reader know perfectly well all the other items which are needed to make the list absolutely complete. The only occasion when this is likely to be true is if you have given the complete list earlier. If you are tempted to use *etc* ask yourself if you can think of any more items. If you can, write them down instead of *etc*. If you cannot, do not write *etc* hoping that the reader will think you could. He will almost certainly assume the opposite.

(d)   Do not forget that items in a simple list are separated by commas except for the last two which are joined by 'and'. If the items in a list consist of more than a couple of words, or if one of them includes the word 'and', use **semicolons** instead of commas. For example:

A competent payroll clerk should be able to deal with piecework pay; deduction of tax and national insurance; joiners and leavers; and preparation of P60s.

8.3 Get things right and do them properly

Often you will want to say something descriptive about the things or the actions in your sentences. You do this by using one or other of two types of *description word*, depending on whether you are describing a thing or an action. One of the most common mistakes that people make is to use the wrong sort of description word.

The basic rule is that if you are describing an *action* the word you use ends with *-ly*.

Example	Explanation
These figures are incorrect.	'incorrect' describes the figures
These figures have been added up incorrectly.	'incorrectly' describes the adding up
That is bad English.	'bad' describes the English
That is badly written.	'badly' describes the writing
Get things right	'right' describes the things
Do them properly	'properly' describes how they are done

Description words that describe *actions* usually say *how* the action is done or *where* it is done or *when* it is done.

8.4 Most common or commonest?

Do you say that something is *more common* than something else or do you say it is *commoner*? The basic rules for deciding whether to add *-er* and *-est* to a word or use *more* and *most* are as follows.

(a)   If the word has only one syllable add *-er* and *-est: harder, longer, biggest, highest* and so on.

(b)   If the word has two syllables and ends in *-y, -er, -le* or *-ow*, add *-er* and *-est: likeliest, happiest, lazier, idlest, cleverest, narrower* and so on. Also add *-er* and *-est* if using the *un-* form of these words: *unlikeliest, unhappier* and so on.

(c)   Otherwise use more and most: *more difficult, more probable, most intelligent, most infuriating* and so on.

With some words you can either add *-er* and *-est* or use *more* and *most* (*common* is such a word), but if you apply the rules above you should never make a mistake.

8.5 Who's who?

Sometimes you can find yourself using words like *he, she, it* and *them* (pronouns, if you want the technical term) so much in a passage of writing that it is not clear what they refer to.
For example, consider this:

Tom, Dick and Harry were talking about their work and Tom said to Dick that he thought he was great.

Does Tom think Dick is great? Or that he is great himself? Or is he saying that Dick thinks highly of himself or, perhaps, of Harry? Or is it that Tom thinks Harry appreciates Dick? There are even more possibilities than these.

You need to read your writing carefully to check whether it contains this sort of ambiguity. To get round the problem you usually have to identify one or more of the people or things involved, using a name or description instead of, or as well as, the word he, she or it.

Jo thought <u>his supervisor</u> was great. He also thought <u>he, Jo,</u> was great.

8.6 I and me

While we are on the subject of words like *he, she* and *it* we may as well remind you about *I* and *me*. Quite simply, use the form *me* if somebody else is doing the action to you.

The company gave Lucy and me a big pay rise.

The company is doing the giving.

If you are doing the action use the form *I*.

I got a big pay rise and so did Lucy.   OR   *Lucy and I got a big pay rise.*

Here it is you who is doing the getting. The question 'Who is doing the action?' is very often the key to a good sentence, as the next few paragraphs illustrate.

8.7 Who's doing what?

Which of the following sentences is correct?

1   *The best guide are accounting standards.*
2   *The problem here is the words are and is.*

The words are and is are the problem. Do you make your action words (or verbs) singular or plural when the first thing is singular and the second thing is plural?

The answer is that it depends which comes first. Sentence 2 is the correct one. If you look carefully at sentence 2 and then go on to the sentence below it beginning 'The words ...' you will see that they say the same thing, except that the order of the words has been changed round. The use of the singular is or the plural are depends on whether what comes first is singular or plural.

If there are two things doing the action and one is singular and the other is plural what happens to the action word? For example is the following sentence correct?

References and an application form has been sent to Mr Slater.

If you think about it, Mr Slater will receive both the references and the form. In other words there are two things performing the action of being sent so the action word must be plural: in the sentence above has should say have.

Be careful not to be distracted by words that just happen to come between the thing doing the action and the action word itself.

The source of the mistakes were not known.

It is tempting in a sentence like this to make the action word fit in with the word nearest to it (mistakes), but give it a moment's thought and you will realise that it is not the mistakes (plural) that are unknown but their source (singular): were should therefore say was.

If a word like *who* or *which* gets in the way be careful. Is this sentence correct?

An accountant is one of those professionals who helps to run businesses and gets well-paid for it.

In fact the words helps and gets are both wrong. It is professionals who help and professionals who get well-paid. The accountant is just one of these people.

8.8 Which hunting

Which is one of the most overused words in bad writing. The rules are quite complicated but most people know them instinctively even though they abandon them when they are writing. Here is a simple explanation.

(a)   Generally if you would *say* 'that' in speech you should *write* 'that' (it is *correct* to do so, it is not, as some people think, more colloquial).

The invoice that we sent you last week contained an error.

BUT

I posted that transaction to the sales ledger, which was a mistake.

Technically, *that* is used when it begins a series of words that *define* what has gone before. In the first example above the words beginning with *that* give information that distinguishes the invoice containing the error from any other invoice. In contrast *which* is used when the sentence changes direction slightly.

You will often see this 'rule' broken (there is sure to be an example somewhere in this book), even by the best writers. We suggest you simply follow the rule that if you would say *that* if you were speaking the words then you should use *that* when writing them.

(b)   If it sounds better to join up the bits of your sentence with a simple *and* or *but* or to write two separate short sentences you should probably do so. Both of the following are correct but the second is better.

You will be sent two invoices which you may pay together if you wish.

You will be sent two invoices but you may pay both together if you wish.

Don't worry unduly about this: simply be aware that if which is badly used it can get you into all sorts of difficulties that could easily have been avoided.

8.9 Who and whom

Strictly, when *who* is the person having an action done to them the form to use is *whom*.

The customers to whom these invoices were sent have all complained.

If you are confident about using whom then do so by all means. In speech, though, you would probably have said 'The customers who these invoices were sent to have all complained'. Likewise in modern business writing it is probably not worth worrying unduly about whom. So long as you are keeping things short and simple it will not offend many people if you break the rule.

A related problem is whether it is allowable to end a sentence with what is technically known as a *preposition*: a 'position' word like *to* or *with* or *from*. In general try to avoid doing so, but do not worry unduly about it. There is a famous example of how badly wrong you can go if you try too hard to avoid it.

That is something up with which I will not put.

This is taking the rules to extremes. It makes it harder, not easier, for people to follow your writing. In fact it is something that readers should not be expected to put up with!

8.10 Do you or are you doing?

What is the difference between *I write* and *I am writing*? This is a frequent problem for people who learned another language before they learned English, because other languages do not make a distinction. Sometimes it doesn't matter which form you use, but sometimes it does. If you are not sure which is correct instinctively, follow these simple rules and you will never make a mistake.

(a) If you are actually doing the action at the time when you are saying that you are doing it, use the *I am doing...* form.

(b) If you do the thing as a normal ongoing part of your life but you are not actually doing it at the time when you are talking or writing use the *I do* form.

Here is an example.

We <u>are investigating</u> your complaint and will write to you again when we have completed our enquiries.

We <u>investigate</u> all complaints fully and offer compensation if we prove to be at fault.

Similar rules can be applied to *I was doing* and *I did* (the first takes you back to a time when the action was actually being done; the second makes you think that though someone did it in the past it is now finished) but in this case either form is usually acceptable.

8.11 To boldly go

One of the forms of an action word is the *to* form: *to do, to calculate, to be, to decide* and so on. The *to* should be regarded as something that cannot be separated from the main action word. You do not write *to <u>quickly</u> calculate*. The correct form is *to calculate <u>quickly</u>*.

Most people break this rule in everyday speech and many people break it in their writing arguing that the rule is unnatural for English. However many others – quite possibly including some of the people that you write to – get annoyed by it. The safest option, therefore, is not to break the rule.

It is sometimes better to avoid the problem by changing the *to* form to something else.

We used to regularly send out statements, but this tends to get neglected now.

You could correct this by changing it to: *We used to send out statements regularly ... .* This is fine, but another possibility, if you wanted to leave *regularly* where it is, would be the following.

At one time we regularly sent out statements ...

8.12 Going too boldly

Never write *to* when what you mean is *too.* If your work is typed up always check that the typist has not typed *to* when you want *too.* This point is made again in the section on spelling but it is such a common mistake that it is worth giving you advance warning.

8.13 Try to get it right

You might often say to someone *I'm going to try and do that*. This is wrong because *and* is a word used to join up two separate things, whereas the *trying* and the *doing* are not two separate things. What you mean is that you are going to *try to do* whatever it is.

RIGHT   *Go and see what the matter is*   Going *and* seeing are two different things
WRONG   *Try and improve your writing skills*   Trying *to* improve is all one action

8.14 Should have

It is very easy to write *I should of done that by half past three*. You write this because it is exactly what you think you say. In fact in terms of pronunciation it *is* exactly what you say. It is never, ever correct, though, whatever your ears tell you.

What you really mean is *I should <u>have</u> done that ...* . The same problem arises and the same mistake is often made with *could*.

WRONG   *I could of finished that if the phone had not rung.*
RIGHT   *I could have finished that if the phone had not rung.*

8.15 Off with of

Since we are on the subject of *of* it is worth saying that just because you go *down to* the shops or *out of* the country or *up to* someone in the street, you do not get *off of* a bus. The word *off* is always quite happy on its own: you *get off a bus*. It is never correct to write *off of*, so you do not *collect the papers off of Mr Jones*, you collect them *from* Mr Jones. Try to get out of the habit of saying *off of* when you are talking.

8.16 Should and would

Since we are also on the subject of *should* it is worth mentioning the conventional way to ask someone to do something in business writing.

I <u>should</u> be grateful if you <u>would</u> settle this account.

Note that should is used with I and would is used with you. This is because should has the sense of ought to and would has the sense of be willing: using should and would like this is just a way of being polite. However so many people write I would be grateful nowadays that this, too, has become perfectly acceptable.

8.17 The silliest mistake of all

The silliest mistake of all is using *their* when you mean *there* or using *they're* when you mean *their* or any other permutation of this error. Always check your writing to make sure that you have got these words right. This is not just a spelling problem: the three words have completely different meanings.

For a start you can make life a little easier for yourself by not using the form *they're* (they are) in formal writing: then there is one fewer to get wrong.

You probably know which spelling is right in different contexts, but it is very easy to write the wrong one as a slip of the pen. Here are some checks you can carry out to avoid this.

Their   in front of a word is a neater way of writing *belonging to them* after it. If your sentence becomes nonsense when you cross out the word *their* and put in the words *belonging to them* you have the wrong word.

Which of the following sentences is wrong?

Students should always check there writing for common mistakes.

Their is a good reason for checking words like this.

The first sentence could be reworded Students should always check the writing **belonging to them** for common mistakes. The word there should therefore be spelled their. In the second sentence you cannot fit in the words belonging to them at all: it doesn't make sense. The word their should therefore be spelled there. Both of the sentences are wrong.

There   is the word to use if the next word is *is* or *are. There* can often be thought of as a similar word to *here*: in fact of course, it is just *here* with a *t* in front, and it indicates that something exists.

There are the papers you asked for.	*Here are the papers ...*
There are six students who always get this wrong and they will have to pay me £5 every time they do it in future!	*Six students exist who ...*

You probably think that we have made a bit of a meal of this simple point. If so, we challenge you never to make mistakes with these words again!

9 Punctuation

9.1 Capitals

Use a capital letter only in the following situations.

(a)   At the beginning of a sentence

(b)   For names of people and institutions: Peter, Jo, Nicole, Barclays Bank plc, Berisford Limited, the Foreign Office

(c)   For titles: Inspector Morse, Sir Humphrey Appleby, Mr Gomez

(d)   For places and nationalities: Manchester, Japan, Italian

(e)   Where convention demands it: I, God. (Not using capitals for *plc* is also a convention)

Do not use capital letters otherwise. For example the following (taken from a piece of writing produced by a student working for a professional qualification) is wrong.

At the end of the day Invoices and Statements are run off on the Printer.

The only capital letter that is correct here is the one at the beginning of the sentence: invoices, statements and printer are general words, not names of things that are special to this particular accounting department. Capitals where they are not needed distract and irritate your readers.

9.2 Consistency

There are, however, some circumstances in which it is neither right nor wrong to use capital letters. For example you might be inclined to use capital letters for someone's job title (*Mr Akashi, the Sales Director*) or for the name of a department (*the Payables Ledger Department*). Whatever decision you make about capitals in these cases you must be consistent within a single document: either *always* use capitals whenever you refer to them or *never* use capitals, but do not do one thing in one paragraph and another in the next.

9.2.1 Quotation marks ('inverted commas')

The main thing to remember about quotation marks is that you should hardly ever use them in business writing.

(a)   It is a very common and very irritating mistake to use them when you are not sure that you have chosen the right word, or when you think you are using a word in a colloquial way. It is also common, but wrong, to use them when you are referring to something that you think is unusual in context, or when you are trying to emphasise something. Avoid these errors in the following ways.

(i) Choose another word that is more appropriate.

(ii) Do not use highly colloquial expressions in formal written English. Ask yourself if you would use the expression if you were talking to a senior person in your organisation and wanted to make a good impression. (Would you say to your company's managing director 'Yo, MD! What's happening?' If not, do not use the expression.)

(iii) If your reader will understand the word you are using, even though it seems a bit wacky, there is no need to use quotation marks. (Find the example in the preceding sentence.)

If you are unsure, just consider whether quotation marks will *help* your reader. Putting them round the word 'wacky' does not help anybody to understand what it means. Quotation marks do not turn informal words into formal words.

(iv) Quotation marks are *never* used for emphasis. Use *italics* for emphasis if typing and underline the word if writing by hand.

(b) The only circumstances in which quotation marks *must* be used are these.

(i) Use them when you are quoting the words that someone actually said.

'I'm fed up with students who put quotation marks all over the place', said the tutor.

One commentator was bullish about the prospects for holders of ACCA qualifications: 'This new emphasis on financial management skills could mean that DipFM holders become one of the highest paid groups in society.'

It will be fairly rare for you to quote direct speech in business communications.

(ii) Use them when you are discussing a word or phrase *as a word or phrase*, probably prior to explaining its meaning. Really this is just a variation on the use of quotation marks for quotations.

This technique is known as 'double entry', and it involves ...

The term 'double entry' means ...

(c) In BPP books we always use single quotation marks unless there is another set within the first set. If this happens the second set are double quotation marks.

The lecturer said 'This technique is known as "double entry", and it involves ...'

In other books, and as a general rule in newspapers, you might see the opposite approach, with double being the more frequent. Either approach is acceptable as long as you consistently follow one or the other throughout a piece of writing.

9.2.2 Apostrophes

In modern English apostrophes are used for two different purposes.

(a) To show that something belongs to somebody or something: *employees' pay records* (meaning the *pay records of employees*).

(b) To show that a letter has been missed out in a word such as *haven't* (short for *have not*) or *they're* (short for *they are*).

9.2.3 's or s'

If the word is plural the apostrophe comes after the *s*. If the word is singular the apostrophe comes before the *s*. This is simple enough but people very often get it wrong. This is probably because they do not check. The rule, if you do not want people to think you are thick, is: *always check that your apostrophes are in the right place!*

9.2.4 Do'nt and Don't

It is best not to use forms like *don't* and *isn't* and *aren't* in formal writing. If you use them in informal communications, get the apostrophe in the right place. It goes in the place where the letter has been omitted. For example *don't* is short for *do not*: the apostrophe takes the place of the missing letter *o*.

9.2.5 Its and it's

These two words do not mean the same thing. You will always pick the right one, though if you simply remember that an apostrophe between two letters means that something has been left out between those two letters. Test by inserting the word *is* and seeing if your sentence still makes sense.

It's time you got to grips with double entry	MEANS	*It is time ...*
It's a sunny day today	MEANS	*It is a sunny day ..*
Tell me the account code and its balance	DOES NOT MEAN	*... and it is balance.*

As we have already said, an even easier way to get this right is to avoid using the form it's completely. Say it is instead.

9.2.6 Whose and who's

Apply the same rule as you apply for *its* and *it's*. If you can insert the word *is* and your sentence still makes sense the form to use is *who's*. Better, use *who is*.

9.2.7 Shop windows

People who write things in huge white letters on shop windows appear to have learned this skill at a special school that required them to make at least one mistake per window. How often have you seen something like this?

HUNDRED'S

OF

BARGAIN'S!!

Both of the apostrophes here are wrong. *Hundreds* and *bargains* are just the plural of *hundred* and *bargain*.

It is probably the word *of* that causes the confusion. If you are guilty of this error try to remember the following examples.

Dozens of students

Dozens of students' pay packets

Whenever *'s* or *s'* is used there *must* be something else in the sentence that belongs to the word with the apostrophe. In the first sentence the students are penniless so they have no apostrophe. In the second sentence the pay packets belong to them so they celebrate by adding an apostrophe.

9.2.8 Commas

Some people use commas to mark places in their sentences where they would pause for breath. This is totally wrong. The people who read your report will breathe as and when they need to: otherwise you would be able to suffocate people by writing extra long sentences.

(You may find that people in authority (your boss, your tutor) believe that punctuation marks are breathing marks, probably because that is what they were taught at school. Tell them to buy a little Penguin book by E V Carey called *Mind the Stop* if they will not believe BPP.)

Commas are used to make the logic of your sentence clearer. Since you will be writing relatively short simple sentences in all your business communications you should not need to use them very much at all.

Here are some simple rules for using commas. These cover the most common uses.

(a)   Use commas in lists of items.

... red, white, blue and green.

... nominal ledger, sales ledger and purchase ledger.

The usual convention is not to put a comma before and and the last item, the argument being that the other commas are used in place of and. Sometimes this rule may need to be broken to make things clear, though:

... accounting firms such as Deloitte and Touche, Arthur Andersen, and Ernst and Young.

Without the comma a reader who is not familiar with these names might think that there was a firm called Arthur Andersen and Ernst.

(b)   Use commas when there are bits of your sentence that could be missed out without making the sentence incomplete.

Debits, which go on the left, are assets of the business.

He said that debits go on the right, which is incorrect.

Mrs Chomsky, one of our leading customers, has cancelled her order.

Here you could miss out the words that are underlined and still have complete sentences.

There are sometimes odd individual words which you could leave out without damaging the sense of your sentence, but putting commas round them is overdoing it.

The payroll records, which were usually kept in the Personnel Department, had completely vanished.

Here you could miss out the words usually and completely but to put commas round them would distract your reader unnecessarily. The logic of the sentence is clear without them.

(c)   Use commas between bits of your sentence that could stand alone as independent sentences but which happen to be joined together with a connecting word. This is usually only necessary with fairly long sentences.

It was suggested that the discrepancy had occurred because entries in the accounting records for the second half of the year had been posted to the wrong accounts, but this proved not to be the source of the error once a more thorough investigation had been carried out.

The general rule, with the exceptions above, is to write simple sentences and use commas as little as possible.

9.2.9 Exclamation marks

Do not use exclamation marks in formal business writing. In informal writing there is no reason to use more than one.

9.2.10 Colons: introductions

The colon is two full stops, one on top of the other. You might want to use this occasionally to introduce things.

There are two types of accounting entry: debits and credits.

You may sometimes see a colon with a dash after it (:-). This is old-fashioned. You may find that older people use it. The dash is not necessary, so leave it out.

It is very easy to type a semi-colon (;) when you mean to type a colon (:) because the two are on the same key on a typewriter. Be aware of this and check carefully that writing that has been typed up has the punctuation mark you intended.

9.2.11 Separations and semi-colons

A semi-colon is a comma with a full stop on top of it. You might want to use these in lists where each item in the list is more than a few words, especially if there are also commas within items in the list.

Attending the meeting were: the managing director, who did not vote; Mr Smith, representing his wife; various small shareholders, most of whom wanted to raise specific issues; and a large man, who was sheltering from the rain.

It is unlikely that you would want to write like this in a business context. It is usually clearer and simpler to have separate lines for each thing in the list.

The meeting was attended by the following people.

- *The managing director, who did not vote*
- *Mr Smith, representing his wife*
- *Various small shareholders, most of whom wanted to raise specific issues*
- *A large man, who was sheltering from the rain*

9.2.12 Dashes

The dash is a multi-purpose punctuation mark and because of this it can make your writing sloppy – you can easily end up dashing about all over the place – not having a clear idea of where your sentence is going – not knowing quite where to finish – and leaving your reader in doubt as to what the point of your sentence was in the first place – if there was a point. The previous sentence illustrates these evils.

Dashes are fine if you know how to use them correctly. On the other hand anything you can do with a dash you can do equally well with other punctuation marks. It is probably best to avoid the problems and dangers by not using them at all.

9.2.13 Brackets

Brackets are used to include bits of extra information within the main sentence. The rules to remember are as follows.

(a) Think of brackets as a form of double entry. For every opening bracket there must be an equal and opposite closing bracket. When you are checking your writing, the first thing you should do when you see an opening bracket is look for the closing one.

(b) If there are too many brackets you will confuse your reader. Try to have no more than one set of brackets per sentence.

(c)   It should be possible to cross out the part of your sentence that is bracketed without upsetting the sense of the main part of the sentence.

Which of the following sentences is correctly punctuated?

This is the main (not the bracketed part) of the sentence.

This is the main (not the bracketed) part of the sentence.

If you cross out the bracketed part of the first sentence you are left with *This is the main of the sentence.* This does not make sense. The second version is the correct one. You should always check that you would be left with a full sentence if you cross out the part you have put in brackets.

9.2.14 Full stops, commas and brackets

The rules are simple.

(a)   If the bracketed part of a sentence is right at the end of the sentence the full stop comes *after* the closing bracket (like this). The full stop is normally part of the main sentence, not the bracketed part (see (d)).

(b)   Never put a comma, a colon or a semi-colon before an opening or closing bracket. Both of the commas in the following example are wrong and should be deleted.

... the receivables ledger, (part of the accounting system,)

(c)   Commas can come after a closing bracket. As usual, try crossing out the bracketed part: if the comma that follows it would be necessary in the main sentence it is correct.

Dogs (which have four legs), ducks (which have two), and spiders (which have eight) were all on the menu that evening.

(d)   If you put brackets round an entire sentence the sentence should begin with a capital letter and end with a full stop, just like any other sentence.

(The whole of this sentence is in brackets.)

It is unusual to put brackets round a whole sentence.

10 Spelling problems

A lot of bad spellers could very easily be good spellers. These are people who know there are rules about, say, dropping the *e* at the end of a word when *-ing* is added to it (*care/caring*), or doubling the *l* when a word ending in *-ful* has *-ly* added to it (*careful/carefully*). Troubles start when people forget that there are exceptions to the rules, or they get confused about when to apply the rules, or they apply them too enthusiastically.

Unfortunately there is no easy way to improve your spelling. The most pleasurable way is to read a great deal: subconscious learning is probably the main way that you have learned to spell over the years. The problem is that this process works relatively slowly.

10.1 Computer spell checking

Any decent word processing package includes a built-in dictionary. If you type something on a word processor you can then click on a button and the program will work through your document pausing at any word that does not appear in its dictionary and offering you the opportunity to correct your spelling or choose an alternative word.

If you have such a tool available you would be foolish not to use it. Make it your habit always to use the spell checking facility just before you close a document.

Remember, on the other hand, that there are certain mistakes that the spell check does not pick up. For example, if you type *form* but meant to type *from* the computer will not recognise your mistake. All it is doing is seeing if the words you have typed are spelled like that in the dictionary. Other examples are typing *i* when you mean *it* (the computer thinks you mean *I*) or typing *n* when you mean *in* or *on* (because individual letters of the alphabet are valid entries in the dictionary).

You cannot rely on the computer to do all your spelling for you or to correct badly written sentences. In other words, spell checking should not be regarded as a substitute for checking through a piece of word processed material on paper with the naked eye.

We suggest that you read through a printed out version of your answers to the projects, looking for typographical errors, and, to be on the safe side, ask someone else to read it too. A fresh pair of eyes can often spot a mistake that you have missed countless times through familiarity.

11 Language

When starting your research work and planning for your project, you may feel that 5,000 words is a lot, and wonder how you will manage to produce that much. By the time you come to write it, you may wonder how you are going to manage to say everything you need to within *only* 5,000 words.
One way to keep your word count under tight control is to be as efficient as possible in your use of language. Practise the use of concise and precise language in all your written work, not just this report.

11.1 Stylistic requirements

There are certain stylistic requirements in the writing of reports, formal or informal.

Coupled with this, you may have time management problems with your writing. In the context of this Report, however, you do have the luxury of taking as much time as you need, unlike in your DipFM exams.

Consider the following actual extract from an exam script submitted for a past exam paper for the Chartered Institute of Marketing (Pearson, 1993). Note in particular the writing times.

(a) Proposals for change in the organisational structure.

(b) Creation of 'strategic business units' centred around each terminal

This would allow each terminal to be represented at board level with each manager having his own operational and commercial staff beneath him. This will involve a huge restructuring of the organisation and individual job roles/responsibilities, however this move is necessary in order that commercial and operations staff work alongside each other and cooperate to solve problems in the most effective way, to the benefit of EAL in serving the needs of its customers. All commercial versus operations conflicts would be solved lower down the hierarchy which will in turn be flattened out as a result of restructuring. Each terminal general manager must have beneath him his appropriate support staff for his commercial and operations roles eg catering manager, retail operations manager, quality control engineers.'

Total words = c 140   **Total writing time = 8 minutes**

Keeping the same heading we might change the section to read as follows.

> Each terminal to become an SBU under a general manager with his own support staff (catering, retail operations, quality control etc).
>
> BENEFIT
>
> Although requiring much restructuring and reformulation of job descriptions:
>
> (a) Commercial and operations staff would work together in meeting the needs of the customer
>
> (b) All commercial v operations conflicts would be solved lower down the hierarchy
>
> (c) Each terminal would be represented at board level
>
> Total words = c 70   **Total writing time = 4 minutes**

The re-wording cuts the original word length in half.

- It is **easier to understand and mark.**
- **It takes half the time to write, leaving you more time to think and to make extra points**.
- It takes up less of your precious ration of words.

11.2 Basic principle: 'Less is More'

	Example	
Rule	**No**	**Yes**
Keep words simple	Expenditure vs	Cost
	Aggregate vs	Total
Short words are quicker to write	Terminate vs	End
Avoid words you don't need to write	I would be grateful	Please
	Due to the fact that	Because
	In the not too distant future	Soon (better: give a time scale)
	At this point in time	Now (or currently)
	In the majority of instances	In most cases (or usually)
	It is recommended that A Ltd should consider	A Ltd should consider
	36 words (55 syllables)	14 words (18 syllables)

11.3 Jargon

Be **careful** of jargon: jargon is **technical language with a precise meaning** and therefore has its uses. Keep in mind the needs and likely response of your audience. Do not try to blind the assessor with technological jargon. If you do, the assessor may question whether you understand it yourself.

Be precise. Be careful of 'very' 'fairly' 'partly', unless you are unable to state facts.

Avoid patronising language

(a) There is a fine line between explaining technical vocabulary or situations which may not be familiar to the reader, and 'dumbing down'. By that we mean reducing the level of your writing to something well below the assumed competence of your audience.

(b) You do not need to explain routine technical terms. You can assume that your audience has a reasonable awareness of factors such as the current state of the domestic and international economy, the debate over the UK's adoption of the Euro, the advance of e-commerce, the now tempered enthusiasm for dot com start ups and so forth.

(c)   Your meetings with your mentor and your peer group presentation could provide a suitable forum for you to discuss the style of language which you have adopted. You could receive some constructive feedback.

11.4 Grammar checkers

Having reached the stage you have in your academic and professional careers, your standard of grammar should be quite high. It is still worth running the grammar check over your report, however, as it enables you to stand back and see the wood from the trees.

The grammar check will perform tasks such as:

(a)   Detecting sentences where you have omitted the verb

(b)   Detecting sentences where you have used mixed singular and plural subject and verb (for example 'two of the main reasons for the development of the multinational company is ....'.)

(c)   Indicating sentences which are unduly long or have too many clauses, potentially confusing the reader

You can specify in the grammar check what style of language you are using, such as 'casual' 'technical' and 'standard'. You can also use a grammar option that gives the readability statistics of your work. This is a useful tool in that it can indicate when your language is becoming over obscure.

11.5 Thesaurus

If you think your use of words is becoming repetitive, try the thesaurus. This will suggest alternatives and can also supply meanings.

Chapter Roundup

- Each project requires an answer, often in report format, approaching 5,000 words. The requirements may be clearly split into the two subject areas, or they may be more integrated with each other.

- Planning such large answers is all-important, and you are likely to produce several drafts.

- Ensure that your report or answer follows a logical structure, with a clearly-identifiable introduction, main content and conclusion and/or recommendation.

- Spelling, punctuation and grammar are all vital if your assignment answers are to give a professional impression.

Part C
ACCA projects

ACCA Live Project – Spring 2005: Module A

Topic list
1 Spring 2005 Project: Module A
2 Suggested approach
3 Suggested answer
4 Examiner's comments

Note. we reproduce in this chapter the questions that were set in the Spring 2005 Module A Project, however we do not reproduce the supplement that was also supplied, containing the financial statements of New Look.

You will need to download this from the ACCA's website:

www.accaglobal.com/students/diploma_fm/module_a/pastpapers/feb05supp

If you do not have internet access please contact our Customer Services department on 020 8740 2211 for hard copy.

As the 2002/2003 Annual Report of New Look was originally issued under UK Accounting Standards and in UK accounting format it has not been altered to reflect the internationalisation of the DipFM syllabus. The answer to this project is therefore based upon the original UK financial statements. However the approach to the answer and the answer itself contain references to international terminology and standards where appropriate.

1 Spring 2005 Project: Module A

Diploma in Financial Management

PROJECT DA2, INCORPORATING SUBJECT AREAS
- **INTERPRETATION OF FINANCIAL STATEMENTS**
- **PERFORMANCE MANAGEMENT**

All questions are compulsory and MUST be answered

The project MUST be written in English.

The maximum word count (including appendices and tables but excluding references and bibliography) is 5,000.

The project MUST be TYPED in black ink, one-sided, double-spaced, using a minimum 12-point font size and a 1-inch margin at each side. HANDWRITTEN SUBMISSIONS WILL NOT BE ACCEPTED. The project must be submitted by post, electronic submissions are not acceptable.

The project should be submitted on A4 paper with your student number, project name, date and page number at the top of each page.

A project submission form MUST be completed for each project submitted and attached to the front of the project.

The Association of Chartered Certified Accountants

BPP)))
LEARNING MEDIA

Incorporating subject areas – Interpretation of Financial Statements and Performance Management

BOTH questions are compulsory and MUST be attempted

Introduction

In recent years a number of previously listed companies have 'gone private'. In many cases it is the original founder of the company who has taken a controlling interest.

One example of this trend is the fashion retailer New Look. In early 2004, Tom Singh, who founded the company, stated that he wished to acquire the company in order to focus on long term development without having to meet the short term demands of stock market investors.

This comment highlights the fact that the objectives of various groups of shareholders may be quite different.

At the same time as Mr Singh was negotiating to purchase the company, the chief executive of New Look reported that the company's strategy was:

'to drive sustainable earnings growth through:

–   the continuing expansion of our trading space, and especially the development of larger stores in key markets.

–   the ongoing development of comprehensive product ranges with broad customer appeal and good potential to increase market share

–   the progressive improvement of our cost to sales ratio

–   and the development of our business in France, where we have identified opportunities for growth'.

Role

In completing this project you are to assume that you are employed by a firm of investment advisors. Your role is to provide advice to both investors and managers of companies in the retail sector. You have been approached by a group of investors who are contemplating investing in a retail group with a profile similar to New Look. They wish to use that company as a template for assessing their options and planning their management approach on the assumption that they successfully complete the investment. You are due to meet with the investors in the near future and they have asked you to provide them with a briefing paper for their review prior to the meeting.

Information

Please note that **under no circumstances** should you contact New Look.

Required

1   Based on the 2002/03 Annual Report of New Look, prepare a briefing paper for the investors which:

   (a)   Compares and contrasts the needs of:

      (i)   Institutional investors and   (3 marks)

      (ii)   Private shareholders with a long-term perspective   (3 marks)

   (b)   Assesses the performance of the company using a maximum of five ratios (or other measures) for each group of investors identified in (a). (NB you should justify your choice of each ratio), and   (32 marks)

   (c)   Illustrates how basing the assessments on published financial information limits the conclusion which can be drawn.   (12 marks)

                                                 (50 marks)

2   Following the completion of the acquisition by the investors, you have been asked to make recommendations with regard to a management reporting package. The package is intended to assist managers in assessing the company's performance. You have initially suggested that the company should complement the financial reporting system with an internal reporting system which will focus attention on factors which are critical for success as this will assist in achieving the goal of delivering long term shareholder value.

You have also indicated that benchmarking would be a worthwhile exercise. You have been invited to make a presentation to the investors to develop your suggestions.

Required

Prepare a presentation (including appropriate visual aids) to the investors which:

   (a)   Outlines how shareholder value can be measured, and its relevance for the investors

                                                            (8 marks)

   (b)   Identifies and explains the significance of a range of non-financial performance measures which can be used to monitor the performance of the company, and

                                                          (24 marks)

   (c)   Explains how benchmarking can assist in managing performance and identifies activities which should be benchmarked, together with the specific measures which should be used.   (18 marks)

                                                 (50 marks)

2 Suggested approach

The entire project, covering both subject areas, Interpretation of Financial Statements and Performance Management, is set in the context of the New Look scenario set out on the first page and the New Look 2002/2003 Annual Report provided in the supplementary information.

Start by reading through the 'introduction' and 'role' sections on the first page of the project. Read this carefully and take note of the context of the scenario – ie the move from a company owned by institutional investors to private investors. Clearly the differing objectives of these two types of investors forms some sort of theme for the project.

Note also the company's strategy as reported by the Chief Executive. The examiner for Module A is always looking for assessment of performance in the context of corporate strategy.

Note also your role as an employee of a firm of investment advisors working for a group of investors who are contemplating investment in a retail group similar to New Look.

Requirements

Move onto the requirements section of the project. You will see that there are two distinct questions. Question 1 relates to Interpretation of Financial Statements whereas Question 2 is to do with Performance Management.

At this stage read through the requirements briefly so that you know roughly what you are being asked to do.

The examiner often comments that the word count in candidates' projects does not always relate to the mark allocation. He has made it quite clear that the mark allocation is an accurate guide to the number of words required for each part of the project. Therefore it is worthwhile at this stage just calculating the approximate number of words required for each part of the project.

Question 1

(a)	(i)	$3/100 \times 5,000$	=	150 words
	(ii)	$3/100 \times 5,000$	=	150 words
(b)		$32/100 \times 5,000$	=	1,600 words
(c)		$12/100 \times 5,000$	=	600 words

Question 2

(a)	$8/100 \times 5,000$	=	400 words
(b)	$24/100 \times 5,000$	=	1,200 words
(c)	$18/100 \times 5,000$	=	900 words

Supplementary information

Turn now to the supplementary information and read through it quite quickly. Scan the numbers for any obvious trend that you can see but do not start doing any calculations at this stage. The idea here is to familiarise yourself with the information available rather than to come up with any material for your project or to draw any conclusions.

At this stage it might be worth taking a break so that you can mull over the supplementary information provided and the overall requirements of the project for a short while.

Question 1

Once you are ready to start on your project return to the requirements again.

What are you being asked to produce? Note that this is a **briefing paper** not a report so the format is less structured.

Part (a)

This requires you to 'compare and contrast the needs' of institutional investors and private shareholders – note however that it is private shareholders 'with a long-term perspective'.

Re-read the introduction to the project as this may give you some ideas in this area and then think carefully about the 'needs' of these two types of investors. The supplementary information will not help you with this part of the question so individual thought is what is required. Remember though that the examiner is only expecting about 150 words for each of these types of investors so you are not being required to write too much. In fact you may find that it is easy to overrun on these two short parts so watch your word count carefully. Remember that if you produce more than 5,000 words in total the marker will not mark anything that comes after word 5,000.

Part (b)

Read the requirements here very carefully:

- assess the performance of the company
- for each group of investors from part (a)
- using a maximum of five ratios for each group
- justify your choice of ratio

A few pointers:

- from your thoughts and comments in part (a) hopefully you can now see that the needs of the two groups of investors are different. Therefore it is likely that the ratios that will be of use to each group will be different.

- you may initially calculate more than 10 ratios but make sure that when you finalise your project answer you are only using a maximum of five per group otherwise you will be wasting your precious word count.

- take note that you must justify your choice of each ratio. The examiner consistently complains about the lack of justification of ratios in project answers even when it is specifically asked for, as in this question.

At this stage turn to the supplementary information and calculate any ratios that you think will be useful in assessing company performance – remember that this is a retailer so ratios such as debtors (receivables) days will not be relevant. You may not eventually use all of these ratios but it will give you a feel for company performance and allow you to choose the best ratios when you actually write up your assessment of the company's performance.

Once you have your list of ratios take some time to consider them. Remember the links between ratios such as ROCE, asset turnover and net profit margin. Think about the context of the financial statements in that we are dealing with a retail group and think about which ratios might apply to institutional investors and which to private, long term investors.

Finally before you can begin your actual answer to this part of the project think about how you will approach the performance assessment. You might wish to assess the performance firstly from an institutional investor's perspective using the five ratios chosen and then from a private investor's perspective using their relevant five ratios. Alternatively you may wish to carry out an overall performance assessment referring where necessary to the interests of institutional or private investors. However you decide to approach it, remember to justify each ratio chosen as part of your answer.

Part (c)

This is a fairly common topic for Module A projects: the limitations of using published financial information for performance assessment. However the examiner does not like answers that appear to come straight from a textbook. Make sure that you set your answer in context of New Look and answer the question that is set ie 'illustrate'.

Question 2

In question 2 we are moving onto the Performance Management area of the syllabus. You are required to prepare a presentation to the investors in the retail company (on the assumption that their proposed investment went ahead).

Note that this presentation is to include visual aids. The examiner noted that despite the evident requirement a number of candidates did not provide any visual aids in their project. Visual aids have been asked for in a number of Module A assessments now and the examiner has made it clear that marks are allocated to them and therefore marks are lost if they are not prepared. In fact the preparation of visual aids can help you to plan your answer as most visual aids will be lists of the key topics to be considered or breakdowns of points within a topic. They will then need to be padded out with narrative but can be a good starting point for your answer.

Part (a)

The two main elements of this part of the question are how shareholder value can be measured and its relevance for investors. However a good starting point might be to define what is meant by shareholder value.

Visual aids might be: 1   What is shareholder value?
2   How is it measured?
3   Relevance

Part (b)

This is all about non-financial measures so do not be tempted to include any financial measures in this part. Remember also that it is all based upon the New Look scenario so the measures you come up with must be relevant to a retail organisation.

These types of measures are not the sort you will necessarily find in a textbook so you will have to think carefully about the retail market and put yourself in the position of a manager in the company. What factors would appear to be critical for success?

For each measure you choose you are to **identify** it, which will include explanation of how it is to be measured, and **explain its significance**.

Part (c)

Before setting out on this final part of the project you might find it useful to revise the subject of benchmarking from your BPP Study Text. In this part of the question you are to:

- explain how benchmarking can assist in managing performance
- identify activities that should be benchmarked
- for each such activity explain the specific measures that should be used.

3 Suggested answer

Question 1

(a) (i) **Institutional investors**

Institutional investors will tend to have two major annual commitments. Firstly to report consistently good performance on their portfolios each year and secondly a commitment to meet their outgoings. For example insurance companies and pension funds will require income from their investments to pay claims and pension benefits. It can be argued that these two major needs of institutional investors mean that they will tend to take a short-term view of company performance and make short term demands on the companies in which they invest.

The need to report consistently good returns, even when the stock market is generally performing badly, means that institutional investors look to their investments for high short term earnings and return on capital employed rather than longer term growth. The need for income from their investments means that they are perhaps more concerned about dividend payouts than about the company retaining funds for future re-investment and growth.

(ii) **Private investors with a long term perspective**

Some private investors will have the same needs as those of institutional investors particularly with regard to dividend income as they have made their investment in the expectation of regular dividend payments. However, in many cases private investors invest in companies for the long term and will therefore have different needs.

A private investor is likely to have fewer investments in his/her portfolio and therefore is likely to have a more personal commitment to the company. In some cases, as with Tom Singh, the investor may even be the original founder of the company. This degree of commitment to the company will mean that the investor is looking at the long term growth and stability of the company in accordance with the strategies of the directors of the company.

In many cases such an investor will also play a part in the management of the company which will further increase his commitment longer term. This level of personal interest and commitment is not a factor with institutional investors and plays a large part in their different perspectives of company performance.

(b) In this part of the briefing paper the performance of New Look for the year 2002/2003 will be assessed based upon the Annual Report for that financial year. The assessment will be carried out using accounting ratios included in the appendix to this briefing paper and from the perspective of both institutional investors and private investors with a long term perspective.

The paper will start with justification of five ratios chosen to assess performance from the perspective of each type of investor mentioned above and will then assess the actual performance of the company using those ratios.

Institutional investors

Institutional investors will largely be considering the short term return on their investment but will also be interested in the longer term position of the company to some degree.

Return on capital employed

The most important ratio to most institutional investors will be the overall return on capital employed. This figure relates the profits the company is making to the amount of capital invested and for the institutional investor gives a return on his investment which can be reported to his investors. It can also be used to compare to other investments in his portfolio, to the market returns in general and to other companies in the same industry.

Net profit margin

Return on capital employed is affected by the level of profitability of the company and by its use of its assets as measured by asset turnover (see below). Therefore comparison of the overall profit as a percentage of revenue from one year to the next provides important information about the overall return as measured by ROCE. Any adverse changes in net profit margin will affect the overall return.

Earnings per share

Traditionally this has been a key figure for institutional investors as it provides valuable information about the earnings available for its investors independent of the dividend policy of the company. These earnings are available either to earn future profits for investors by re-investment in the company or to provide income in the form of dividend. Allied to this figure, institutional investors will also be interested in dividend per share as this is the income that they will be receiving and will require for other purposes.

Working capital cycle

Institutional investors are often interested in short–term profitability levels and this can be dramatically affected by a worsening of the working capital cycle. This is the amount of time that cash is tied up in the working capital of the business before being received as cash from turnover (revenue). Particularly in an industry like the fashion industry where stocks (inventory) should be moving quickly and debtors (receivables) are virtually non-existent any worsening of the working capital cycle will have an immediate effect on profit.

Gearing

Gearing measures the degree of risk to investors due to the commitments to providers of debt capital both in terms of interest that must be paid before profits are available for equity investors and also in terms of risk if the company were to be wound up. Gearing is a measure of financial risk and institutional investors, although able to diversify risk through their portfolio holding, will wish to monitor the risk of individual investments.

Private investors with long term perspective

Private investors with a long term interest in a company will of course be interested in short term profits and returns but will have more interest in financial ratios which indicate the future of the company and the achievement of its objectives.

Trend in turnover (revenue)

In a fashion retailer such as New Look the ability to generate sales is the key to success. Therefore the increase in turnover year on year is an important indicator to a private long term investor of the operating health of the company.

Gross profit margin

Clearly a yearly increase in sales is not enough to ensure the success of a company. These sales must also be made at a reasonable profit level. Therefore the gross profit margin, the margin over cost at which the goods are being sold, and the trend of this margin gives an investor important information about the ability of the company to achieve and to continue to achieve profits.

Asset turnover

Increase in profitable sales however is only part of the picture for long term health. The private, long term investor will also be concerned as to how efficiently the company has used its assets to achieve the level of turnover. This is measured by asset turnover and this efficiency is just as important as profit levels in achieving the overall return on investment. In a company such as New Look which has a stated objective of 'continuing expansion of our trading space, and especially the development of larger stores' it means that the expenditure on additional stores and fixtures must be efficiently used to turn into turnover and profits. The investor may also be interested in fixed (non-current) asset turnover which more accurately reflects the efficiency of usage of the fixed (non-current) assets of the business.

Dividend cover

A private investor with a long term perspective will have a particular interest in dividend cover. This measures the proportion of net profit in the company which is paid out as dividend and, perhaps more importantly, the proportion which is retained within the company for re-investment and long-term growth. The private investor would like to see a high dividend cover which indicates that dividend levels are safe for those interested in them but also that large amounts of profits are being retained within the business.

Stock (inventory) turnover

Although stock (inventory) turnover is usually seen as a short term measure, in a business such as the retail industry it is a key indicator of the financial health of the business and is therefore important to an investor with a long term interest in the company.

Assessment of performance of New Look

Profitability

The overall measure of profitability is the return on capital employed which has increased marginally from 61.6% to 62.3%. However from either a short term or a long term perspective this is a healthy return although it would be useful to be able to compare it to the ROCE of other similar high street fashion retailers. It is also interesting to note that this level of profitability has not always been evident in the company as it still has a debit balance on its profit and loss account (retained earnings) reserve. However it does indicate that in more recent times profitability is not an issue.

The ROCE is made up of two elements – the level of **profitability** and the efficient use of the capital employed or net assets. From the profitability perspective, the gross profit margin and net profit margin have increased, indicating good control of purchasing and other expenses. This improvement in profitability is also reflected in increased **earnings per share** which will be of interest to both long and short term investors. It is also interesting to note that diluted earnings per share is very similar to the basic earnings per share indicating that for long term investors there is no risk of any substantial dilution of the value of their holding in terms of earnings.

The other element of ROCE is the **efficient use of the assets** of the business. Both asset turnover and fixed (non-current) asset turnover have shown a marked reduction from last year. This will probably be of concern to short-term investors who may feel that their return could have been even higher if the assets had continued to be used as efficiently as before. However a long term investor, aware of New Look's policy of expansion of trading, may look at this differently. This will indicate, together with the significant expenditure on fixed (non-current) assets, that the company is investing in new assets which although not yet providing a full return, as they may not have been operational for the entire year, leaves the company well-placed for future growth.

Working capital

New Look has seen a growth in sales turnover for the last year of almost 10% however from the five year summary it can be seen that this is in fact a significantly lower level of increase than in the previous four years. However it is still a healthy increase and long term investors will be pleased with this year on year position.

As turnover grows however it is important both from a long term and short term perspective to keep control of working capital. The stock (inventory) turnover period has remained constant at 30 days although the overall working capital cycle has increased by 4 days. This may be of concern to those interested in short term profits but if the creditors (payables) payment period is looked at this increase is entirely down to paying creditors (payables) four days earlier. As the gross profit margin has increased it is likely that this shortening of the creditors (payables) payment period has been in response to negotiated lower prices or discounts with suppliers which is beneficial from both a short and long term perspective.

Financial structure

As gearing is a measure of financial risk it will be of interest to both short and long term investors. However in New Look it should not cause any problems. Not only is gearing at a low level of 11% but it has also been reduced from 24% the previous year largely due to the increase in retained earnings. From a profit and loss account (income statement) perspective interest cover is very high in both years indicating no real issues with financial risk.

From a short term investor's viewpoint the dividend policy of New Look would appear to be satisfactory as there has been an increase in both dividend per share and dividend cover. Although dividend cover has increased from 2.8 to 3.2 this still might appear quite low to a long term investor interested in the long term growth of the company through profitable reinvestment of retained earnings, as this means that one third of profits are being paid out as dividend.

Conclusion

From the limited information available it would appear that New Look's performance has improved over last year from either a short term or long term investor's perspective.

(c) **Limitations of using published financial information**

Trends

Most of a published annual report for a company is made up of the current year financial information and the same comparative information for the previous year. This means that the only comparison between financial ratios that can be made is the current year to the previous year rather than any longer term trend. For example from New Look's accounts it can be calculated that the ROCE has increased by 0.7% from 61.6% last year to 62.3% this year. On its own this is not a very impressive increase but if similar increases had taken place over the last few years this provides much more positive information.

The exception to this is that a five year summary of results is included, as in New Look's financial statements, but this only provides profit and loss account (income statement) information therefore no ratios which require links to the balance sheet can be calculated for this extended period.

Strategy

It can be argued that the performance of a company can only be properly assessed if that is done in the context of the strategy of the company. Although some information about strategy is often available in the Chairman's statement or Chief Executive Officer's report there are often only vague statements of strategy with little detail. For example we know that New Look's strategy is to 'continue expansion of our trading space' and to develop 'key markets' but we have little idea what these key markets are and are not able to assess the growth in trading space from the financial information.

Benchmarks

When using published financial information for assessment of performance the only figure with which to compare the current year figure is the previous year rather than any external or definitive benchmark. For example New Look's gross profit margin has increased from 22.3% to 23.7%

which on the face of it appears to be good. However if the general gross profit margin for similar companies is 28% then New Look is not performing as well as it might.

Accounting treatments

Although all companies must prepare their financial statements in line with accounting standards there are accounting treatments and policies which can affect the financial ratios used to assess performance. For example New Look has a significant number of operating leases for fixed (non-current) assets. The accounting treatment for these is that the rental is charged against profit but the assets themselves do not appear in the balance sheet and therefore are not part of the asset base or capital employed. This can have the effect of overstating ROCE compared to the assets truly being used within the business.

Similarly the depreciation policy of New Look states that fixtures and fittings, which make up the vast majority of the fixed (non-current) assets are depreciated over a period of 'three to fifteen years'. The period of depreciation chosen within this range will have a significant effect on the reported profit.

Share price information

The financial statements do not normally contain any information on the company share price therefore it becomes impossible to calculate measures such as dividend yield and P/E ratio which would be useful information for current and prospective shareholders.

APPENDIX

New Look Annual Report 2002/2003 – Ratio Analysis

	2003	*2002*
Increase in turnover		
(643.4 – 585.4)/585.4	10%	
Gross profit margin		
Gross profit (note 3)/turnover × 100		
152.5/643.4 × 100	23.7%	
130.6/585.4 × 100		22.3%
Net profit margin		
Operating profit + interest receivable (note 4)/turnover × 100		
84.6 + 1.9/643.5 × 100	13.4%	
63.7 + 0.9/585.4 × 100		11.04%
Dividend cover		
Profit attributable to shareholders/dividends		
55.5/17.4	3.2	
39.3/14		2.8
Earnings per share		
– basic	27.9p	19.8p
– diluted	27.4p	19.5p
Dividend per share	8.75p	7.0p
Return on capital employed		
Operating profit + interest receivable (note 4)/shareholders funds and bank loans		
84.6 + 1.9/130.6 + 8.3 × 100	62.3%	
63.7 + 0.9/88.7 + 16.2 × 100		61.6%
Asset turnover		
Turnover/Capital employed		
643.4/130.6 + 8.3	4.63	
585.4/88.7 + 16.2		5.58
Fixed (non-current) asset turnover		
Turnover/fixed (non-current) assets		
643.4/116.9	5.50	
585.4/99.8		5.86
Stock (inventory) turnover		
Stock (inventory)/cost of sales (note 3) × 365		
40.3/490.9 × 365	30 days	
37.7/454.8 × 365		30 days
Creditors (payables) payment period		
Trade creditors (payables)(note 15)/cost of sales × 365		
19.2/490.9 × 365	14.3 days	
22.7/454.8 × 365		18.2 days
Working capital cycle		
Stock (inventory) turnover – creditors (payables) payment period		
30 – 14.3 days	15.7 days	
30 – 18.2 days		11.8 days
Gearing		
Long term creditors (payables)/shareholders funds		
13.7/125.0 × 100	10.96%	
20.6/85.5 × 100		24.09%

Question 2

Presentation to investors – Management reporting package

(a)

Slide 1

WHAT IS SHAREHOLDER VALUE?

= RETURN TO SHAREHOLDERS

= DIVIDENDS + CAPITAL GROWTH

It is a generally accepted business maxim that the aim of a business is to maximise shareholder wealth. So how is shareholder wealth or shareholder value to be defined? It is made up of two elements:

- dividend income
- increase in share price = capital growth

Slide 2

HOW IS SHAREHOLDER VALUE MEASURED?

- **profit**
- **earnings per share**
- **dividend per share**
- **economic value added**
- **share price increase**

There are a variety of ways in which shareholder value can be measured:

Profit

Profit can be measured by ROCE. If a company is making profits then it will be in a position to pay dividends to shareholders and is also likely to attract new investors leading to a rise in share price.

Earnings per share

A company may be profitable but it is important for shareholders to appreciate how much of that profit belongs to them. In a growing company profits may be increasing but new shares may be issued as well. Earnings per share relates the profits earned to the number of shares in issue and effectively shows the current year profits that relate to each one of the investor's shares.

Dividend per share

This is a more direct way of measuring shareholder value as it measures directly the amount of dividend income that will be received for each share owned.

Economic value added

The measures already discussed are based upon book values. However for a truer measure of shareholder wealth, economic value added (EVA®) could be used. This is the excess of reported profit over and above an economic profit which is based upon the economic value of the assets employed.

Increase in share price

Capital growth can be measured by periodic changes in the share price of the company's shares. However this information cannot be found in the financial statements of the company but instead from stock market records.

Slide 3

RELEVANCE?

OTHER STAKEHOLDERS

It was stated earlier that the assumed purpose of a business was to maximise the wealth or value of its shareholders. However in practice it is now recognised that a company, to be successful, must meet the needs of a variety of stakeholders of which the shareholders are just one. However it is possible to reconcile this with shareholder value. For example one of the major stakeholders will be the company's customers and if their needs are met through quality and service then this will more than likely feed through to greater shareholder value.

(b)

Slide 4

NON-FINANCIAL PERFORMANCE MEASURES

RETAIL INDUSTRY

Footfall

Total sales area

Sales per square foot

Customer satisfaction

New markets

Market share

New products

Manufacturer's quality

Footfall

The number of customers entering a store gives an indication of the effectiveness of advertising and brand name and also of the corporate and individual store display. The higher the number of customers, or footfall, the higher the probability of sales being made. Without customers, sales cannot be made.

The major problem here is the measurement of footfall. The basic measurement is the number of customers entering each store on a daily basis. This could be based upon estimates from the sales staff or more technical, electronic methods of measuring each customer entering the doors.

Total sales area

One of the stated aims of New Look is 'the continuing expansion of our trading space, and especially the development of larger stores in key markets'. Therefore measurement of total sales area must be critical in meeting this strategy of trading area growth. The more stores that are available to customers the more likely it is that potential customers will find a store local to them and will purchase from it.

Measurement should be a straightforward total of the floor space of all the active stores. A further associated measure that might also be of use is the average floor space per store – ie the total floor space divided by the number of stores. As there is an emphasis on the development of larger stores one would expect to see the average floor space per store increasing over time.

Sales per square foot

Getting customers into the store is one matter but making the sale is the most important factor. The fixed costs of store space will be a major element of costs and it is important that this expensive store space is used effectively. It could also be useful to compare not only total sales per square foot in stores but also an analysis between different product lines of sales.

This would be simply measured for each store as sales value divided by floor area. If further analysis is required per product line then estimates of the floor area taken up by each product line must be made.

Customer satisfaction

One theoretical method of measuring customer satisfaction is a measure of the amount of repeat business and the amount of business referred from satisfied customers. However in a retail situation this is very difficult to measure in practice. However customer satisfaction is an important factor in the success of any retail organisation and can perhaps be measured in different ways.

One method of measuring customer satisfaction is to measure the level of customer returns and reasons for returns. This will help to assess whether the company's quality standards are being met. This could be measured either as the number of items returned as a percentage of the number of items sold or as the value of items returned as a percentage of the value of items sold. Both measures should yield similar percentage results.

New markets

New markets could be defined in opening stores in new towns or shopping centres in the UK or could be looked at in terms of opening up new markets in other countries, particularly as the Chief Executive states the objective of 'the development of our business in France, where we have identified business opportunities'. The wider the market, in the UK or elsewhere, ie the number of stores available for customers to visit the higher will be the footfall and therefore the potential sales.

This could be measured by the number of new stores opened each month. The measure could further be analysed into new stores in a new geographical area in the UK and in another country.

Market share

In a competitive market such as high street retail, one major method of achieving growth is to attract a higher volume share of the market. This is an important indicator of the success of attracting customers and making sales.

This would be measured as New Look's share of the total high street retail clothing market as a percentage.

New products

In a retail environment it is important to customers that there are new products in store. Therefore it is important to measure the number of new product lines introduced as this will maintain customer expectations and encourage them to visit the store more frequently. This can be measured by the number of new product lines introduced per week.

It is also important that when a new fashion trend is determined the time between agreeing the new product idea and getting it into the stores is minimised. This can be measured by the number of days between a new product being agreed and it being displayed in store.

Manufacturer's quality

Customer satisfaction with the products on offer is, as we have seen, an important factor in retailing success. The process of ensuring customer satisfaction can begin at the goods inwards stage as customer satisfaction can only be effectively achieved if the goods received from the manufacturers are of sufficient quality. If large levels of returns have to be made to suppliers then this will affect the stock (inventory) of the stores and if goods are not available may lead to loss of goodwill from customers. If the number of items which do not meet the required production standards are measured at the goods inwards stage then the reliability of individual suppliers can be assessed and their use evaluated. Also to assess the quality at the goods inwards stage rather than to wait for returns from customers will have a less negative effect on customer goodwill.

The returns to suppliers can be assessed as the number of items returned as a percentage of the number of items purchased or alternatively the value of items returned as a percentage of the value of items purchased.

(c) **Benchmarking**

Slide 5

BENCHMARKING AND MANAGEMENT PERFORMANCE

Improvement of performance

Store comparison

Motivation

Range of areas

Benchmarking is a method of comparing results to a pre-set target or benchmark as opposed to comparing results from one period to another. This is done with key areas of performance in order to improve that performance by comparison to a realistic and relevant target. Ideally benchmarks should come from a competitor or an average figure for the retail industry, but in such a competitive market as retail it may be difficult to find realistic competitor figures. Care should be taken with using average industry figures as this might mean that targets are set which are too low.

Another way in which benchmarking can be used internally is in store comparison. The benchmark figure for a performance area could be the best performing store in this area which other stores should aspire to.

If used carefully, benchmarking should not only improve performance but should also act as a motivational factor as store managers attempt to meet these benchmark targets, provided that they are viewed as realistic.

Care should however be taken to ensure that a range of outcomes are measured in order that decisions are not taken that will improve one benchmarked figure but lead to a downturn in overall performance.

Slide 6

BENCHMARKING ACTIVITIES

Customer satisfaction

Store sales and efficiency

Stock (inventory) management

Activities that could be usefully benchmarked in a retail organisation such as New Look can be classified under these three headings. Some of these were justified earlier but some are additional measures that will be justified in this section.

Customer satisfaction

Level of customer returns as a percentage of sales

Customer complaints procedure

It is important that customer complaints are dealt with promptly and if possible at store level in order to minimise any loss of customer goodwill.

This aspect could be measured by the number of customer complaints for each store unresolved after 24 hours. Alternatively the number of unresolved complaints as a percentage of total complaints could be measured to give a relative measure of the success in dealing with complaints.

Customer requests not met

This is the situation where a customer wishes to purchase an item but it is not in stock in the store or cannot be supplied to the customer quickly. Not only will this lead to a lost sale but also a loss of customer goodwill.

This could be measured by keeping a record of the number of items requested by customers but not in stock for each store. This would also help in decisions regarding stock (inventory) control.

Store sales and efficiency

Footfall – the number of customers through the door each day/week.

Sales per square foot – total sales divided by stores floor area.

Average spend per customer.

The more that customers spend on average the more this is an indication of customer satisfaction and sales efficiency.

This could be measured by the total sales for a period divided by the number of transactions in that period.

Sales achievement

In a retail environment high stock turnover over all ranges of products means higher profits. A comparison could be made in each store to determine the number of lines sold in comparison to the number of lines stocked. This would give an indication of how efficiently each store is set out and is presenting its goods to customers.

Stock (inventory) management

Stock (inventory) turnover period

In the fashion retail industry short stock (inventory) turnover periods are essential. This measure must be monitored at store level and stores compared and any deterioration highlighted and dealt with quickly.

This is measured as closing stock (inventory) as a percentage of stock (inventory) received during the period in the store × 365 (in order to measure it in days.)

Discounted sales

If items are being sold at less than their original full retail price then these sales will reduce the gross profit margin and overall profitability therefore it is important that they are carefully monitored.

This could be measured as the percentage of sales revenue per stores at less than full retail price and this will indicate whether stores have allowed surplus or slow moving items to build up.

In conclusion always remember that no performance measure should be looked at in isolation. Instead the management reporting package should include a range of key performance indicators which should be reviewed by managers on a regular basis in order to improve the performance of the organisation.

4 Examiner's comments

Examiner's comments. The theme of the examiner's comments remains that many candidates do not specifically address the scenario that is given in the project. Generalised, text book answers are not enough to gain good marks and the analysis provided must be based upon and justified by the scenario and the information provided in the supplement.

The examiner's comments are set out below.

General comments. The purpose of the project is to provide candidates with an opportunity to prepare answers free of the time-constrained environment of the examination hall. This freedom is intended to allow the development of analytical and critical thinking. It was pleasing that a good number of candidates took this opportunity and produced work of a very high standard.

The **best answers** presented tended to demonstrate both awareness and application of a number of key issues. These included:

Evidence of good answer planning

The best answers clearly showed that candidates had taken time to consider the questions and develop answers which avoided repetition, with successive parts of the answer building on common analysis and observations in earlier parts.

Attention to the relative importance of each part of the question

The mark allocation is intended to assist candidates to discern how much they are expected to write. The best answers used the 5,000 word allowance over the parts of the question relative to the number of marks allocated to that part.

Reading beyond the basic texts

A number of candidates produced observations and analysis which demonstrated that they had read (and more importantly, understood) material from relevant publications beyond the basic texts.

Clear understanding of context

Answers that considered the context in which the analysis was placed, and which used the context as the basis for analysis, tended to score well.

Unfortunately a number of candidates did not produce work with the qualities already noted. As a consequence, such work did not gain high marks. Typical **weaknesses** in such answers were:

Lack of proofreading

It was clear that some candidates had not carefully read through their final report prior to submission. This meant that what may have been a good piece of work was spoilt by poor presentation. In one or two extreme cases, it was clear that material which the writer had intended to include had somehow been left out, as sentences at the end of a page were unfinished even though the page numbers were consecutive. It goes without saying that such proofreading would also provide an opportunity for a critical reading through referred to above. Of course it is only possible if careful planning has been undertaken, with time allocated to this activity.

Weak conclusions

A sound conclusion will address the question asked and will follow logically from the data to the analysis of such data. Too many candidates included vague statements which did not follow in a logical fashion from the analysis of data.

Lack of visual aids

Question 2 specifically asked for visual aids. This requirement had also been included in recent projects. This has been a deliberate policy as the ability to make presentations is now regarded as an essential skill for a manager. As this approach had been introduced previously, a small number of marks were allocated to the quality of the visual aids. Candidates should note that the number of marks allocated to this area may be greater in future projects.

Poor planning

Some answers suggested that candidates had decided to write as much as possible about one or two areas in the hope of gaining enough marks to compensate for the weaker areas of their answer. This is often an unproductive strategy as the marking scheme is designed to reward candidates who take time to research relevant theory before producing answers. In many cases, lack of planning led to opportunities for gaining marks being rejected. For example, some answers to part (b) of Question 2 included less than 600 words, even though it was worth 24 marks. On the basis of the words in total this would represent 1,200 words. It is inconceivable that an answer of such brevity could contain sufficient material to obtain high marks.

Context

In some cases there was evidence that candidates had not given their answers much thought even though a considerable amount of supplementary information was provided. Naturally not all of this could be used. Part of the reason for providing so much information is to allow candidates to develop their approach to answering the questions. Another reason is to attempt to replicate the 'real world' where managers are required to exercise choice and discretion in deciding what information is relevant – and what information can be ignored. The chosen company in this case was a fashion retailer and although this may be stating the obvious it was an important piece of information. Unfortunately for some candidates it was information which was ignored. This meant that in Question 1, one of the ratios included for consideration was the debtors collection period, while in Question 2 performance measures which would have been relevant to a manufacturer were considered.

Question 1

Lack of justification of measures used

Even though the question specifically required candidates to justify their choice of measures a number of candidates did not do so. This is particularly surprising as this point has been the subject of an article in *Finance Matters* and has been referred to in reports on previous sittings. In this context candidates should note that a statement such as 'Return on capital employed is a key ratio' is not justification because it begs the question 'why is it a key ratio?'. What is required is a clear statement as to why the measure is important for the specific company being assessed. Other examples attempted to avoid the need to think and analyse by stating that certain ratios 'are relevant to investors' but did not explain why. One technique for avoiding this tendency is for candidates to critically read through their work prior to final submission, and put themselves in the place of the marker. Attempt to identify where the marker is likely to think 'why have you said that?' and provide evidence for the comment.

Descriptive comments

At this level it is taken for granted that candidates know that if ROCE has moved from say 24% to 26% that this is an improvement. What is expected of candidates is that they consider the extent to which such an improvement meets the stated objectives of the company, and the possible reasons for the change.

Too many candidates seem to think that by using the ratios included in the text and describing the results of the calculation they will pick up marks. This is a mistake, as marks are only allocated to analysis not to description. That is not to say that description is irrelevant. Unless candidates actually include points that may be regarded as descriptive (or obvious) the marker will not be able to appreciate the argument that is being developed. While a basic descriptive comment is a necessary part of an answer, the answer must move beyond description if marks are to be awarded. The same comments can be applied to internally-generated measures of performance.

In some extreme cases, candidates did not provide even descriptive comments on the ratios.

No link between ratios

One of the best ways of developing an analysis of either financial ratios or internal performance measures is to consider the elements of the measure and to consider these in turn. The most obvious example of this is the fact that asset utilisation and profit margin combine to produce return on capital employed. This is consistent with a key issue in business performance – managing both the level of activity and the profit margin on each transaction.

Question 2

Balanced scorecard

It was extremely surprising how many candidates treated Question 2 as a question on the balanced scorecard. While it would have been relevant (but not essential) to refer to the balanced scorecard as a structured methodology for performance measurement, there was no basis for providing descriptive comments about the scorecard or its historical development.

It is probably the case that any reference to the scorecard was likely to reduce the opportunity to gain marks. The main reason for this is that the scorecard attempts to take performance measures beyond the use of financial measures but does not eliminate the use of financial measures. Without exception, those candidates who referred to the balanced scorecard provided a potential scorecard including financial measures. The question, however, specifically required that non-financial measures of performance were considered. Therefore this approach bore all the hallmarks of candidates answering their own question rather than the one that was actually asked, or relying on studies rather than some hard thought and analysis to produce an answer. While this approach is sometimes understandable in the pressure of an exam room (although invariably non-productive) it is totally unacceptable in the context of the project where candidates are not under such pressures.

Measures

Perhaps the most common reason for candidates not gaining marks in Question 2 was a lack of thought when proposing measures of performance. This has been a weakness at successive sittings with candidates noting the area in which measurement is required but failing to provide any specific method of measurement.

ACCA Live Project – Spring 2005: Module B

7

1 Spring 2005 Project: Module B

Diploma in Financial Management

PROJECT DB2, INCORPORATING SUBJECT AREAS
- FINANCIAL STRATEGY
- RISK MANAGEMENT

All questions are compulsory and MUST be answered

The project MUST be written in English.

The maximum word count (including appendices and tables but excluding references and bibliography) is 5,000.

The project MUST be TYPED in black ink, one-sided, double-spaced, using a minimum 12-point font size and a 1-inch margin at each side. HANDWRITTEN SUBMISSIONS WILL NOT BE ACCEPTED. The project must be submitted by post, electronic submissions are not acceptable.

The project should be submitted on A4 paper with your student number, project name, date and page number at the top of each page.

A project submission form MUST be completed for each project submitted and attached to the front of the project.

The Association of Chartered Certified Accountants

Incorporating subject areas – Financial Strategy and Risk Management

This ONE question is compulsory and MUST be attempted

Emmanuel Hire plc

Emmanuel Hire plc operates a chain of tools and equipment hire branches throughout England and Wales. In the past ten years it has grown rapidly through a process of acquisition and organic growth and now, with more than 150 branches, is one of the leading tool hire businesses in Europe. The customer base is largely local tradesmen and DIY enthusiasts and the tools and equipment hired range from carpet cleaners through to excavators. However, drills, breakers and concrete mixers are the core revenue producers for the company. The company operates a fleet of delivery vehicles and all branches have vehicles for delivery purposes. The company has high service standards and has acquired a good reputation. As a result, more than 60% of the revenue generated comes from repeat business.

The most recent financial statements of the business are set out below.

EMMANUEL HIRE PLC
DRAFT BALANCE SHEET
AS AT 31 JANUARY 2005

	£'000	£'000
Non-current assets (at written down values)		
Goodwill		4,560
Freehold land and buildings		1,920
Leasehold land and buildings		130
Hire equipment		13,230
Motor vehicles		960
Fixtures and fittings		2,370
		23,170
Current assets		
Inventory	220	
Receivables	10,540	
Cash in hand	4	
		10,764
		33,934
Capital and reserves		
£0.50 ordinary shares issued		10,000
Retained earnings		16,164
		26,164
Non current liabilities		
7% Loan stock (secured on freehold building)		1,500
Current liabilities		
Trade payables	3,520	
Tax	1,100	
Dividends	1,650	
		6,270
		33,934

EMMANUEL HIRE PLC
DRAFT INCOME STATEMENT
FOR THE YEAR ENDED 31 JANUARY 2005

	£'000	£'000
Revenue		35,730
Cost of sales		7,080
Gross profit		28,650
Less		
Selling and distribution expenses	3,350	
Administration expenses	19,845	
		23,195
Operating profit		5,455
Finance expenses		105
Profit before tax		5,350
Tax (25%)		1,337
Profit after tax		4,013
Dividends		1,337
Profit for the year		2,676

Emmanuel Hire plc uses the straight line method of depreciation and depreciation charges for the year to 31 January 2005 were £3,850,000. The company, which is listed on the London Stock Exchange, has a price earnings (P/E) ratio of 12 times and has a policy of maintaining a dividend cover ratio of 3.0 times.

The hire market is very competitive and there are many small businesses operating within the industry. However, there has been a trend towards consolidation over recent years with many small businesses being either taken over or forced out of business by their larger rivals. Emmanuel Hire plc has acquired five small businesses over the past three years and expects to acquire further businesses in the future in order to increase both market share and geographical coverage. To this end, Emmanuel Hire plc is now in the final stages of negotiation for the purchase of the assets of Hughes Hire Ltd, which operates more than 40 branches in Lanarkshire. The most recent financial statements of this company are as follows.

HUGHES HIRE LTD
DRAFT BALANCE SHEET
AS AT 31 JANUARY 2005

	£'000	£'000
Non-current assets (at written down values)		
Freehold land and buildings		700
Hire equipment		4,280
Motor vehicles		390
Fixtures and fittings		960
		6,330
Current assets		
Inventory	70	
Receivables	3,850	
		3,920
		10,250
Capital and liabilities		
£1 ordinary shares		1,000
Retained earnings		4,015
		5,015
Non-current liabilities		
5% loan stock (secured on freehold buildings)		2,200
Current liabilities		
Trade payables	1,280	
Tax	555	
Dividends	1,200	
		3,035
		10,250

HUGHES HIRE LTD
DRAFT INCOME STATEMENT
FOR THE YEAR ENDED 31 JANUARY 2005

	£'000	£'000
Revenue		12,810
Cost of sales		2,480
Gross profit		10,330
Less		
Selling and distribution expenses	1,260	
Administrative expenses	6,740	
		8,000
Operating profit		2,330
Finance expenses		110
Profit before tax		2,220
Tax (25%)		555
Profit after tax		1,665
Dividends		1,200
Profit for the year		465

The company uses the straight line method of depreciation and depreciation charges for the year to 31 January 2005 were £960,000.

An inspection of the branches of Hughes Hire Ltd by the operations director of Emmanuel Hire plc revealed a lack of investment over recent years. The delivery fleet is in need of replacement, the hire equipment is in poor condition and the quality and presentation of the branches are well below the standards of the prospective new owner. Assuming the acquisition goes ahead, an investment of approximately £4 million will be required to bring the newly-acquired operations up to the required standards. However, no new investment will be made during the first year of operations. The operations director of Emmanuel Hire plc believes that the potential of the branches has not been fully exploited. He estimates that, following acquisition, sales can be increased by 20% per year. Furthermore, selling, distribution and administrative expenses relating to the newly-acquired branches can be reduced by 10% per year through better monitoring and control systems.

The price paid for the assets of the company is likely to be £12 million and will be paid in cash. The purchase negotiations concern the assets of Hughes Hire Ltd only. The owners of Hughes Hire Ltd will take responsibility for the payment of any outstanding liabilities before winding up the company. To finance the purchase, Emmanuel Hire plc will make either a 2 for 5 rights issue of ordinary shares or an issue of loan capital at par.

The board of directors of Emmanuel Hire plc is due to meet shortly to discuss the proposed acquisition and there are a number of items on the agenda for discussion. One of the more important items concerns the financing of the purchase. If loan stock is used to help finance the bid, the finance director is keen to hedge against interest rate risk. The company has a good credit rating and can raise fixed rate loan capital at 6.5% and floating rate loan capital at LIBOR plus 0.7% from its bank. The company want to use long term, floating rate finance to help fund the purchase of Hughes Hire Ltd and has been offered a five-year swap arrangement by a bank. The bank has identified Fitzwilliam plc as a counterparty to the agreement. Fitzwilliam plc is a large soft drinks company that can raise fixed interest loan capital at 8.1% and floating rate loan capital at LIBOR plus 1.4% from its bank. The swap bank will arrange the swap agreement and act as guarantor for both parties for an annual total fee of 0.3%. The two companies will pay to, or receive from, the swap bank a fixed amount and will receive, or pay, LIBOR in return. It has been estimated that LIBOR will be 5.8% for the whole of next year.

Recent reports suggest that the tool and equipment hire market will remain unchanged for the foreseeable future. A succession of rises in interest rates over the past two years has led to stagnation in the home improvements market and, as a consequence, the market for tool hire has also stagnated. However, the directors of Emmanuel Hire plc are confident that sales (excluding the acquisition of Hughes Hire Ltd) can be increased next year by entering new markets. The company has begun to forge links with construction companies and is now about to sign a contract with one large construction business that is likely to increase sales by £3 million per year. The gross profit margin from this agreement will be the same as for the business as a whole and there will be no additional selling, distribution or administration costs as a result of the agreement.

The directors are keen to standardise the credit period allowed to credit customers following the takeover of the assets of Hughes Hire Ltd. As a result, they have agreed that customers for both Emmanuel Hire plc and Hughes Hire Ltd will all be given three months' credit. The only exception to this policy is the construction business, which has negotiated a credit period of four months. Trade payables are expected to be 40% of total trade receivables at the year end.

Emmanuel Hire plc was created by David Emmanuel in 1992 and he was both chief executive and chairman up until his retirement at the end of January 2005. After his retirement, a new chief executive was appointed and a non-executive chairman was also appointed. David Emmanuel was extremely entrepreneurial and, in the early years, the company benefited from his flair and appetite for risk. However, in more recent years, this entrepreneurial style has become less successful. The company, although still growing, appears to have entered a new, more mature, phase in its development. There have been increasing calls from institutional investors for the company to be managed more strategically and for risk management to feature more strongly in the decisions made by the directors. The finance director has pressed for some years for the business to adopt a risk-based management approach to decision-making but was consistently rebuffed by David Emmanuel. However, the new chief executive is keen to adopt this approach.

Required

(a)   **Evaluate the acquisition of Hughes Hire Ltd from the viewpoint of shareholders in Emmanuel Hire plc**   (18 marks)

(b)   **Set out the factors to be considered when deciding between ordinary share capital and loan capital to finance the purchase of Hughes Hire Ltd**   (7 marks)

(c)   **Assuming the purchase of Hughes Hire Ltd is financed by an issue of loan capital**

   (i)   **set out the details of the swap arrangement showing how it can benefit both companies and showing the total interest rate to be paid by Emmanuel Hire plc in the first year.**

   (ii)   **suggest an alternative method by which interest rate risk may be managed and compare this with a swap arrangement.**   (10 marks)

(d)   **Assuming that the various proposals are undertaken at the beginning of the year to 31 January 2006:**

   (i)   **prepare a forecast cash flow statement and forecast income statement for Emmanuel Hire plc under each of the financing options identified for the year to 31 January 2006**

   (ii)   **calculate the effect on the profitability and gearing of the company under each of the financing options identified for the year to 31 January 2006**

   (iii) **comment on the findings in (i) and (ii) above**   (25 marks)

(e)   **Set out the main advantages of a risk-based management approach to decision-making and identify the key tasks that should be carried out to implement such a system.**   (20 marks)

(f)   **Identify the key operational risks that confront Emmanuel Hire plc as a result of the purchase of Hughes Hire Ltd and state how these might be managed.**   (20 marks)

(100 marks)

Notes

1 All recommendations must be supported by reasoned arguments
2 All key workings must be shown and key assumptions must be clearly stated
3 Workings should be in £'000s
4 Ignore inflation
5 Assume that tax is payable nine months after the year end.

2 Suggested approach

The scenario given, Emmanuel Hire plc, covers both subject areas for Module B – Financial Strategy and Risk Management.

Start by reading through the scenario. At this stage do not worry about the numbers; just read through the information so that you have a broad overview of the situation.

Now turn to the requirements and read them through carefully together with the notes at the end of the requirements section.

Bearing the requirements of the project in mind now read through the scenario again, possibly highlighting areas that you think might be relevant.

Part (a)

This is a very open ended question as you are simply being asked to 'evaluate' the acquisition from the perspective of the acquirer's shareholders. You might want to start with an attempt to value Hughes Hire Ltd. Any estimated value put on Hughes Hire can then be compared to the suggested purchase price.

However you need to take your evaluation further. Emmanuel Hire is acquiring Hughes Hire in order to run it as a going concern. Therefore consider the effect that Hughes Hire might have on Emmanuel Hire. What is the profitability level of Hughes Hire? What is its working capital management like? Are these likely to alter when acquired by Emmanuel Hire? You could investigate all of this by carrying out some basic ratio analysis on Hughes Hire. Remember also to take into account the narrative information that you have been given about Hughes Hire.

Part (b)

This is a standard question on the factors involved in a decision between raising the funds for the acquisition by an issue of ordinary shares or an issue of loan capital. Try to make seven valid points as there are seven marks available. Think about all aspects of the raising of the funds from the initial availability through to costs and the effect on the financial structure of the company.

Part (c)

Part (i) requires you to deal with the numerical aspects of an interest rate swap. If you are not confident about this area, study it in the BPP textbook before you have a go at the numbers.

For part (ii) the most obvious examples are either a forward rate agreement or an interest rate option. Whichever you choose, try to illustrate the difference between it and the interest rate swap.

Part (d)

This is the big number crunching section which will take time but the figures are not too complex. Note precisely what you have to do:

- forecast cash flow statement and forecast income statement under the share capital option
- forecast cash flow statement and forecast income statement under the loan capital option

- the effect on profitability (ie ratios) and gearing under each option
- commentary on your findings.

When preparing the cash flow statement and income statement under each option you will find it easier to do the income statement first as you will need the operating profit figure as a starting point in your cash flow statement.

Remember to state all of your assumptions – the golden rule is that if you think you are making an assumption then state it!

Part (e)

Here you firstly have to set out the advantages of a risk-based management approach to decision-making. This is fairly textbook stuff so you might find that a re-read of the first 4 chapters of the BPP textbook is useful, taking notes as you go through about areas that you think would be relevant to this answer.

You then have to identify the key tasks that should be carried out to implement such a system. Again you should be able to get ideas about this from the BPP textbook.

Part (f)

Finally, you are required to consider the operational risks that might exist as a consequence of Emmanuel's takeover of Hughes. Operational risks can be viewed as all risks other than financial risks. You will need to re-read the scenario to remind yourself of the details of the takeover and consider the possible problems/risks that Emmanuel might face.

Note that you not only have to identify these operational risks but also state how they might be managed.

3 Suggested answer

(a)   **Evaluation of acquisition of Hughes Hire Ltd**

Emmanuel Hire plc is proposing to acquire the assets of Hughes Hire Ltd for an expected cash price of £12 million.

Book value of Hughes Hire Ltd

The book value of the assets of Hughes Hire Ltd is £10.25 million. Book values often bear little indication of the true value of the assets of a business. In this case it is likely that the value of the freehold land and buildings may be considerably higher than the figure in the balance sheet of £700,000 as these assets are clearly recorded at historical cost as there is no revaluation reserve. The other assets are either in need of replacement or in poor condition so there is little evidence as to whether their book values reflect their true value. The trade receivables figure is high, representing 110 days or over three and a half months of sales ($3,850/12,810 \times 365$) therefore it is possible that there are some bad debts included in that amount. It is also likely that there is some goodwill in Hughes Hire which is a valuable asset but is not recorded in the balance sheet.

Therefore on the basis of book values £12 million appears to be a reasonable price.

Earnings based valuation of Hughes Hire Ltd

However the book value is often viewed as being of little relevance as these are accounting values. A fairer view of the value of Hughes Hire will be given by valuing its shares on the basis of earnings.

If the P/E ratio of Emmanuel Hire is used to value the shares in Hughes Hire the following value per share can be calculated.

EPS of Hughes Hire   =   £1,665/1,000 shares
                        =   £1.665

Value of share in Hughes Hire = £1.665 × 12

                                  = £19.98

However we have used a quoted company's P/E ratio here to value a private company's shares. Therefore this estimate of share value should be reduced to recognise the lack of marketability of the shares in Hughes Hire and the difference in size of the two companies. A suitable discount might be 30% giving the following share value:

Value of share in Hughes Hire = 70% × £19.98

                                  = £13.99 say £14.00

Emmanuel is paying a price of £12 per share (£12 million/1 million shares) for shares valued at around £14.

Operating characteristics of Hughes Hire Ltd

On the face of it this would appear to be a good deal. However the characteristics of the business that Emmanuel Hire is purchasing must also be considered. This can be done by carrying out some basic ratio analysis based upon the draft financial statements given.

	Emmanuel Hire	Hughes Hire
Gross profit margin		
Gross profit/revenue × 100		
28,650/35,730 × 100	80.2%	
10,330/12,810 × 100		80.6%
Net profit margin		
Operating profit/revenue × 100		
5,455/35,730 × 100	15.3%	
2,330/12,810 × 100		18.2%
Return on capital employed		
Operating profit/capital and non-current liabilities × 100		
5,455/26,164 + 1,500 × 100	19.7%	
2,330/5,015 + 2,200 × 100		32.3%
Return on shareholders funds		
Profit after interest and tax/shareholders funds × 100		
4,013/26,164 × 100	15.3%	
1,665/5,015 × 100		33.2%
Gearing		
Non-current liabilities/shareholders funds × 100		
1,500/26,164 × 100	5.7%	
2,200/5,015		43.9%
Asset turnover		
Revenue/capital and non-current liabilities		
35,730/26,164 + 1,500	1.3 times	
12,810/5,105 + 2,200		1.8 times
Receivables collection period		
Receivables/revenue × 365		
10,540/35,730 × 365	107 days	
3,850/12,810 × 365		110 days

It would appear from this analysis that Hughes Hire is certainly a profitable company.

Its gross profit margin is slightly higher than that of Emmanuel Hire and its net profit margin is significantly higher, although the difference here is largely caused by depreciation policies.

Emmanuel's depreciation charge is approximately 20% of the book value of non-current assets whereas Hughes's depreciation is only 15% of the book value of non-current assets.

However when return on capital employed is considered there is a very big difference with Emmanuel at 19.7% and Hughes at 32.3%. This is partly due to the better net profit margin as discussed above but also due to the fact that Hughes has an asset turnover of 1.8 times compared to that of Emmanuel of 1.3 times.

This, however, is probably not due to the fact that Hughes is more efficient in its use of its assets than Emmanuel but due to the fact that the assets of Hughes have low book values due to their age and condition. The lack of investment in Hughes over recent years means that capital employed is low therefore giving high figures for returns on capital and asset turnover.

The other major difference between the two companies is the level of gearing. Hughes has a high level of gearing of 44% of capital and reserves whereas the level for Emmanuel is just over 5%. However as Hughes would appear to be borrowing at just 5% per annum ($110/2,200 \times 100$) and earning net profits considerably in excess of this figure this reflects in the return on shareholders' funds being 33.2% in Hughes and just 15.3% in Emmanuel.

Therefore it would appear that Hughes Hire Ltd is a profitable company although its returns on capital are inflated somewhat due to the lack of investment in the business in recent years.

Future prospects

Although Hughes is clearly profitable the operations director of Emmanuel expects sales to be increased by 20% after acquisition and selling, distribution and administration expenses to be reduced by 10%. This will make Hughes even more profitable.

However it would appear that the quality of the assets that Emmanuel is taking over is not high and that £4 million will need to be spent in future on these assets.

Conclusion

From the information available and the analysis carried out it would appear that Emmanuel Hire will be acquiring a profitable company with good future prospects at a very reasonable price.

(b)   **Ordinary share capital v loan capital**

The factors to be considered when deciding between ordinary share capital or loan capital in order to raise the funds for the purchase of Hughes Hire Ltd are detailed below.

Market conditions

Market conditions at the time of raising the finance will affect the choice as to which type of capital. If interest rates are generally expected to rise in the near future then the rate of interest on loan capital will tend to be higher to compensate for this. However in this case Emmanuel is being offered an interest rate swap which will effectively mean that for the next year the company will pay an interest rate of 6.2% (see part (c)) compared to the rate of 7% that it appears to be paying on its current loans ($105/1,500 \times 100$).

If ordinary shares are to be raised with a rights issue there is some risk if the company's share price falls between the announcement of the rights issue and the rights issue itself. If Emmanuel's share price falls below the rights issue price then the issue will fail as the rights will not be taken up.

Security

For an issue of loan stock Emmanuel will almost certainly have to provide fixed or floating rate security whereas this will not be necessary for a rights issue. However as the level of gearing in Emmanuel is currently low and the non-current assets have relatively high book values (and possibly higher market values) the availability of security should not be an issue.

Cost of issue

In general the costs of a rights issue will be higher than the cost of issuing loan stock as the rights issue will involve legal fees, adviser's fees, printing costs and advertising costs.

Cost of servicing finance

The cost of servicing the loan finance is the interest cost which will be 6.2% (see part (c)) for the coming year. The cost of servicing the additional shares will be the cost of paying additional dividends. The current dividend per share is 6.68 pence (£1,337/20,000) and the current market value of the share can be estimated at £2.41 using the P/E ratio of Emmanuel (4,013/20,000 × 12). Therefore the current cost of dividend payments is just 2.8% (0.0668/2.41 × 100).

Availability of profits and cash

If loan finance is to be raised the company must be certain that it has the cash flows necessary to pay the annual interest costs and to eventually redeem the loan stock. If additional shares are issued then the company will still wish to continue paying dividends but must have both the cash and distributable profits available. As retained earnings are high this would not appear to be a problem but if Emmanuel is to continue its policy of maintaining a dividend cover ratio of 3.0 times then annual profits need to be high enough to do this without there being a fall in dividend value.

Dilution of control

The issue of loan finance will have no effect on control of the company which will still be in the hands of the current shareholders. If the rights issue is taken up in full by the existing shareholders then again there will be no change in the control of the company. However if the existing shareholders do not take up their rights and sell them on then they will see a dilution in their control of the company as new shareholders are introduced.

Risk

The issue of additional loan finance of £12 million will significantly increase the gearing level of Emmanuel. The effect of this is that the financial risk of the company will be perceived to have increased. This may affect the required return of the equity shareholders which may increase which could lead to a fall in the share price. The greater financial risk may make it more difficult to raise loan finance in future.

Loan covenants

The issue of loan stock may include covenants which either restrict the issue of further loan stock in future or impose limits on management's ability to make decisions.

(c)   (i)   **Overall benefit of swap**

Borrowing rates:

	Fixed %	Floating %
Emmanuel	6.5	LIBOR + 0.7
Fitzwilliam	8.1	LIBOR + 1.4
Difference	1.6	0.7

The benefit of the swap can now be determined:

	%
Overall benefit – interest rate differential (1.6 – 0.7)	0.9
Bank fee	(0.3)
Benefit to swap companies	0.6

Benefit split:

	%
Emmanuel	0.3
Fizwilliam	0.3
	0.6

Terms of swap

As Emmanuel has the larger comparative advantage with fixed rate borrowing so the company should borrow at fixed rate. As the benefit to Emmanuel of the swap arrangement is 0.3% then the final outcome is that Emmanuel must pay floating rate interest of LIBOR + 0.4% (0.7% – 0.3%). Emmanuel's payments and receipts in percentage terms would be:

	%
Borrows fixed rate	(6.5)
Pays to swap bank	(LIBOR)
Receives (bal fig)	6.1
Net payment	LIBOR + 0.4

Interest paid by Emmanuel Hire plc

	£000	£000
Borrow at fixed rate (£12m × 6.5%)		780
Pay to swap bank (LIBOR) (£12m × 5.8%)	696	
Receive from swap bank (£12m × 6.1%)	(732)	
Net swap receipt		(36)
Net interest payment (LIBOR + 0.4% = 6.2%)		744

Two possible alternative methods of managing interest rate risk are a forward rate agreement or an interest rate option. Both of these will be considered below but only one was required for the project.

Forward rate agreement

A forward rate agreement (FRA) is used to manage short term interest rate risk. It is essentially a forward contract on an interest rate for a short term loan or deposit used to lock-in an interest rate now for a future loan or deposit. An FRA is not an actual loan or deposit but an agreement about an interest rate in the future based upon a notional amount of principal.

Emmanuel wants to borrow at a floating rate but to hedge against interest rate risk. Therefore Emmanuel will borrow at LIBOR + 0.7% and pay interest on the loan at that rate.

It will then, as a separate transaction, buy an FRA from a bank with a notional principal of £12 million with an agreed rate of interest known as the settlement rate or reference rate. At the settlement date if LIBOR is higher than the FRA rate the bank pays the difference to Emmanuel. If however LIBOR is lower than FRA rate Emmanuel pays the bank the difference.

Interest rate option

An interest rate option grants the holder the right, but not the obligation, to deal at an agreed interest rate, known as the strike rate, at a future maturity date. In this case Emmanuel would take out a borrower's option with a bank which would give it the right, but not the obligation, to obtain a notional loan on a specified principal amount (£12 million) at a fixed rate of interest for a fixed cost or premium.

If at the expiry date of the option LIBOR + 0.7% is lower than the option strike rate then Emmanuel will let it lapse and will only incur the cost of the option, the premium.

If at the expiry date LIBOR + 0.7% is higher than the option strike rate Emmanuel will receive the difference between the market rate and the strike rate from the bank. Again the premium will already have been incurred.

With an interest rate option the holder can benefit from lower interest rates but is protected against higher interest rates but the cost of this is the premium.

(d) (i) **Share capital option**

Rights issue

Current market value of Emmanuel shares	=	P/E ratio × EPS
	=	12 × (£4,013/20,000)
	=	£2.41
Number of shares to be issued	=	20,000 × 2/5
	=	8,000
Issue price to raise £12 million	=	£12,000/8,000
	=	£1.50

FORECAST INCOME STATEMENT
FOR THE YEAR ENDED 31 JANUARY 2006

	£000	£000
Revenue (35,730 + 3,000 + (12,810 × 1.20))		54,102
Cost of sales (bal fig)		10,651
Gross profit ((35,730 + 3,000) × 80.2%) +		
(12,810 × 1.20) × 80.6% part (a))		43,451
Selling and distribution expenses (3,350 + (1,260 × 0.90))	4,484	
Administrative expenses (19,845 + (6,740 × 0.90))	25,911	
		30,395
Operating profit		13,056
Finance expenses		105
Profit before tax		12,951
Tax (25% × 12,951)		3,238
Profit after tax		9,713
Dividends (9,713/3)		3,238
Retained profit		6,475

FORECAST CASH FLOW STATEMENT
FOR THE YEAR ENDED 31 JANUARY 2006

	£000	£000
Operating profit (see income statement)		13,056
Add: depreciation (3,850 + 960)		4,810
		17,866
Decrease in trade receivables (W1)	615	
Increase in trade payables (W2)	1,990	
		2,605
		20,471
Interest		(105)
Tax (prior year being paid)		(1,100)
Cash flow from operations		19,266
Cash flows from investing activities		
Acquisition of Hughes Hire		(12,000)
Cash flows from financing activities		
Issue of shares	12,000	
Payment of dividend (prior year amount)	(1,650)	
		10,350
Net cash inflow		17,616

Loan capital option

FORECAST INCOME STATEMENT
FOR THE YEAR ENDED 31 JANUARY 2006

	£000	£000
Revenue (35,730 + 3,000 + (12,810 × 1.20))		54,102
Cost of sales (bal fig)		10,651
Gross profit ((35,730 + 3,000) × 80.2%) + (12,810 × 1.20) × 80.6% part (a))		43,451
Selling and distribution expenses (3,350 + (1,260 × 0.90))	4,484	
Administrative expenses (19,845 + (6,740 × 0.90))	25,911	
		30,395
Operating profit		13,056
Finance expenses (105 + 744 (part (c)))		849
Profit before tax		12,207
Tax (25% × 12,207)		3,052
Profit after tax		9,155
Dividends (9,155/3)		3,052
Retained profit		6,103

FORECAST CASH FLOW STATEMENT
FOR THE YEAR ENDED 31 JANUARY 2006

	£000	£000
Operating profit (see income statement)		13,056
Add: depreciation (3,850 + 960)		4,810
		17,866
Decrease in trade receivables (W1)	615	
Increase in trade payables (W2)	1,990	
		2,605
		20,471
Interest (105 + 744)		(849)
Tax (prior year being paid)		(1,100)
Cash flow from operations		18,522
Cash flows from investing activities		
Acquisition of Hughes Hire		(12,000)
Cash flows from financing activities		
Issue of loan stock	12,000	
Payment of dividend (prior year amount)	(1,650)	
		10,350
Net cash inflow		16,872

Assumptions

1   As stated in the scenario the sales of Hughes can be increased by 20%

2   The existing gross profit margins of Emmanuel and Hughes remain the same

3   As stated in the scenario selling, distribution and administrative expenses of Hughes can be reduced by 10%

4   Any costs involved in the issue of the shares has been written off to the share premium account

5   The tax rate remains at 25%

6   Dividend cover remains at 3.0 times

7   Depreciation of Hughes Hire's non-current assets remains at the rate charged by Hughes themselves and is not adjusted to reflect the rate of depreciation charged by Emmanuel

Workings

1   *Decrease in trade receivables*

	£000	£000
Opening trade receivables (10,540 + 3,850)		14,390
Closing receivables		
Construction contract (3,000 × 4/12)	1,000	
Other ((54,102 – 3,000) × 3/12)	12,775	
		13,775
Decrease		615

2   *Increase in trade payables*

	£000
Opening trade payables	3,520
Closing trade payables (40% × 13,775)	5,510
Increase	1,990

(ii) **Effect on profitability and gearing**

	Share capital option	*Loan capital option*
Earnings per share		
Earnings/number of shares		
9,713/(20,000 + 8,000)	34.6 pence	
9,155/20,000		45.8 pence
Return on shareholders funds		
Profit after tax/Shareholders funds × 100		
9,713/(10,000 + 12,000 + 16,164 + 6,475)	21.8%	
9,155/(10,000 + 16,164 + 6,103)		28.4%
Gearing		
Non-current liabilities/shareholders funds × 100		
1,500/(10,000 + 12,000 + 16,164 + 6,475)	3.4%	
1,500 + 12,000/(10,000 + 16,164 + 6,103)		41.9%
Interest cover		
Profit before interest/interest		
13,056/105	124.3 times	
13,056/849		15.4 times

Commentary

The forecast income statements and cash flow statements under each of the financing options indicate the following:

•   under both options the company continues to show healthy levels of profit and strong cash inflows

•   the loan option increases the gearing of the company but still leaves a comfortable level of interest cover of 15.4 times

- earnings per share are lower if the additional share capital is issued but if all shareholders take up their rights this will have no effect on the overall amount of earnings for each shareholding

- as the loan capital is being raised at 6.2% (see part (c)) and it is being used to earn profits that are significantly higher than this, the issue of the loan capital has a beneficial effect on the return on shareholders' funds

- the cash flow statement shows net cash inflows of around £17 million for 2006 and therefore consideration should be given as to how to invest the surplus cash

- the cash flow statement shows that with a net cash inflow from operations and after the payment of dividend of around £17 million that Hughes Hire could in fact be bought for cash without the need to raise long term funds by either method.

(e)   **Advantages of a risk-based management approach to decision making**

A risk-based management approach is designed to help management to achieve the organisation's performance and profitability targets, prevent losses of resources, ensure effective reporting and compliance with laws and regulations. A risk-based management approach helps the organisation to get where it wants to be and to avoid many pitfalls and surprises along the way. The main advantages of such an approach are expanded upon below.

Flexibility and responsiveness

A successful risk-based management approach can make a business more flexible and responsive to a changing environment. The establishment of the system provides the top-down coordination within the business which is necessary to make the various individual functions work efficiently. Therefore it increases organisational efficiency.

This is achieved by focusing management attention on risks and identifying and managing multiple and cross-enterprise risks, where there are risks affecting different parts of the entity. In these situations managers can understand and aggregate connected risks. A risk-based management system can also help the business to seize new opportunities as it may be able to identify and exploit opportunities as well as risks.

Improving the responses of the business to risk

A risk-based management system will provide the framework to identify and select among alternative risk responses which will help the business to either reduce, eliminate or transfer the risk.

Strategic goals

Such a system can ensure that the business gains an improved capability to identify potential events and establish responses to those events which should reduce surprises and any associated costs or losses and thereby help in the achievement of the business's strategic goals.

Link between risk and return

Risk cannot be wholly eliminated from a business but a risk-based management approach can help the business to strike an appropriate balance between the risks and returns associated with a particular decision or course of action.

Making the risk appetite explicit

The risk appetite of a business is the amount of risk that it is prepared to tolerate. A risk-based management system is a top-down system in which the risk appetite of the business will be determined usually by the board of directors in the light of what the organisation is trying to achieve.

Align risk appetite with strategic goals

If the risk appetite of the business is defined by the senior management then this will be in line with the strategic goals of the business which are also set by the senior management. This in turn should increase the likelihood of achieving strategic goals.

Better use of capital

A risk-based system should improve the use of the business's capital as there will be a better understanding of the true risk and return economics of the business which means that the company can take more of the profitable risks and less of the less profitable ones.

Stability of earnings

A risk-based approach to decision making should reduce losses, lead to lower volatility in earnings (more stability) and therefore improve shareholder value. This can happen by taking a portfolio view of all the business's risk and managing the linkages between risk, capital and profitability.

Cost of capital

The lower volatility of earnings, or greater stability, should reduce the cost of capital as the business as a whole is perceived as less risky by the providers of capital.

Key tasks in implementing a risk-based management system

Internal environment

From the top of the organisation the risk management philosophy and risk appetite must be set together with the integrity and ethical values of the business. This must be communicated to everyone in the organisation in the form of a risk policy document. It may be necessary to change the culture of the organisation in order to align with the risk appetite and risk policies.

Setting objectives

The key objectives of the business must be chosen in line with the business's mission statement and being consistent with its risk appetite. This will involve the development of a risk management strategy.

Event identification

Internal and external events affecting the achievement of the business's objectives must be identified, distinguishing between risks and opportunities.

Risk assessment

The risks facing the business must be analysed by considering their likelihood and their impact as a basis for determining how they should be managed.

Determining risk response

Management must select risk responses such as avoidance, reduction, sharing or acceptance which are then developed into a set of actions to align the risks with the risk appetite of the business.

Controls

The internal control system must be reviewed to ensure that it supports the risk policies. If it does not then procedures must be established and implemented to help ensure that risks are identified and that the risk responses are carried out effectively.

Information

A reporting system must be set up that identifies, captures and communicates relevant information. Senior management must have a reporting system that allows early warning of problems.

Communication

There must be communication flowing up, down and across the business. For a risk-based approach to management to be successful it must embrace the whole entity. Therefore there should be widespread consultation with staff concerning the risk appetite of the business and the risk management policies as well as reporting of potential risks to more senior management.

Monitoring

The risk management processes must be continually monitored and modified if necessary.

(f)   **Operational risks as a result of purchase of Hughes Hire Ltd**

Operational risks are the risks that an organisation faces which are not financial risks such as interest rate risk or exchange rate risk. If the strategic decision has been made to purchase Hughes Hire Ltd then operational risks cannot be avoided entirely. Instead they must be identified and managed effectively in order to reduce the risk as much as is possible.

The main operational risks that Emmanuel Hire plc may have to confront as a result of the purchase of Hughes Hire Ltd are detailed below together with a suggestion as to how each operational risk should be managed.

Tangible assets

One of the major problems identified in the scenario is that of the quality and condition of the tangible assets of Hughes Hire Ltd. The delivery fleet needs replacing, the hire equipment is in poor condition and the branches need substantial renovation.

There is little choice but to accept this risk and to deal with the improvement as soon as possible. It would appear that the management have already done this by accepting that the improvements necessary will cost £4 million over a period of time.

Lack of controls

It is likely that the control systems of Hughes may not be up to the standards of Emmanuel being a much smaller company. However Hughes certainly seems to be profitable and therefore this may not be too significant a risk. If new controls are to be installed however there is always the risk of them not being accepted or implemented by the Hughes employees.

It would appear that management have decided to manage this risk by installing better monitoring and control systems resulting in the expected reduction in expenses of Hughes of 10%.

No increase in sales or reduction in costs

Emmanuel is hoping to increase sales in Hughes by 20% and decrease costs by 10%. There is of course always the risk that this may not happen.

In order to ensure that these changes do happen there must be regular monitoring of the results of Hughes by senior management of Emmanuel and appropriate actions taken where necessary.

Personnel problems at Hughes

When one business takes over another there are often considerable problems with personnel. Emmanuel may be concerned that the workforce of Hughes is not up to the standards of its own workforce and therefore has a negative impact on Emmanuel's own goodwill. There is the risk that key staff at Hughes may leave as a result of the acquisition by Emmanuel. Even if staff do not leave there is a risk of hostility from the workforce towards the new management.

There are a variety of ways in which Emmanuel can manage these risks. Training can be organised for the Hughes workforce in order to ensure that they provide the same level of service as the workforce of Emmanuel. If the potential loss of key staff is a problem then contracts could be negotiated with them as an inducement to stay. However the costs and benefits of this would have to be considered carefully.

The problem of hostility from the workforce is harder to manage but could be managed by employee empowerment. The principle is that the people closest to the job, those actually doing it, are the ones best placed to decide how it should be done and therefore they should have the freedom and authority to do it as they think best. This will lead to more job satisfaction and a benefit to the business as a whole. However for this to work Emmanuel will have to ensure that the employees of Hughes are competent, that they know and accept that they will be held accountable for what they do, that they are aware of risk and that they take ownership of the risks that apply to what they do. It is also of great importance that these employees are monitored carefully by senior management and corrective action is taken where necessary.

Culture of the organisation

In many cases takeovers of companies fail as the acquirer is unable to integrate the acquired company into its own culture. It is usually possible to change the culture of an organisation but it will not happen overnight.

This risk can be managed largely by the leadership of management. The beliefs of management can be used to condition the employees of Hughes into their own beliefs and the management of Emmanuel can provide leadership for cultural change in regards to attitudes to trust, control, formality, participation and innovation. This can be done by providing the employees of Hughes with a vision or a sense of mission which is set out by the management of Emmanuel. It is also possible for the reward system for Hughes employees to encourage and reinforce the new attitudes and behaviour.

Customer reaction

It is likely that Hughes Hire Ltd has a loyal customer base who may react adversely to the new ownership. In particular Emmanuel intend to introduce a three month credit period policy for all credit customers. At the current time Hughes Hire's receivables collection period is 110 days and this will therefore be reduced by Emmanuel to 90 days. This is likely to be unpopular, although does not appear unreasonable, with many customers.

In order to manage this Emmanuel's credit control team must be polite, firm and effective in reducing the credit period that has been allowed not only to its own credit customers (107 days) but also to those of Hughes Hire Ltd.

Lack of management skills within Emmanuel

The integration of Hughes's 40 branches in Scotland is a huge management task and one risk that is faced by Emmanuel is that it does not have the levels of management skills to manage this integration process.

This could be managed by either recruiting new management or using expert consultants for the time scale for which they are required.

4 Examiner's comments

Examiner's comments

General comments

The performance of candidates was generally satisfactory and this was reflected in the pass rate on the whole. Marks were not widely dispersed. There were few projects of a very low standard but equally few projects of a very high standard. Virtually all the projects submitted contained a reasonable attempt at two or more parts of the question and so few very weak projects could be found. However certain parts of the question required a more considered, and sometimes more creative, approach than was usually found – and so few outstanding projects could be identified.

It is pleasing to report that problems that have been raised in previous reports concerning the failure of candidates to show key assumptions and workings, and to address the issues posed, were less evident on this occasion.

Questions

The case study, on which the question was based, concerned Emmanuel Hire plc, a tool-hire business which was in the final stages of an agreement to acquire the assets of Hughes Hire Ltd a smaller tool-hire business based in Lanarkshire, Scotland.

Part (a) carried 18 out of the 100 marks for the whole project and required candidates to evaluate the acquisition of Hughes Hire Ltd from the viewpoint of the shareholders of Emmanuel Hire plc. The general standard of answers to this part was disappointing, with few candidates managing to gain high marks. Although various approaches may have been employed to answer the question, a good starting point was to undertake ratio analysis of the financial statements of Hughes Hire Ltd, using the financial statements of Emmanuel Hire plc as a basis for comparison. This approach would have provided insights into the financial health of the target company. However surprisingly few answers offered a serious attempt at analysing the position and performance of Hughes Hire Ltd.

Some consideration of the price paid in relation to the benefits gained was also an important issue. Calculating the value of shares in Hughes Hire Ltd based on both a P/E ratio basis and on underlying net assets would have revealed that Emmanuel Hire plc acquired a profitable business at a fairly cheap price. Although many candidates made an attempt at valuing the shares of Hughes Hire Ltd, their conclusions were not always clear. Some candidates felt that this part could be answered without any attempt at numerical calculation and instead chose to focus exclusively on strategic and other issues. This approach was disappointing. Given the information available in the case study, some form of numerical analysis should have been undertaken and candidates who failed to do so lost an opportunity to gain higher marks.

Part (b) carried seven marks and required candidates to identify the factors to be considered when deciding between ordinary shares and loan capital as a means of financing the acquisition of Hughes Hire Ltd. This part was usually done well. Most candidates were able to discuss the advantages and disadvantages of these two main forms of long-term finance and marks awarded were generally high.

Part (c) carried 10 marks and required candidates to set out details of a swap arrangement, based upon the details contained in the case study, on the assumption that the purchase would be financed by loan capital. This part also required a discussion of an alternative to interest rate swaps as a means of hedging against interest rate risk. Once again, the general standard of answers to this part was good with many candidates gaining maximum marks for their efforts.

Part (d) carried 25 marks and required candidates to evaluate the effect of the purchase of Hughes Hire Ltd on Emmanuel Hire plc by preparing a forecast cash flow statement and forecast income statement under each financing option and then to evaluate the impact of the acquisition on the future profitability and gearing of Emmanuel Hire plc. This part was rarely answered well with many failing to achieve a pass mark. Although reasonable marks were often gained in preparing forecast income statements, few managed to achieve similar marks when preparing forecast cash flow statements. This often reflected a failure to understand the main elements and structure of cash flow statements.

For some reason a number of candidates prepared a forecast balance sheet under each financing option in answering this question, even though this was not required. Their efforts were unrewarded and it is worth repeating the point made in previous reports that candidates must **read each part of the question carefully**.

Part (e) carried 20 marks and required candidates to set out the main advantages of a risk-based management approach and to identify the key tasks to be carried out when implementing such a system. Answers to this part, although rarely of a very high standard were satisfactory, with the majority of candidates gaining a pass mark.

Part (f) carried 20 marks and required candidates to identify key operational risks confronting Emmanuel Hire plc and to state how these might be managed. Once again, the marks awarded were often satisfactory but with few of a very high standard. Generally speaking, candidates needed to reflect more on the nature of the risks that were being faced and to put forward more considered explanations concerning the ways in which the risk could be managed. Many of the answers provided were **perfunctory** and required more **depth of analysis** in order to gain higher marks.

ACCA Live Project – Autumn 2005: Module A

Topic list
1 Autumn 2005 Project: Module A
2 Suggested approach
3 Suggested answer
4 Examiner's comments

Note. we reproduce in this chapter the questions that were set in the August 2005 Module A Project, however we do not reproduce the supplement that was also supplied, containing the financial statements of Stagecoach.

You will need to download this from the ACCA's website:

http://www.accaglobal.com/pubs/students/study_exams/qualifications/ diploma_fm/module_a/project_da2/projects/da2_2005_aug/da2_aug05 _1.pdf

If you do not have internet access please contact our Customer Services department on 020 8740 2211 for hard copy.

As the 2003/2004 Annual Report of Stagecoach was originally issued under UK Accounting Standards and in UK accounting format it has not been altered to reflect the internationalisation of the DipFM syllabus. The answer to this project is therefore based upon the original UK financial statements. However the approach to the answer and the answer itself contain references to international terminology and standards where appropriate.

1 Autumn 2005 Project: Module A

Diploma in Financial Management

PROJECT DA2, INCORPORATING SUBJECT AREAS
– INTERPRETATION OF FINANCIAL STATEMENTS
– PERFORMANCE MANAGEMENT

All questions are compulsory and MUST be answered

The project MUST be written in English.

The maximum word count (including appendices and tables but excluding references and bibliography) is 5,000.

The project MUST be TYPED in black ink, one-sided, double-spaced, using a minimum 12-point font size and a 1-inch margin at each side. HANDWRITTEN SUBMISSIONS WILL NOT BE ACCEPTED. The project must be submitted by post, electronic submissions are not acceptable.

The project should be submitted on A4 paper with your student number, project name, date and page number at the top of each page.

A project submission form MUST be completed for each project submitted and attached to the front of the project.

The Association of Chartered Certified Accountants

BPP LEARNING MEDIA

Incorporating subject areas – Interpretation of Financial Statements and Performance Management

This ONE question is compulsory and MUST be attempted

Introduction

In order to complete the project you should refer to the data provided in the appendix.

You have been approached by a group of potential investors. They are investigating the potential benefits of investing in Stagecoach Group plc (hereafter referred to as 'the Group').

As part of their investigation, they have asked you to prepare a presentation which assesses the performance of the Group for the year to 30 April 2004. You have obtained the data which is contained in the appendix.

Required

Prepare a presentation (including appropriate visual aids and a full text of your speech) which:

(a)   discusses the importance of relating performance management to the organisational mission statement, strategy and objectives;   (4 marks)

(b)   selects six ratios or other measures from the appendix which can be used to assess the performance of the Group in the 12 months to 30 April 2004 from the perspective of a potential investor, and clearly explains why these are appropriate measures of performance of the Group;   (12 marks)

(c)   based on the measures you have selected in (b) above, assesses the Group's performance in the context of the stated strategic objectives;   (30 marks)

(d)   indicates how your assessment of performance of the Group is limited by using information which is available in the published financial report;   (8 marks)

(e)   indicates how an internal management team can improve performance management through the use of a balanced scorecard;   (10 marks)

(f)   outlines the possible content of a balanced scorecard for use in the Group (your outline should include specific performance measures which should be reported, and these measures should be justified in the context of the stated strategy and objectives of the Group).   (36 marks)

(100 marks)

2 Suggested approach

The entire project, covering both subject areas, Interpretation of Financial Statements and Performance Management, is set in the context of the Stagecoach Group plc information which you are provided with. This supplementary information is extracts from the 2004 Annual Report of Stagecoach Group plc and a number of key ratios and other measures of performance for the last five years for both Stagecoach Group and a key competitor in the same industry.

Start by reading through the "introduction" section on the first page of the project. This makes it quite clear that your role is to advise a group of potential investors in the Group. You should bear this in mind throughout this project.

Requirements

Move onto the requirements section of the project. The first important point to note is the requirement is to prepare a presentation which will include appropriate visual aids and also the full text of your speech. The examiner has commented in the past that despite the evident requirement a number of candidates did not provide any visual aids in their project. Visual aids have been asked for in a number of Module A assessments now and the examiner has made it clear that marks are allocated to them and therefore marks are lost if they are not prepared. In fact the preparation of visual aids can help you to plan your answer as most visual aids will be lists of the key topics to be considered or breakdowns of points within a topic. They will then need to be padded out with the full speech but can be a good starting point for your answer.

The examiner often comments that the word count in candidates' projects does not always relate to the mark allocation. He has made it quite clear that the mark allocation is an accurate guide to the number of words required for each part of the project. Therefore it is worthwhile at this stage just calculating the approximate number of words required for each part of the project.

(a) $4/100 \times 5{,}000$ $=$ 200 words
(b) $12/100 \times 5{,}000$ $=$ 600 words
(c) $30/100 \times 5{,}000$ $=$ 1,500 words
(d) $8/100 \times 5{,}000$ $=$ 400 words
(e) $10/100 \times 5{,}000$ $=$ 500 words
(f) $36/100 \times 5{,}000$ $=$ 1,800 words

Read through the individual requirements so that you have an idea of what areas are being tested in this project.

Part a) concerns the organisational mission statement, strategy and objectives. Part (b) is concerning choosing ratios which can be used to assess the performance of the Group and part (c) is to assess the Group performance on the basis of these measures. Part (d) is the last part of the project concerned with Interpretation of Financial Statements and considers the limitations of the information available.

Parts (e) and (f) return to the Performance Management element of Module A and both parts are concerned with the balanced scorecard and how this can be used to improve performance management and which performance measures should be reported for the Group.

Supplementary information

Turn now to the supplementary information, of which there is a lot, and read through it quite quickly. Scan the numbers for any obvious trend that you can see but do not start doing any calculations at this stage. The idea here is to familiarise yourself with the information available rather than to come up with any material for your project or to draw any conclusions.

At this stage it might be worth taking a break so that the supplementary information provided and the overall requirements of the project can be mulled over for a short while.

The project

Once you are ready to start on your project return to the requirements again.

Part (a)

Think about this one carefully. It is not specific to Stagecoach but a generalised question requiring you to discuss how performance management should be related to the organisational mission statement, strategy and objectives. As this is generalised and not specific you will not need to refer directly to the Stagecoach supplementary information but you will need to put some thought to this area.

This area of the syllabus comes from the Performance Management section of Module A and you might like to remind yourself about this area and the related areas of mission statements and strategy by reviewing chapter 1 of the Performance Management Study text before starting your answer.

Maybe start with your first visual aid which may mention the key matters in the requirement of performance management, mission statement, strategy and objectives. Then consider how you would discuss the importance of relating performance management specifically to the mission statement, strategy and objectives. Remember that this is only 200 words so you do not need to go into too much detail.

Part (b)

In this part you are required to select just 6 appropriate ratios from those given in the supplementary information in order to assess the performance of the Group from the perspective of a potential investor.

The examiner commented that the purpose of providing a large number of ratios and then asking candidates to select just 6 was to "highlight the need to be selective and to ensure that ratios chosen would assist in assessing the performance" in the next part of the project.

The examiner also comments that, as in the past, many answers read like extracts from a study text, and there were many occasions when answers were too generalised and not specific to the particular scenario set, in this case Stagecoach Group. Note that you are also clearly asked to explain why each of your ratios is an appropriate measure of performance of the Group.

Part (a) should give you some clues here. In the previous part you considered the importance of performance management within the context of the overall mission statement and associated strategies and objectives. Therefore a starting point would be to discover the mission and objectives of the Group which should help in the selection of appropriate performance measures.

Read through the Chairman's statement, Chief Executive's review and the operating review and you should get an overall feel for the strategies of the group although the mission statement is not stated specifically. However there are a number of themes which come out from these three documents which can be used in selection of measures.

Then carefully consider each of the performance measures that have been given in the supplementary information in the light of the objectives of the Group. Ask the question – will this performance measure help to assess whether the objectives of the Group are being met?

Part (c)

In this part you are required to use the 6 measures chosen in part (b) in order to assess the performance of the Group in the context of the stated objectives. If you have thoroughly justified your choice of measures in part (b) then you will know why you are using them and what you wish to assess in your use of these measures.

The examiner commented that the key to maximising marks in this section was to take on board that the assessment required is within the context of the stated strategic objectives.

Remember that you are not only given the relevant figures for the Group for five years but also for a key competitor for the same time scale. Therefore in your performance assessment do not just compare the measures for the Group over time but also compare to the competitor.

Do not necessarily confine yourself to the summary of performance measures given. You are given the financial statements and notes for the Group for 2004 and these may provide additional useful information for your assessment. Therefore spend some time analysing the financial statements themselves for any information that will help with your assessment. In particular the Chairman's and Chief Executive's reviews are useful areas of information with key elements of the financial statements being highlighted here.

Part (d)

Limitations of assessing a company's performance using the published financial statements is a fairly standard topic. However in order to gain good marks in this section it is necessary to apply these limitations to the assessment you have just performed rather than just to give a generalised answer.

Also remember that you are providing the assessment for a potential investor in the Group as this may help you when you consider the limitations.

Part (e)

We now move onto the Performance Management element of the syllabus. In this part of the project you are being asked to show how a management team can improve performance management through the use of a balanced scorecard. You will obviously need to know what is meant by a balanced scorecard approach so it may be worthwhile revising this area from the Study Text before starting this part of the project.

Make sure, however, that you do not fall into the trap of just describing a balanced scorecard. Although this part of the project does not necessarily refer to Stagecoach Group the requirements are specific in that you are being asked how the technique can be used to improve performance.

Although this is a more generalised part of the project the examiner did note that those candidates who related the issue to the Group did tend to score higher marks.

Part (f)

In this final part of the project there are a number of requirements in the one sentence:

- the possible content of a balanced scorecard
- specific performance measures
- justification of the measures.

This should all be done in the context of the stated strategy and objectives of the Group.

This is therefore a very specific area of the project and you must relate everything to the Group. Start with the strategic objectives identified earlier and think about how these could be achieved. Break down the achievement of these strategic objectives into the actual operations that must be carried out in order to achieve these objectives and consider the types of performance measures that could be used to measure the success of these operations. Use the four perspectives of the balanced scorecard to help you to determine the types of performance measures that would be useful within the Group.

3 Suggested answer

(a) Good morning ladies and gentlemen.

I have been asked to talk to you this morning about the potential benefits of investing in the Stagecoach Group, which from now on I will refer to as the Group.

However we will start with more general discussion of how important it is to relate performance management to the organisational mission statement and associated strategy and objectives. This discussion should give us a basis for consideration of the performance of the Group later on this morning.

Slide 1

Organisational Mission statement	Strategy	Objectives
	Performance Management	

First we shall ask the question of what is performance management?

Performance management is where managers in a business use a variety of performance measures in order to take new planning decisions or control actions in order to improve the future performance of the organisation.

So performance management is about making decisions in order to improve performance. But what is meant by improvement in performance? Does this mean growth in market share or reduction of costs and improvement in profit margin? Does it mean internal improvements in operating policies or does it mean growth by acquisition?

These questions can only be answered in the context of the overall aims of the organisation. These will have been set at Board level and will usually be in terms of the mission statement of the organisation. This overall mission statement gives the reason for the existence of the organisation and will then be converted into the strategies and objectives of the organisation. Only when the overall aims of the organisation are known and the methods or strategies of achieving those aims are understood will management be able to make effective decisions that will take the organisation closer to those overall aims.

(b)

Slide 2

Stagecoach Group – Objectives

- generate increase in shareholder value
- profitable growth – both organic and by acquisition

The two main aims of the Group would appear to be to generate increases in shareholder value and to achieve profitable growth both through the organic growth of existing operations and through acquisition.

Subsidiary to these overall aims are a number of other aims:

- to lead the way in innovative public transport services,
- to pursue a progressive dividend policy,
- to achieve a more efficient capital structure,
- to identify new ideas and growth opportunities at an early stage and to deliver them quickly,
- to provide high quality bus and rail services,
- investment in research to drive growth,
- to retain a commitment to good environmental stewardship,
- getting the basics right and applying entrepreneurial skills in core geographic markets,
- encouraging more people to use public transport,
- making sure that the Group has the right employees on board to satisfy customer needs.

A wide range of objectives indeed!

> **Slide 3**
>
> **Performance measures**
>
> - Profit margin
> - Return on Shareholders Funds
> - EBITDA margin
> - Turnover per employee
> - Profit per employee
> - Gearing

Profit margin

The Group aims to increase shareholder value by profitable growth therefore the profit margin is one aspect of this. As we will see later the overall profit on the investment made by shareholders will be measured by the Return on Shareholders Funds but an important element of this figure is the profit margin made. This allied with the effective use of the assets of the business, measured by the asset turnover, determines the overall profit to the shareholders.

Return on Shareholders Funds

Return on Shareholders Funds (ROSF) gives a measure of the overall profit or return from the investment made by the shareholders in the Group. The Group strategy is to increase this return by profitable growth therefore this is a key measure to determine whether there has been an improvement. The ROSF measures the effectiveness of the use of the funds invested by shareholders.

EBITDA margin

The EBITDA margin is the measure of the earnings before interest, tax, depreciation and amortisation. By taking out non-cash charges such as depreciation and amortisation this figure gives an indication of the underlying ability of the company to earn profits from its operations. As the objective of the Group is to provide profitable growth (as opposed to unprofitable growth) then this is an important figure to consider. We would expect to see an improvement of this measure over time.

Turnover per employee

Growth will almost inevitably lead to an increase in the number of employees. However such increases must be managed to ensure that these employees are being used effectively. By considering sales revenue per employee we can assess the overall success in managing the growth of the Group.

Profit per employee

Although growth in turnover is an important aspect of overall growth the aim of the group is profitable growth. An increase in turnover and employees is not what is wanted if this is allied with a reduction in profitability. Ideally we would like to see an increase in both turnover per employee and profit per employee. Therefore profit per employee will indicate how the Group has managed the growth in operations as a whole.

Gearing

Growth will require additional investment which could be in the form of additional equity finance or in the form of additional debt finance. It is widely thought that excessive levels of debt finance or gearing are not to be desired and indeed one of the stated aims of the Group is to achieve a more efficient capital structure. Therefore the measurement of gearing will help in the assessment of the success of this aim.

(c)

Slide 4

Assessment of performance measures

- Profit margin
    - variable but 2004 improvement
    - 2004 higher than competitor

- Return on Shareholders Funds
    - variable but 2004 improvement
    - 2004 in line with competitor

- EBITDA margin
    - variable but 2004 improvement
    - 2004 slightly higher than competitor

- Turnover per employee
    - general improvement over 5 years
    - considerably higher than competitor

- Profit per employee
    - variable but 2004 improvement
    - by 2004 considerably higher than competitor

- Gearing
    - increasing to 2003 but improvement in 2004
    - now considerably lower than competitor

Profit margin

The most obvious comment about all of the profitability measures in general and profit margin in particular is that the figures have fluctuated wildly over the five year period. Indeed in 2001 and 2003 the figures were in fact negative indicating losses rather than profitability.

However by 2004 the profit margin has become 6.38% which although an improvement is still lower than the figure in 2000. From the information in the financial statements it is difficult to assess the reasons for these fluctuations in profitability. However from the Chairman's statement we are told that the restructuring of the North American operations 'has resulted in a more predictable business' and the Chief Executive's review claims that in 'North America we now have an established core of more robust businesses'. It is also noted that the operating profit of the North American business has been maintained on a significantly smaller base of operations. The Chief Executive believes that this area of the business 'can make an increased contribution to earnings moving forward'.

Therefore it would appear that one cause of the evident improvement in 2004 may be that the restructuring of the North American operations has been completed during the year and it is stated that as a result of this the Group has 'excellent potential to deliver good returns to shareholders'.

A further important point about the profit margin is that the profit margin of the competitor has gradually fallen over the five year period and in 2004 is considerably lower than that of the Group at 4.95%. It is possible that this position has been achieved by the sales of non-core businesses as well as the North American restructuring in order to remain with operations with healthier profit margins than the competitor.

These figures would seem to demonstrate that over the five year period the position has been far from the profitable growth which is the stated objective although with some considerable improvement in the current year.

If turnover is considered as an indication of growth although total turnover is less than 2003 by about 14% if the impact of the disposed businesses is excluded turnover in 2004 compared to 2003 did in fact grow by 4.9%. Therefore there is some evidence of growth in the core, retained businesses.

The history of profitability within the Group is not good but the evidence of the current year figures allied with the optimism of the Chairman and Chief Executive do bode well. However to base any form of conclusion on just the 2004 figures would not be wise. As a potential investor a continued improvement in profitability year on year would be required.

Return on Shareholders Funds

As with the underlying profit margin, ROSF has been volatile with two years of negative figures. However by 2004 ROSF has become 24.56% which is the highest that it has been over the five year period.

When compared with the competitor figures for ROSF the competitor has shown some fluctuations in ROSF but nowhere near to that of the Group and has always been profitable. This would indicate that the problems with the ROSF of the Group have been caused by factors internal to the Group operations rather than factors affecting the industry as a whole. Despite the recovery of the Group ROSF in 2004 it is still considerably below that of the competitor at 34.74% despite the Group having a higher profit margin.

The reason for the Group having a lower ROSF than the competitor despite the higher profit margin must therefore lie with the asset turnover. With the figures for profit margin and ROSF available it is possible to calculate the asset turnover which measures the efficiency with which the resources of the Group have been used. This has improved from 1.38 times in 2000 to 3.84 times in 2004 indicating a significant improvement which may be as a result of the rationalisation of the Group. However if the 2004 asset utilisation of the competitor is calculated this is 7.02 times indicating that there may still be significant areas where improvements can be made.

EBITDA margin

Again as this is a profitability measure it is showing the same signs of volatility as the other profitability measures already considered. However the EBITDA margin has not fluctuated quite as wildly as other profit measures which indicates that the volatility has perhaps largely been due to the restructuring. By 2004 the EBITDA margin is 14.76% compared to that of the competitor of 12.73%. Indeed the EBITDA margin of the competitor has fallen from 14.01% in 2000 and 15.76% in 2001 to 12.73% in the current year.

This is perhaps further evidence that the recent restructuring of the Group has placed it in good stead for future profitable growth and increases in shareholder value. This is emphasised in the Finance Director's review where the increase in profit before goodwill amortisation and exceptional items is noted which reflects 'growth in profits in our continuing operations more than offsetting the impact of disposals'.

Turnover per employee

Although it has been noted that turnover overall decreased in 2004 although showing a slight increase if the disposed businesses are excluded, turnover per employee in the Group has not only grown considerably year in year out over the five years but also the turnover per employee is almost 30% higher than that of the competitor whose figures actually show very little growth in this area. From the Chief executive's review it is clear that the workforce are an important aspect of the performance of the Group and therefore there is some indication here that there should be optimism for the future growth of the Group. Control of the workforce expenses is particularly important as staff costs form almost half of the operating costs of the business.

Profit per employee

Although there has clearly been growth in turnover per employee the aim of the Group is profitable growth therefore profit per employee is also important. Again there is some reason for optimism when this figure is considered.

As with all of the profitability measures profit per employee fluctuates over the five years however by 2004 it is 74% higher than that of its competitor which has in fact seen profitability per employee decline over the five year period. This is encouraging for the Group.

Gearing

One of the aims of the Group was to achieve the most efficient capital structure and to this end there has been a significant decrease in the gearing level during the current year from 311% to 190%. Although this would appear to be high in absolute terms there is no definitive right or wrong capital structure and this will differ from industry to industry. Organisations such as the Group with high levels of physical assets such as buses and trains will often tend to have higher levels of gearing than organisations with lower levels of physical assets.

The normality of high levels of gearing in this business is perhaps borne out by considering the competitor whose gearing level is 250% in 2004 which is only slightly less than in 2000 at 275%.

Much is made in the Finance Director's review of the substantial decrease in net debt by £492.4m or 87.9% from 2003. This is partly due to the strong cash flow position with net cash inflows of £347.4m and free cash flow of £209.5m although this is clearly partly due to the disposal of non-core operations. However the result is that the book gearing level (net debt divided by net assets) is 17.3% compared to the 2003 figure of 176.6%.

However we must note from the Chairman's statement that the Board proposes to return £250 million of capital to shareholders which will reduce shareholders funds and thereby increase the gearing levels again. The reason for this is that the Board believes that this will lower the Group's overall cost of capital and therefore generate further shareholder value.

Conclusion

Clearly the Chairman and Chief Executive are very positive about the position of the Group at the end of 2004 and believe that after the restructuring and rationalisation the Group has 'good prospects for further growth and increased shareholder value'. From the evidence of the five year figures this is not really borne out but there is clear evidence that there has been a significant improvement in the position in 2004 and that in comparison with its competitor it would appear that the Group's fluctuating profitability was due to internal management policies which have perhaps been overcome with the sale of businesses and restructuring. However in order to be confident that this is the case one would hope to see similarly improving figures over a sustained period.

(d)

Slide 5

Limitations of published financial statements

- Historic information
- Trend
- Benchmark figures
- Evidence

Historic information

By their very nature published financial statements comprise historic information. Therefore as a tool for predictive purposes they are very limited. My assessment of performance has been done for you, potential investors, and the question that a potential investor will want answering is how is the Group likely to perform in the future?

The Chairman's review and Chief Executive's review are certainly optimistic about the future but there is no particular evidence from the financial statements that these understandably upbeat comments are factual in nature. In the case of the Group it would certainly appear that the restructuring has improved the Group position but whether this will lead to increased shareholder value in actual fact is impossible to tell from the information in the financial statements alone.

Trend

Although we have been provided with performance measures for five years for the Group the financial statements themselves only cover the current and previous year. With only two years of financial information available it is not possible to establish any form of trend in performance.

However as we can see from the five year performance measurement figures the performance of the Group has fluctuated over this period so that in this case even with more years of figures it may still be difficult to establish any form of trend.

Benchmark figures

To look at the figures of an entity in isolation, with no regard to the type of industry in which it operates, means that only limited information can be taken from the financial statements and conclusions drawn may not be valid.

For example the Group gearing figure at 190% does seem high but when this is compared to the competitor figures which we have been given then maybe this is a normal part of the operations of this type of business. However the financial statements themselves do not provide any such benchmark figures.

Evidence

Much of the positive information from the financial statements comes from the reviews by the Chairman and Chief Executive. However unfortunately there is little evidence within the financial statements themselves to support the claims and optimism.

(e)

> **Slide 6**
>
> **Balanced scorecard and performance management**
>
> - Link between strategy and operations
> - Non-financial performance measures
> - Critical success factors
> - Specific activities

The balanced scorecard approach to performance measurement is one which provides a clear link between the strategy of the entity and its actual operations. This is done by measuring and monitoring performance measures which relate directly to the strategic objectives of the organisation. Thereby the focus of the operational managers is in line with the requirements of the Board in terms of overall strategy.

The balanced scorecard approach recognises that for an entity to achieve its objectives there must be a balance to what is controlled and monitored in the organisation. To this end the balanced scorecard recognises four 'perspectives' which must be measured. These four perspectives are customer, internal processes, learning and growth, and financial.

As you can see only one of these perspectives is 'financial'. A further aspect of the balanced scorecard is that it attempts to move management away from only considering financial performance measures and the financial implications of operations. Therefore the focus of performance reporting is moved towards non-financial measures.

The balanced scorecard also effectively reduces the amount of information that management are required to monitor by focusing on critical success factors. For each perspective only a limited number of objectives are set which are deemed to be critical success factors. For each of these areas a performance target will be set and will then be measured and monitored.

The choice of these specific activities to be monitored will be based upon the strategic objectives of the organisation but in many cases much thought will have to go into them. For example in the context of the Stagecoach Group the strategic objectives are to increase shareholder value and to maintain profitable growth. An obvious way of attempting to measure the attainment of these objectives is to consider profit margins and return on shareholders funds as we have already done. However these are purely financial measures and only relate to the financial perspective of the balanced scorecard.

The achievement of these strategic objectives must be broken down further to see how they can in fact be achieved in operational terms. For example if there is to be organic growth within the Group then this will require more customers to use the Group's public transport facilities. This in turn will only be possible if the needs of customers are being met. Therefore measures of customer satisfaction such as comfort, safety and ease of access should be monitored. If customers are satisfied with the performance of the Group in these areas then this should in turn lead to increases in customers and growth, increased profits and increased shareholder value.

Therefore by considering, measuring and monitoring lower level critical activities the higher level strategic objectives can be achieved.

(f)

Slide 7

Strategic objectives

Specific activities

Performance measures

Perspectives

The starting point to determining the possible content of a balanced scorecard for the Group is to consider its strategic objectives. These were considered earlier in this presentation and were determined to be the increase in shareholder value and profitable growth both organically and by acquisition.

The subject of acquisition is a strategic and not operational issue so not relevant to the balanced scorecard. However organic profitable growth leading to an increase in shareholder value is our starting point for considering the specific activities and performance measures that will play a part in achieving these objectives.

Therefore we need to consider in more detail what is meant by profitable organic growth in the context of the Group. One of the stated aims of the Group is 'encouraging more people to use public transport' not only for the growth prospects of the Group but also from a corporate social responsibility aspect. Therefore we need to consider what the Group needs to do in order to achieve this greater use of its buses and trains.

The crux of the situation is what the Group needs to do in order to attract more passengers. One answer is to meet passenger needs and another is to acquire more routes and services.

From this basis we need to consider specific performance measures and how they should be measured using as a basis the four perspectives of the balanced scorecard. What is also important is that the performance measures are limited in order not to overload managers of the business.

Slide 8

Customer perspective

- Customer satisfaction
- Customer retention
- Customer growth

If more customers are to be attracted in order to generate organic growth then customer needs must be satisfied. One of the ways of measuring this is fairly negative but it involves measurement of the number of complaints received. It is almost inevitable that on occasions complaints will be made. These could be complaints to the Group itself or complaints to a higher authority, the industry Regulator.

The key issue here is to manage any complaints to the Group effectively as even a customer complaint, if dealt with satisfactorily, can be turned into a positive situation with possible repeat business. However a complaint not dealt with satisfactorily by the Group may result in a complaint to the Regulator. Therefore it is important to measure the ratio of complaints to the Group compared to complaints to the Regulator as an indicator of levels of customer dissatisfaction and conversely satisfaction.

If the Group is to grow organically then at the very least it must retain its current customer base. Therefore a measure of customer retention is important. This can be achieved by measurement of the number of repeat sales ie sales of bus/train fares to repeat customers. This will be easier to establish for sales on credit cards – largely train customers – but harder for cash customers for example on bus journeys.

Once customers have been retained by good service the next element of growth will be in the form of new customers. A measure of the number of first time customers should assess this aspect.

Slide 9

Internal perspective

- Reliability
- Capacity utilisation

One of the key factors that public transport users will consider is the reliability of the service so a key customer requirement that must be dealt with by internal procedures is that the transport arrives at the stated time or within a short time scale of the stated time. A measure of this is perhaps the percentage of arrivals within a stated number of minutes of the scheduled time. The question is then how management deal with this performance measure. There are likely to be factors outside the Group's control which will affect arrival times but the Group must do everything in their power to manage the factors which are within their control in order to achieve reliability of their services. Whether the Group's public transport services are on schedule will be a major factor in their goodwill from customers. If customers stay loyal to the Group's services then this will contribute to profitable growth and an increase in shareholder value.

Capacity utilisation is a key factor. If there is to be organic growth then this must come from utilising the current routes more fruitfully by attracting more customers. This could be measured in two ways:

- percentage of available seats occupied – the more seats that are filled the more profit will be made from each journey. Each additional passenger has a nil marginal cost until capacity is reached therefore 100% capacity is the aim of any such organisation.

- ratio of passenger miles to staff – it has been noted that due to the nature of the business staff costs are a major element of the cost structure. Therefore it is vital that the staff are utilised as effectively as possible. This measure and its monitoring should ensure that the staff resource is being used to maximum efficiency.

Slide 10

Learning and growth perspective

- Safety
- Route expansion
- Staff capacity
- Employee retention
- Research and development

Within the transport industry safety is clearly a very important issue. Accidents will inevitably take place but the Group needs to demonstrate the highest possible safety standards. This is a tricky one in that an excellent safety record will not necessarily lead to more customers and profitable growth and increase in shareholder value but the converse is inevitably the case. A poor safety record or a high profile accident will definitely lead to a loss of current customers and fewer new customers. Therefore a measure such as the number of accidents per 1,000 passenger miles will be a good indicator of the Group's success in this vital area.

As already mentioned organic growth can also be achieved through expansion of routes and services and both the Chairman's review and Chief Executive's review refer to this as a strategy of the Group. This can simply be measured by the number of new routes or services introduced in each period but this must also be tempered by basic cost control measures. Any new routes or services must also be cost effective if they are lead to profitable growth.

It has already been noted that the staff of the Group are key to its success or failure. It is the staff who are in constant communication with the customers and therefore are the human face of the Group. As has been recognised by both the Chairman and Chief Executive in their reviews it is the workforce base which drive the Group. A key element in achieving customer satisfaction and therefore growth is ensuring that the staff are seeking constant improvement and are aware of the corporate goals and requirements from themselves. Staff need to be well trained in order to provide a better service for the customer. This could be measured by the number of training hours per employee with the intention that increased training will both retain and attract customers leading to growth and increases in shareholder value.

Having invested in the training of staff as well as them imbibing the corporate culture it is also important to retain such staff. Staff turnover levels will therefore be an important element in achieving the corporate objectives. Low staff turnover generally indicates high levels of staff satisfaction and also benefits the customer. The retention of staff will have a positive effect on customers and will therefore contribute to profitable growth and increases in shareholder value due to the retention of customers. Equally, and related to the previous point, low staff turnover minimises the very important staff training costs.

In order to stay ahead and achieve the strategically required growth the Group are aware of the importance of research and development. The Chief Executive in his review states that 'our focus on new business development through investment in research is driving growth' and cites in particular the megabus.com and Yellow Taxibus initiatives. Such research and innovation must continue and could be measured by research costs as a percentage of sales.

> **Slide 11**
>
> **Financial perspective**
>
> - Customer growth
> - Operating costs

The entire point of the balanced scorecard is to get away from purely financial performance measures. However in any control aspect of an entity it will be necessary to monitor financial aspects as well as non-financial aspects. Therefore clearly the financial element has to come into play. For the Group the key factors are profitable growth therefore the financial elements which are key to this are growth in customers (organic growth) and profitability maintained by control of costs.

Although we have considered growth in the measures already discussed, such as increasing number of routes and increasing passenger numbers there is little point in such growth unless it leads to increases in revenue and profits.

Customer growth could be measured by revenue earned per available passenger mile and this will be a measure of the real growth achieved. Allied to this however is the cost of each passenger mile available. Only if costs are controlled can an increase in profitability and shareholder value ensue.

4 Examiner's comments

Examiner's comments. The overall performance of candidates was sound with some very good answers being presented. However, the number of candidates achieving very high marks is not as high as might be expected. The reason for the high expectation is that candidates have a reasonable amount of time between the issue of the project and the deadline for final submission. This time should allow candidates an opportunity to assess the information provided, consider the issues involved, read around these issues, plan their answer, and include a fully-developed analysis.

Those candidates who use this opportunity invariably gain high marks. Conversely, those who do not avail of the opportunity do not gain good marks.

The single most disappointing aspect of reviewing projects which did not obtain a high mark is that such candidates have clearly not taken account of the comments in previous examiners' reports, nor do they appear to have read the question carefully. These candidates therefore present material which could have been taken from any decent textbook, but has little or no link to the material provided.

QUESTION 1

This was well answered by the majority of candidates. The best answers made a strong link between the mission statement, strategy and objectives, and discussed the necessity of placing performance management in the context of both strategy and objectives.

The issues considered in this question also provided the basis for the answers to subsequent questions, and should have assisted candidates in avoiding the trap of 'generalism'.

QUESTION 2

While many candidates demonstrated careful choice of the ratios and measures which might be considered relevant, too many candidates appear to have opened a textbook and paraphrased material on various ratios, with no consideration of which ratios may be of particular importance. This renders such answers general, rather than applied to the material provided in the supplement booklet. It also reduces the number of marks that can be awarded. This is a specific example of the tendency to produce general material. It is a matter of surprise that some candidates still persist in this practice. It is even more surprising when the question specifically asked for each ratio or measure selected to be justified. The main reason for restricting the choice to six was to highlight the need to be selective and to ensure that ratios chosen would assist in assessing the performance in the next question.

QUESTION 3

For candidates who are prepared to go beyond basic and general comments, there were a good number of marks to be obtained in this question. While a number of candidates did this, there were still others who did not and their answers did not score high marks. The key to maximising the marks awarded on this question was to consider why the results were as calculated. Candidates who scored good marks had clearly taken on board the part of the question which stated that the assessment should be 'in the context of the stated strategic objectives'. The need to set any assessment in the context of the company's strategy is implicit in any question of this kind. It is therefore difficult to award marks to answers which do not do so when it is explicitly asked for.

QUESTION 4

Most candidates were able to offer observations as to how an assessment is limited by using information in published reports in general. To obtain maximum marks, it was necessary to consider how the assessment carried out in the previous questions was limited by the published financial report of this company. Perhaps the best way to do this was, as many candidates did, to select particular items from the report and discuss them.

QUESTION 5

Unlike the previous three questions, this question did not require a consideration of the specific company or industry. Although many of the better answers did so, and consequently gained very good marks, this was not a necessity.

However, this does not mean that the question could be answered by a general description of the balanced scorecard. Unfortunately a number of candidates did not appreciate this point, and therefore did not gain many marks.

The question was general in the sense that it concerned the balanced scorecard, but it was specific in the sense that it asked how the technique can be used to improve performance.

QUESTION 6

This question moved from a consideration of how the balanced scorecard may be used by any company to how it might be used by a specific company. Those candidates who used the strategic objectives which had been considered in the earlier questions as the basis of the items to be included in the balanced scorecard, and whose answers indicated that they had thought about how to actually measure such items, scored good marks. The main reasons for answers not obtaining good marks was the failure to provide a basis for actually measuring the items included in the balanced scorecard or including measures that had not been related to the strategic objectives of the company.

ACCA Live Project – Autumn 2005: Module B

1 Autumn 2005 Project: Module B

Diploma in Financial Management

PROJECT DB2, INCORPORATING SUBJECT AREAS
- FINANCIAL STRATEGY
- RISK MANAGEMENT

All questions are compulsory and MUST be answered

The project MUST be written in English.

The maximum word count (including appendices and tables but excluding references and bibliography) is 5,000.

The project MUST be TYPED in black ink, one-sided, double-spaced, using a minimum 12-point font size and a 1-inch margin at each side. HANDWRITTEN SUBMISSIONS WILL NOT BE ACCEPTED. The project must be submitted by post, electronic submissions are not acceptable.

The project should be submitted on A4 paper with your student number, project name, date and page number at the top of each page.

A project submission form MUST be completed for each project submitted and attached to the front of the project.

The Association of Chartered Certified Accountants

Incorporating subject areas – Financial Strategy and Risk Management

This ONE question is compulsory and MUST be attempted

Plutus plc

Plutus plc is a manufacturer and retailer of premium confectionery and cakes. The company began in 1989 when Arthur Plutus set up a small manufacturing operation to produce confectionery and cakes for shops in the county of Lincolnshire. The operation was an immediate success and the company quickly established a strong reputation for the quality of its goods, which are sold under the Plutus brand. The company now operates a large manufacturing facility in Lincolnshire and has one hundred and fifty shops throughout the UK. Around 40% of the confectionery and cakes is sold through the company's shops and the remainder is sold through the internet, mail order and gift shops. The company was listed on the Alternative Investment Market in 1998.

The draft financial statements for the year that has just ended are set out below:

Draft balance sheet as at 31 July 2005

	£'000	£'000	£'000
Fixed assets (at written down values)			
Freehold land and buildings			11,860
Retail fittings and equipment			3,510
Plant, vehicles and equipment			13,230
			28,600
Current assets			
Stocks		4,650	
Debtors		4,170	
Cash in hand		1,024	
		9,844	
Less Creditors: Amounts due within one year			
Trade creditors	6,848		
Corporation tax	870		
Dividends	622		
		8,340	
			1,504
			30,104
Less Creditors: Amounts due after more than one year			
5% Debentures (secured on freehold buildings)			6,800
			23,304
Capital and reserves			
£0.25 ordinary shares issued			8,000
Retained profit			15,304
			23,304

Draft profit and loss account for the year ended 31 July 2005

	£'000	£'000
Sales		55,460
Cost of sales		26,190
Gross profit		29,270
Less:		
Selling and distribution expenses	19,610	
Administration expenses	5,832	
		25,442
Operating profit		3,828
Finance expenses		348
Net profit before tax		3,480
Corporation tax (25%)		870
Net profit after tax		2,610
Dividends proposed		522
Retained profit for the year		2,088

The Plutus family still owns 40% of the shares in the company but is no longer involved in the day-to-day management of the company. However, the family members still expect to be consulted on any key decisions to be made. A new chief executive, David Ceto, undertook a thorough review of the company's operations soon after taking office. He found that the company had experienced very little growth in recent years as sales of confectionery and cakes have been increasingly concentrated in the hands of large supermarkets. Supermarket sales now account for 50% of total market sales and this percentage is predicted to grow in the future through aggressive advertising and discounting campaigns.

A recent forecast of sales for Plutus plc over the next five years has been produced by the Marketing Director, which provides gloomy reading:

Forecast sales for the year ended 31 July

	2006	2007	2008	2009	2010
Sales (£m)	55.8	52.6	49.5	46.1	42.4

In addition, the Finance Director has provided further forecast information concerning the company for the next five years:

Forecast information for the year ended 31 July

	2006	2007	2008	2009	2010
Operating profit margin (%)	6.5	6.0	5.8	5.6	5.3
Depreciation (£m)	3.1	3.5	4.6	4.6	4.8
Capital expenditure (£m)	4.3	2.5	12.2	3.4	4.6

The prospect of falling sales and falling margins convinced David Ceto that the company needed to seek new strategic directions in order to survive and prosper. Within days of arriving at this conclusion, Plutus plc was approached by another company, Maia plc, with a view to a possible joint venture. Maia plc is a large coffee company, which imports, roasts and blends coffees from all over the world and sells its produce to wholesale distributors, restaurants and retailers. Until recently, Maia plc enjoyed an unrivalled reputation for the quality of its coffee products. However, the company has failed to keep pace with the changing taste of its customers and has suffered a fall in sales and profits as a result. In order to revive the company, the chief executive of Maia plc is keen to diversify by exploiting the growing demand for coffee shops.

In recent years, a number of coffee shop chains originating from the US have flourished in the UK. Although these coffee shops are popular among younger people, they have often been criticised for providing characterless surroundings and for selling inferior quality coffee. The chief executive of Maia plc believes that there is a gap in the market and that coffee shops selling high-quality coffee, confectionery and cakes would be successful. He is therefore keen to build a large chain of coffee shops that will be located in major high streets and in 'up market' stores. The coffee shops will provide surroundings based on those found in cafes situated in fashionable parts of Paris and the ambience provided will be designed to appeal to affluent shoppers over 25 years of age.

The proposed joint venture would involve Maia plc providing the coffee and Plutus plc providing the confectionery and cakes. Maia plc has proposed that a separate company should be formed with 60% of the shares being held by Maia plc and 40% of the shares being held by Plutus plc. The joint venture would last for a five-year period, after which time the chain of coffee shops would be floated on the Stock Exchange with each company retaining a maximum of 10% of the ordinary shares in the newly-floated company.

The proposal interested David Ceto, who immediately began discussions with the chief executive of Maia plc to see whether such a joint venture was feasible. During these discussions, the following forecasts for the proposed chain of coffee shops over the five-year period were provided:

Forecasts for the year to 31 July

	2006	2007	2008	2009	2010
Sales (£m)	8.8	19.6	29.2	36.5	47.5
Fixed overheads (£m)	3.8	7.7	12.2	14.5	21.1
Capital expenditure (£m)	4.8	5.6	10.1	10.8	6.5
Gross profit percentage	60.0	62.0	62.0	63.0	65.0
Variable overheads as a percentage of sales	10.0	11.0	11.0	11.0	12.0

The new chain would trade under the name of Café Crème plc and would be financed by an immediate injection of share capital of £2m in total, consisting of £0.50 ordinary shares. In addition, a further £5m would be raised immediately by a 6%, four-year loan to be guaranteed by Maia plc and Plutus plc. Café Crème plc will issue no dividends, at least for the first five years, and any further finance required will be raised by internal sources or by the issue of further ordinary shares to Plutus plc and Maia plc where there is insufficient cash in a particular year. The fixed overheads mentioned above include depreciation, which is charged at the rate of 15% on cost per year on all fixed assets acquired. This is also the rate for tax purposes.

At the end of five years, Café Crème plc will be floated on the Stock Exchange and Plutus plc is likely to sell the whole of its stake in the company at this point. David Ceto sees the joint venture as a medium-term investment and believes that the coffee shop fad is likely to peak after five years with little prospect of future growth. The offer price for the shares is very difficult to judge, however, analysts have suggested that a price based on a P/E ratio of between 10 and 13 times is possible and that a P/E ratio of 12 times is most likely. Flotation costs are typically around 8% of the capital raised. The shares sold to the public will consist of shares already held by Plutus plc and Maia plc and so flotation costs will be borne by the existing shareholders.

As part of the joint venture agreement, Plutus plc will undertake to supply cakes and confectionery to Café Crème plc at cost price. This trading relationship will have no overall effect on profits or net cash flows of Plutus plc. The undertaking to supply Café Crème plc will end when the company is floated and will not be renewed as David Ceto believes that, in five years' time, Plutus plc will have more profitable opportunities to pursue.

The chief executive of Maia plc is keen to ensure that Café Crème plc implements good corporate governance practice from the outset in order to prepare the company for flotation. To this end, he has suggested a board comprising four executive directors and four non-executive directors. However, David Ceto is not convinced of the need for non-executive directors at such an early stage. The experience of having non-executive directors at Plutus plc has not been a happy one. There has been considerable suspicion and tension between the executive and non-executive directors over a number of years, which have interfered with board decision making. This has led to board resignations and a general feeling among the executive directors that non-executive directors were not adding value to the business. David Ceto felt, therefore, that the speed and quality of decision making would be improved if non-executive directors were not appointed to the board of Café Crème plc until much nearer the proposed flotation date.

A further source of disagreement between the chief executive of Maia plc and David Ceto concerned the way in which the risks associated with the venture should be identified, assessed and managed. Although both recognised the need for carrying out these tasks, they held different views as to how they should be carried out. The chief executive of Maia plc felt that they should be carried out 'in-house' and that a risk manager for Café Crème plc should be appointed as soon as possible. However, David Ceto felt that the risk management problem should be 'outsourced' for the first few years and that a firm of risk consultants should be employed. Three risk consultancy firms have been recommended to David Ceto and he argued that one of these should be appointed.

Although discussions were still at an early stage and final agreement over the proposal was still some way off, David Ceto felt that members of the Plutus family should be consulted over the proposed joint venture. He found that, although they were not opposed to the proposal, they did not want to see an issue of ordinary shares to finance the proposal or for the gearing ratio of Plutus plc to increase to more than 33%. They made it clear that they wished to avoid any dilution of control or to add significantly to the financial risks of the company. They were also keen for the dividend payout of Plutus plc to be maintained.

When carrying out calculations, the following information should be taken into account:

1. Corporation tax is at the rate of 25% on operating profits and is payable nine months after the year end.

2. Plutus plc has an after-tax required rate of return for the investment of 12%.

Required

(a) **Prepare forecast annual cash flow statements for Café Crème plc to show the total amount that Plutus plc would have to invest in ordinary shares in the company over the five-year period.**

(12 marks)

(b) **Assuming a decision to invest in Café Crème plc is made:**

(i) **prepare a forecast annual cash flow statement for Plutus plc for each of the next five years and discuss any financing issues that the company must confront.**

(ii) **suggest how any financing problems experienced by Plutus plc may be overcome, using appropriate calculations to support your arguments.** (16 marks)

(c) **Calculate the net present value of the investment in Café Crème plc from the perspective of Plutus plc and assess the sensitivity of these calculations to possible errors in the predicted P/E ratio on flotation of Café Crème plc.** (12 marks)

(d) **Discuss the possible benefits and problems that may arise for Plutus plc from a joint venture with Maia plc.** (8 marks)

(e) **Discuss the possible reasons why suspicion and tensions may exist between non-executive and executive directors of a company and suggest ways in which such suspicion and tensions may be managed.** (15 marks)

(f) **Outline the benefits and potential problems associated with the use of risk consultants to help in identifying and managing risk and suggest criteria that should be employed in selecting a suitable firm of consultants to help in this process.** (10 marks)

(g) **Identify the key risks associated with the investment in Café Crème plc by Plutus plc and state how these risks should be managed.** (20 marks)

(h) **Outline your views concerning the proposed investment in Café Crème plc and state whether you believe Plutus plc should agree to the proposal.** (7 marks)

Notes

In answering the case study questions:

1.   All recommendations must be supported by reasons.
2.   All key workings and assumptions must be clearly stated.
3.   Workings should be in £millions and should be to one decimal place.
4.   Ignore inflation.

(100 marks)

2 Suggested approach

Start by quickly reading through the scenario so that you have an idea of what it is about. At this stage do not bother looking at any of the numbers, only the overall situation is of importance.

Next move onto the requirements. Again there is no need to read them in detail but just to take note that for parts (a) and (b) forecast cash flow statements need to be prepared and for part (c) the net present value of the investment in Café Crème. Thereafter the requirements are all of a narrative nature which can be dealt with when you come to them.

Now you should concentrate on requirement (a).

Part (a)

You are being asked to prepare forecast annual cash flow statements for Café Crème (the new joint venture) and in particular to show the total amount that Plutus plc would have to invest in ordinary shares in the joint venture over the five year period.

Now read through the scenario again bearing these requirements in mind.

The cash flow forecast itself is fairly straightforward but take care with the tax calculation. Remember that depreciation is not a cash flow and therefore should not appear as an outflow in the cash flow forecast but it is allowable for tax purposes therefore when working out the tax for each year the depreciation charge should be deducted from the net cash inflows.

It is important that you realise that Plutus and Maia have agreed to fund any cash deficits by buying further ordinary shares in Café Crème. That is why you need to show the amount that Plutus would have to invest in ordinary shares over the five year period. These are the additional shares that Plutus will have to buy in order to fund any cash deficit in Café Crème.

Part (b)

For part (b) you now have to look at the project from the perspective of Plutus and to prepare a forecast cash flow statement for Plutus for the next five years. Again read through the scenario to make sure that you have all the relevant information to hand. Information is dotted about throughout the scenario so do read it through very carefully.

In the calculations remember that you will have to include the shares purchased in Café Crème calculated in part (a) as well. Take care when dealing with tax and dividend calculations in particular as to whether you are calculating profits or cash flows as the timings will be different.

There is some overlap between requirements (i) and (ii) here as in (i) you are asked to 'discuss any financing issues that the company must confront' and in (ii) to 'suggest how any financing problems experienced by Plutus plc may be overcome.'

Think carefully about this financing issue. Plutus has a large amount of capital expenditure in 2008 which will mean that financing is required from that point on. What are the main options available to Plutus?

- issue of shares
- loan
- bank overdraft

The family have stated that they do not want an issue of further ordinary shares so this leaves a loan or bank overdraft as the options. As the finance is required for capital expenditure then a medium term loan would appear to be a more appropriate form of financing than an overdraft which is technically repayable on demand. Therefore loan finance is chosen and the final factor is to carry out calculations to ensure that such a loan will not mean that the gearing ratio exceeds 33%.

Part (c)

This time you are required to calculate the net present value of the investment in Café Crème from the perspective of Plutus. Think about this very carefully – what are the cash flows of Plutus in relation to the investment in Café Crème?

The answer is that they are the initial investment, the additional investments in 2008 and 2009 from part (a) and finally the amount that Plutus would get when Café Crème was sold in 2010. The examiner commented that many candidates in fact used the cash flows of Café Crème over the five years as they failed to consider the investment from the perspective of Plutus.

When calculating the final sale price of Café Crème when it is floated it is probably sensible to use the most likely P/E ratio of 12 to estimate the sale proceeds initially. This can then be compared to using the lowest likely P/E ratio of 10 in order to satisfy the second part of the requirements which asks you to assess the sensitivity of the calculations to possible errors in the P/E ratio.

Part (d)

Now move onto the discursive elements of the project. Make sure that you make your answer specific to Plutus and Maia and not just a general discussion of the benefits and problems of joint ventures. As a rough guide this part of the project should be about 400 words (8/100 × 5,000).

Part (e)

In this part take careful note that there are two distinct questions being asked here. Firstly the possible reasons for there being suspicion and tensions between executive and non-executive directors and secondly suggestions of ways in which these suspicions and tensions should be managed.

The examiner commented that the reasons tended to be well-addressed but the ways in which this could be managed generally required more thought.

As a guide you should write about 750 words (15/100 × 5,000) for this part of the project.

Part (f)

Note that there are three parts to this element of the project:

- benefits
- problems
- criteria for selecting a suitable firm of consultants

The examiner commented that it was the third element of these requirements which let a lot of answers down.

Aim for about 500 words for this section (10/100 × 5,000).

Part (g)

There are two aspects to this part of the question – identification of the key risks and how each risk should be managed. If you do not feel confident in this area have a look at the sections in the Study Text on types of risks as this may give you some ideas but do make sure that you relate it all to the scenario and do not just write in general terms about types of risk.

For 20 marks aim for about 1,000 words (20/100 × 5,000).

Part (h)

As the concluding part of this project you are asked to outline your views of the proposal and whether you think Plutus should agree to it. The examiner commented that attention was usually only given to one side of the argument. Therefore a candidate who supported the investment would only set out the arguments in favour of it. The examiner has pointed out that higher marks could have been gained by also pointing out possible arguments against the investment and then going on to state why such arguments should be disregarded or should not be weighed too heavily.

Word count should be about 350 words (7/100 × 5,000).

3 Suggested answer

(a) **Café Crème - Forecast cash flows for year ended 31 July**

	2006 £m	2007 £m	2008 £m	2009 £m	2010 £m
Sales	8.80	19.6	29.2	36.5	47.5
Gross profit	5.3	12.2	18.1	23.0	30.9
Variable overheads	(0.9)	(2.2)	(3.2)	(4.0)	(5.7)
Fixed overheads (W1)	(3.1)	(6.2)	(9.2)	(9.9)	(15.5)
Operating profit (excl. depn)	1.3	3.8	5.7	9.1	9.7
Interest	(0.3)	(0.3)	(0.3)	(0.3)	
Profit before tax (excl. depn)	1.0	3.5	5.4	8.8	9.7
Tax (25% - 1 year delay) (W3)	-	(0.1)	(0.5)	(0.6)	(1.1)
Loan repayment				(5.0)	
Capital expenditure	(4.8)	(5.6)	(10.1)	(10.8)	(6.5)
Net cash flow	(3.8)	(2.2)	(5.2)	(7.6)	2.1
Opening balance	7.0	3.2	1.0	(4.2)	(11.8)
Closing balance	3.2	1.0	(4.2)	(11.8)	(9.7)

Plutus investment in ordinary shares

1 August 2005 – initial investment	£2m × 40%	=	£0.8m
31 July 2008 – cash deficit	£4.2m × 40%	=	£1.7m
31 July 2009 – cash deficit	(£11.8m – £4.2m) × 40%	=	£3.0m

Working 1 – Fixed overheads

	2006	2007	2008	2009	2010
Per question	3.8	7.7	12.2	14.5	21.1
Less: depreciation (W2)	(0.7)	(1.5)	(3.0)	(4.6)	(5.6)
	3.1	6.2	9.2	9.9	15.5

Working 2 – depreciation charges

	2006	2007	2008	2009	2010
Capital expenditure	4.8	5.6	10.1	10.8	6.5
Depreciation charge (15%)	0.7	0.7	0.7	0.7	0.7
		0.8	0.8	0.8	0.8
			1.5	1.5	1.5
				1.6	1.6
					1.0
	0.7	1.5	3.0	4.6	5.6

Working 3 – Tax

	2006	2007	2008	2009	2010
Profit	1.0	3.5	5.4	8.8	9.7
Less: depreciation (W2)	(0.7)	(1.5)	(3.0)	(4.6)	(5.6)
Taxable profit	0.3	2.0	2.4	4.2	4.1
Tax at 25% - 1 year delay	0.1	0.5	0.6	1.1	

(b) (i) **Plutus plc – Forecast cash flows for years ended 31 July**

	2006 £m	2007 £m	2008 £m	2009 £m	2010 £m
Sales	55.8	52.6	49.5	46.1	42.4
Operating profit	3.6	3.2	2.9	2.6	2.2
Add back depreciation	3.1	3.5	4.6	4.6	4.8
Interest (6,800 × 5%)	(0.3)	(0.3)	(0.3)	(0.3)	(0.3)
Cash flow profit before tax	6.4	6.4	7.2	6.9	6.7
Tax (W1)	(0.9)	(0.8)	(0.7)	(0.7)	(0.6)
Operating cash flows	5.5	5.6	6.5	6.2	6.1
Dividends paid (W2)	(0.6)	(0.5)	(0.4)	(0.4)	(0.3)
Capital expenditure	(4.3)	(2.5)	(12.2)	(3.4)	(4.6)
Investment in Café Crème (part (a))	(0.8)		(1.7)	(3.0)	
Net cash flow	(0.2)	2.6	(7.8)	(0.6)	1.2
Opening balance	1.0	0.8	3.4	(4.4)	(5.0)
Closing balance	0.8	3.4	(4.4)	(5.0)	(3.8)

Therefore we can see that Plutus plc will need additional finance from 2008 onwards. The main reason for the additional finance is the large capital expenditure of £12.2m in 2008. Therefore as the expenditure is on fixed assets a medium term loan to finance the purchase of these assets would be more appropriate than an overdraft. As the forecast requirement increases to £5.0m in 2009 then a loan agreement for £5m should be sought.

(ii) It has been noted above that the most appropriate method of raising the additional finance required for the capital expenditure would be to use a loan facility of £5m. However this will only be possible, or acceptable to the Plutus family, provided that the gearing ratio does not rise above 33%.

We must therefore check the gearing ratio under the assumption that £4.4m of the loan facility is drawn down in 2008 and the remaining £0.6m drawn down in 2009. As a loan is likely to have a higher interest rate than the existing debentures then we will assume an interest rate of say 8%.

Gearing ratio

	2006 £m	2007 £m	2008 £m	2009 £m	2010 £m
Opening equity	23.3	25.3	27.1	28.2	29.2
Retained profits (W2)	2.0	1.8	1.5	1.4	1.1
Additional int (8% × 4.4m/5.0m)	-	-	(0.4)	(0.4)	(0.4)
Closing equity	25.3	27.1	28.2	29.2	29.9
Loan capital	6.8	6.8	11.2	11.8	11.8
Total funding	32.1	33.9	39.4	41.0	41.7
Gearing ratio	21.2%	20.1%	28.4%	28.8%	28.3%

Therefore this method of financing should be acceptable to the Plutus family.

Working 1 – tax paid

Tax is paid in the year following that to which it relates.

	2006 £m	2007 £m	2008 £m	2009 £m	2010 £m
2005 charge in P&L account	0.9				
25% × operating profit less interest					
25% × (3.6 − 0.3)		0.8			
25% × (3.2 − 0.3)			0.7		
25% × (2.9 − 0.3)				0.7	
25% × (2.6 − 0.3)					0.6

Working 2 – Dividends paid

We are told in the scenario that the dividend payout ratio is to be maintained. Currently this is 20% (522/2,610). Dividends will be paid in the year after they are proposed.

	2006 £m	2007 £m	2008 £m	2009 £m	2010 £m
Operating profit	3.6	3.2	2.9	2.6	2.2
Interest (6,800 × 5%)	(0.3)	(0.3)	(0.3)	(0.3)	(0.3)
Profit before tax	3.3	2.9	2.6	2.3	1.9
Tax 25%	(0.8)	(0.7)	(0.7)	(0.6)	(0.5)
Profit after tax	2.5	2.2	1.9	1.7	1.4
Dividends (20%)	(0.5)	(0.4)	(0.4)	(0.3)	(0.3)
Retained profit	2.0	1.8	1.5	1.4	1.1
Dividends paid (one year later)	(0.6)	(0.5)	(0.4)	(0.4)	(0.3)

(c) **Plutus plc – Net present value of investment in Café Crème**

	2005 £m	2006 £m	2007 £m	2008 £m	2009 £m	2010 £m
Cash outflows – investment	(0.8)			(1.7)	(3.0)	
Cash inflow – sale (W)						13.6
Discount factor at 12%	1.00	0.89	0.80	0.71	0.64	0.57
Present value	(0.8)			(1.2)	(1.9)	7.8

Net present value = £3.9m positive

However the P/E ratio is not certain and could be as low as 10 rather than 12 as used in these calculations. If the P/E ratio is 10 then the selling price per share will be £1.12 and the amount received by Plutus will be £1.12 x 11m shares x 92% = £11.3m.

The net present value if the sale value is only £11.3m will be:

	2005 £m	2006 £m	2007 £m	2008 £m	2009 £m	2010 £m
Cash outflows – investment	(0.8)			(1.7)	(3.0)	
Cash inflow – sale (W)						11.3
Discount factor at 12%	1.00	0.89	0.80	0.71	0.64	0.57
Present value	(0.8)			(1.2)	(1.9)	6.4

Net present value = £2.5m positive

Therefore a 17% drop in P/E ratio (12 to 10) has caused a 36% drop in NPV (£3.9m to £2.5m).

Working – likely proceeds of sale of Café Crème

The sale in five years time will be based upon a most likely P/E ratio of 12. Therefore we need to find the earnings per share figure for Café Crème for 2010.

	£m
Operating profit for 2010 (9.7 – 5.6 depn) (part (a))	4.1
Tax (4.1 × 25%)	(1.0)
Profit after tax	3.1

Total number of £0.50 shares in issue

($2m + £4.2m + £7.6m) × 2		27.6m shares
Earnings per share	=	£3.1m/27.6m = £0.112 per share
Selling price per share (assuming P/E ratio of 12)	=	12 × £0.112
	=	£1.34 per share
Shares held by Plutus = 27.6m × 40%	=	11m shares
Cash received less costs	=	11m shares × £1.34 × 92%
	=	£13.6m

(d)   There are a number of potential benefits and problems that could arise for Plutus plc in a joint venture such as this with Maia.

In terms of benefits the directors of Maia are offering Plutus an investment opportunity which has not been considered before which on the face of it would appear to be an attractive one (see anticipated net present value from part (c)). The fact that the proposition is a joint venture means that Plutus has the opportunity to enter this new market at a lower cost than if it had ventured into this area on its own. In addition it also means that the burdens of ownership and additional capital commitments to the joint venture are shared and in particular the risks involved in any venture such as this are also shared between Plutus and Maia. A joint venture such as this one also means that the two venturers can bring their own individual expertise or area of operations to the venture and they can both benefit from complementary resources. In this case it is the coffee of Maia and the confectionery and cakes of Plutus.

However despite the optimistic figures and net present value from the joint venture there are also a number of problems which the venturers may come across. The main problem for both Plutus and Maia is that neither company has direct experience of running a chain of coffee shops. Plutus manufactures and sells cakes and confectionery whilst Maia imports, roasts, blends and then sells its coffee to wholesalers, restaurants and retailers. This is very different to owning or leasing a chain of buildings and running a successful chain of coffee shops.

There are also a number of problems that Plutus itself might encounter in the joint venture. Effectively Plutus is the junior partner in the joint venture with only a 40% share compared to the

60% interest of Maia. This may lead to frustrations within Plutus over any restrictions on decision making that the directors of Plutus may feel they are under. It may also lead to accusations and frustrations over the efforts of each party to the joint venture and most importantly the risks incurred by each party in relation to the gains received.

On balance the investment in joint venture looks attractive but the potential problems and risks must also be considered.

(e) It is not uncommon in a group of strong, intelligent, independent minded individuals for there to be tensions and therefore it is entirely understandable that there may be tensions between the executive and non-executive directors on the Board of Plutus plc. Executive directors are hired and promoted to carry out their particular role within the organisation and non-executive directors tend to be chosen for their general background, experience and skills. It is likely that any suspicions and tensions will come from both groups of directors.

In many situations the executive directors may not entirely trust the non-executive directors. It is widely known that the appointment of non-executive directors to a Board is part of the aim for strong corporate governance and to help reduce the likelihood of some of the recent corporate scandals taking place again. Therefore it is possible that the executive directors may view the non-executive directors as having the role of 'policing' their activities and keeping an eye on them.

Non-executive directors, by their very nature, do not have an executive or working role within the organisation. They will be recruited from a wide range of backgrounds and indeed may hold a number of different non-executive director roles. The nature of their role as non-executive directors therefore may lead some executive directors not to trust their ability or their judgement. As they do not actually work within the organisation and may not even have any experience in the particular field in which the organisation works, many executive directors may feel that their knowledge of the business or industry is not great enough. How can they disagree with decisions made by those who work in the business if they know little about the business?

In a similar way executive directors, who often work long hours within the business, may feel that the non-executive directors do not spend enough time in the business, getting to know it and how it works, in order to carry out their role. If the non-executive directors have other non-executive director roles as well then the executive directors may rightly feel that maybe their company is not a priority and the non-executive directors do not have the loyalty to the company that is required.

Equally the non-executive directors may have suspicions and tensions with the executive directors. The executive directors work full time in the business whereas the non-executives only generally work for a few hours a month largely to attend Board meetings. The non-executive directors could rightly feel suspicious that they are being excluded from important matters. They may feel that the executive directors and managers do not provide them with all the information necessary for them to carry out their roles or that this information is not provided at the right times. They may believe that the executive directors specifically withhold information which may alter a decision of the Board. The non-executive directors may also feel that the executive directors hold additional, informal Board meetings and take decisions when they are not around or discuss important matters amongst themselves before the non-executive directors have a chance to consider them at Board meetings. Finally the non-executive directors may feel, on a personal basis, that they are not respected by the executive directors due to their background, professionalism or character for example.

This need not all be bad for a company. In some instances tensions between the two types of directors may help to prevent Board meetings becoming too comfortable and decisions being taken without full and frank discussion. Such tensions can lead to robust debate where all of the issues surrounding the decision are thoroughly debated.

However in the case of Plutus the suspicions and tensions are such that they have interfered with Board decision making and indeed led to Board resignations. There are a number of ways in which such extreme tensions can be managed:

- ensuring that there is a rigorous and thorough recruitment process for both executive and non-executive directors

- ensuring that the right calibre of non-executive director is recruited and that their strengths and experience are communicated clearly to the executive directors

- holding regular, thorough and relevant induction courses to ensure that the new non-executive directors understand fully the nature of the business and their role within the company

- ensuring that there is a free flow of information at all times

- holding board meetings at such frequent intervals that all key issues are raised at these meetings with the non-executive directors and not discussed in periods between board meetings

- monitoring of the performance of all directors, both executive and non-executive, and dismissal of any incompetent individual.

During actual Board meetings themselves the role of the Chairman can be vital in dealing with suspicions and tensions. The Chairman should ensure that all relevant information has been made available to all parties prior to the meeting and should also ensure that the meetings themselves are well run. The meetings should focus on strategic issues rather than operational issues which is where the non-executive directors can bring their skills and background to the fore. The Chairman should encourage open debate at these meetings and ensure that all directors air their views.

(f)   There are disagreements between Plutus plc and Maia plc about how the risks associated with the joint venture in Café Crème are to be identified, assessed and managed. The chief executive of Maia believes that they should be carried out in-house and that a risk manager for Café Crème should be appointed as soon as possible whereas David Ceto feels that the risk management problem should be outsourced to a firm of risk consultants. There are both benefits and potential problems associated with outsourcing this area and using risk management consultants.

The benefits largely centre around the experience and expertise of risk management consultants. They are likely to have a sound understanding of current best practice in this complex area and they should also have up-to-date knowledge of the latest methods of both identifying and assessing risks. They should also have not only experience in the best ways of managing different types of risks but also contacts with the likes of insurance brokers and insurance companies which may be of benefit in managing these risks as cost-efficiently as possible. Risks not only need to be identified, assessed and managed but the risk culture and risk management process also needs to be embedded in the management and culture of Café Crème. Risk management consultants should be well placed, with their experience, to manage this process and ensure that the risk management processes continue within Café Crème. Finally if outside consultants are used for this important process then this frees up the time of directors and managers of Café Crème to carry out other important aspects of the business.

However there are also potential problems associated with the use of outside consultants. One major drawback is likely to be the costs involved. Even taking into account the value of the time spent by directors and managers if the project were done in-house the use of consultants will almost certainly be higher. From a cultural perspective if the directors, managers and employees of Café Crème see that the risk management process is being dealt with from start to finish by external consultants then they are less likely to take on board the risk management processes as part of the corporate culture. Risk management may always be seen to be the responsibility of the consultants rather than the management and workforce.

If a firm of risk management consultants are to be used then a lot of care needs to be taken with their recruitment. The criteria that should be employed in selecting a suitable firm of consultants to provide this service should include:

- the consultants' understanding of this type of business and their past experience of this type of business

- whether the consultants have the requisite experience and skills to undertake the risk analysis and assessment

- whether the consultants have the requisite tools such as computer models and software to carry out the risk analysis and assessment

- the capacity of the consultants to carry out all of the services which are required by Café Crème

- the ability of the consultants to carry out the required services within an agreed budget and to an agreed timescale.

(g) As with most new investments there are a variety of risks associated with the investment in Café Crème by Plutus plc.

Initially there is forecasting risk. One of the major elements of the decision of whether or not to invest in Café Crème will be the outcome of the net present value calculation of the cash flows associated with the investment in Café Crème. All elements of the forecast have some degree of risk attached to them – sales, expenses, additional investment, exit value etc. Therefore Plutus runs the risk of the forecasts being incorrect and the investment not in fact being profitable. However this risk can be managed to a degree by carrying out sensitivity analysis. As we saw earlier if a P/E ratio of 12 is used then the net present value of the investment was £3.9 million and even if the P/E ratio fell to 10 the net present value was still positive at £2.5 million. Therefore even if other figures in the forecasts turned out to be overly optimistic with such a generous positive net present value it would seem unlikely that the investment would not be profitable.

We have already touched on some of the risks of such a joint venture. These are particularly emphasised in the case of Plutus as they are the junior partner in the joint venture with a holding of only 40% compared to the 60% holding of Maia. One way in which this risk can be controlled is by building into the joint venture agreement safeguards regarding risks, returns and decision making responsibilities.

A significant risk that the joint venture runs is that the joint venture will fail to achieve its performance targets. This is an entirely new venture for both Plutus plc and Maia plc and it is entirely possible that the forecast figures could have been overstated and that the results are not as good as expected. Plutus should investigate whether there are any abandonment options available whereby it can realise its investment in the joint venture before the five year period is up if the results are not as expected.

As mentioned in the previous paragraph this is a completely new type of venture for both parties and it is unlikely that either Plutus plc or Maia plc will have much detailed knowledge of their competition in this line of business. Therefore there is an element of competition risk. This may be partly overcome by environmental scanning and by carrying out market research in this area.

In more general terms the joint venture, as with all businesses, runs the risk of a general economic slowdown. As an up-market coffee shop is likely to be a luxury consumer activity then it will tend to be hit quite hard in any general economic downturn as luxury goods or activities will be the first to be cut back by consumers. However as the proposed investment is only for a five year period the investors should have a reasonable view of the economic prospects for most of that period. The usual booms and troughs in the economy tend to occur at seven to nine year intervals.

Both the joint venture in Café Crème and Plutus plc itself are subject to cash flow risk. The detailed forecasts for the results of Café Crème indicate that it will need additional funding in 2008 and 2009 and both Plutus plc and Maia plc must ensure that they have the funds in place at this point in time to provide the funding required. Plutus itself has heavy capital expenditure in 2008 and this combined with the necessity to provide additional funding for Café Crème will be a drain on resources. Plutus should have discussions with its bank or other lenders to try to ensure that when the funds are needed they will be available.

Reputation risk is also very relevant for Plutus plc. It was a family owned business in which the family is still very much involved and the goods that it has sold under the Plutus brand for many years have a strong reputation for quality. Although it is unlikely that the quality of the goods that Plutus plc supplies to Café Crème will alter if the coffee shops are not a success then this will have an overall effect on the Plutus brand. When dealing with the public there is always the risk of bad publicity and to this end it may be wise for Plutus to employ a public relations officer to liaise with the media and mitigate any form of bad publicity.

Again an aspect of working with the public is that Café Crème will be judged as much on the service provided as the coffee, cakes and confectionary provided. Therefore it is vital that the right type of people are employed and retained within the organisation. This is also true of the management team who must be capable of starting up this operation and ensuring that it can deal with the already existing competitive market. The new company will therefore need a strong human resources department to ensure that all of this takes place.

(h) The major argument in favour of the joint venture of Café Crème is the evident level of profitability based upon the forecasts provided by Maia plc. With a most likely net present value of £3.9m and a worst case net present value of £2.5m this is obviously a powerful argument for investing.

However there are also a number of factors which longer term may make the investment seem not quite such a good investment:

- the diversification into coffee shops does not necessarily seem to fit in with the overall strategy of Plutus

- it is not clear from the scenario whether any other investment opportunities have been considered – maybe other avenues should be investigated before a commitment is made

- the approach of investing in Café Crème for five years and then selling through a flotation is typical of a venture capital organisation rather than a manufacturer and retailer

- discussed earlier have been the potential problems and risks of operating the joint venture

The profitability aspect certainly makes the venture appear to be worthwhile however there are a number of risks involved not least of which is the lack of experience of either joint venturer in such a business. Before any final decision is made at the very least other opportunities for diversification and investment should be investigated.

4 Examiner's comments

Examiner's comments. The pass rate for this sitting was satisfactory, with the majority of candidates providing projects of a reasonable standard or higher. As in the previous sitting, however, marks awarded for the projects were not widely dispersed. There were few projects of a very low standard but equally few projects of a very high standard. Although one or two parts of the project question caused difficulties for candidates, most were answered satisfactorily and only a few very weak projects were submitted. Nevertheless, most candidates could have achieved higher marks if they had adopted a more thoughtful approach to some of the issues raised. Principles or points raised should often have taken greater account of the particular circumstances set out in the case study or should have been explored in more depth.

Failure to do this led to answers that often appeared superficial or too mechanical in the approach taken. Those awarded very high marks were able to demonstrate their ability to analyse the issues and problems raised in a considered manner.

SPECIFIC COMMENTS

The case study, upon which the question was based, concerned a proposal for a joint venture to set up Café Crème plc, a chain of upmarket cafes. The proposed joint venture involved Maia plc, a coffee importer, and Plutus plc, a confectionery manufacturer.

Part (a) carried 12 marks out of 100 marks for the whole project and required candidates to prepare forecast annual cash flow statements for Café Crème plc over a five-year period and to identify the amount that Plutus plc would have to invest in the new company.

Most candidates adopted the correct approach to answering this part of the question. The cash flow statements were generally set out using an appropriate format and candidates demonstrated an understanding of what was required. However, many ran into difficulties when calculating particular figures for inclusion in the cash flow statements, such as taxation and depreciation. In addition, few managed to identify correctly the amount of finance that Plutus plc would have to inject in the new company. Nevertheless, the approach taken and the principles displayed ensured that most managed to achieve a pass mark.

Part (b) carried 16 marks and was divided into two sub parts. Part (i) required candidates to prepare forecast annual cash flow statements for Plutus plc over a five-year period and to discuss any financing issues that were revealed by these statements.

Once again, most candidates adopted the correct approach and used an appropriate format when preparing the cash flow statements but, again, errors were often made in deriving certain key figures. Taxation, dividend and depreciation calculations were often the cause of candidates failing to achieve full marks. In particular, depreciation calculations failed to take account of the cumulative nature of the depreciation charge. Nevertheless, this sub-part was answered satisfactorily with most managing to achieve a pass. Part (ii) required candidates to suggest how any financing problems revealed by the forecast cash flow statements could be resolved. Answers to this sub-part produced more disappointing results. Most identified loan capital as the appropriate way of dealing with the shortfall revealed. There was a specific requirement for candidates to provide calculations to support the financing proposals that were made. The case study stated that if new loan capital were used to 'plug' any financing gap, it should not result in a gearing ratio higher than 33%. A good answer to this sub-part should, therefore, have shown the effect of additional loan capital on the gearing ratio for each year over the five-year period to demonstrate that this limit was not breached. Unfortunately, few candidates managed to do this. In some cases, a single calculation was made to show the effect of the additional loan capital in a single year and in other cases no calculations were offered in support of the financing proposal. As a result, marks for this sub-part were not high.

Part (c) carried 12 marks and required candidates to calculate the net present value of the investment in Café Crème plc from the perspective of Plutus plc and to undertake sensitivity calculations to take account of possible errors in the predicted flotation price.

This part was not done well. The main problem was that many candidates failed to recognise that the relevant cash flows to be used in the calculations should have been based on the capital injections made by Plutus plc in Café Crème plc. These cash flows should then have been compared to the cash inflows arising on flotation. Instead, candidates often used the net cash flows generated by Café Crème plc over the five-year period leading up to the proposed flotation. This failed to consider the investment from the perspective of Plutus plc.

Part (d) carried eight marks and required candidates to discuss the possible benefits and problems that may arise for Plutus plc by entering into the proposed joint venture.

On the whole this part was reasonably well answered and most candidates managed to achieve a pass mark. However, more marks could often have been gained if the particular issues raised in the case study were addressed. Too often, candidates provided a list of the general issues and problems associated with joint ventures and made no real attempt to tailor their points to the particular circumstances outlined, such as the lack of knowledge of both parties to the joint venture in operating a chain of cafés.

Part (e) carried 15 marks and required candidates to discuss reasons why suspicion and tensions may exist between executive and non-executive directors and to suggest how these may be managed.

Most candidates were aware of the issues that lead to tension between the two groups and marks awarded for this element were often high (some of the relevant points had been identified in an article that I wrote for *finance matters* and so candidates should have benefited from reading this article). However, the proposals made for resolving tensions and problems were rarely given enough consideration. For nearly all candidates, a more thoughtful and detailed consideration of this element would have yielded higher marks. In particular, the chairman has an important role to play in resolving excessive tension and this role could have been discussed.

Part (f) carried 10 marks and required candidates to discuss the potential problems and issues arising from the use of risk consultants and to suggest criteria that should be employed in selecting a suitable firm of consultants.

Most candidates managed to make a reasonable attempt at discussing the benefits and problems that may arise but some struggled with the criteria for selection. It seemed that some candidates misunderstood what was required when dealing with this particular aspect. The answers provided often discussed the process of employing risk consultants (such as drafting terms of reference and providing letters of appointments etc) rather than identifying what attributes risk consultants should possess. Overall, the marks awarded for this part reflected the total marks for the project: few low marks but also few very high marks.

Part (g) carried 20 marks and required candidates to identify the risks associated with the investment in Café Crème plc by Plutus plc and to state how these risks may be managed.

Although most candidates managed to pick up a reasonable number of marks for this part, the general standard of answers was not high. Once again, a more thoughtful approach to dealing with the issues was often required. The impression was often given that candidates had a list of possible risks confronting any business and used this list without giving any real thought to the particular circumstances outlined in the case study. To achieve high marks, candidates needed to identify the particular nature of the risks being faced, using information from the case study to support the points made. Similarly, when dealing with the management of risk, a more considered approach was often required. Too often, answers were superficial and did not really get to grips with the risks that had been identified.

Part (h) carried seven marks and required candidates to outline their views on the proposed investment in Café Crème plc.

On the whole, this part was done well with most candidates achieving a pass mark, although attention was usually given to only one side of the argument. For example, a candidate that supported the investment in Café Crème plc would simply set out the arguments in favour of the investment. More marks, however, could have been gained by also pointing out possible arguments against the investment and then going on to state why such arguments should either be disregarded or should not be weighed too heavily when making the final decision.

ACCA Live Project – Spring 2006: Module A

This project was originally issued in February 2006, before the DipFIM qualification adopted International Accounting Standards and terminology. The answer to this project is therefore based upon the original project, but it contains references to international terminology and standards where appropriate.

1 Spring 2006 Project: Module A

Diploma in Financial Management

PROJECT DA2, INCORPORATING SUBJECT AREAS
- INTERPRETATION OF FINANCIAL STATEMENTS
- PERFORMANCE MANAGEMENT

All questions are compulsory and MUST be answered

The project MUST be written in English.

The maximum word count (including appendices and tables but excluding references and bibliography) is 5,000.

The project MUST be TYPED in black ink, one-sided, double-spaced, using a minimum 12-point font size and a 1-inch margin at each side. HANDWRITTEN SUBMISSIONS WILL NOT BE ACCEPTED. The project must be submitted by post, electronic submissions are not acceptable.

The project should be submitted on A4 paper with your student number, project name, date and page number at the top of each page.

A project submission form MUST be completed for each project submitted and attached to the front of the project.

The Association of Chartered Certified Accountants

Incorporating subject areas – Interpretation of Financial Statements and Performance Management

This ONE question is compulsory and MUST be attempted

Motorsayles plc

You have recently been appointed to the post of Chief Executive with Motorsayles plc, a retail motor sales group which operates a number of outlets throughout England and Wales. You were appointed when the founder, Malcolm Sayles, retired. The company has achieved strong growth which has been achieved both organically and through acquisitions. The board is continuing to seek opportunities to acquire additional dealerships as well as growing existing outlets.

Malcolm Sayles had often been quoted as saying that the company's strategy was:

'To grow the business through the acquisition of high quality dealerships, and the development of a range of franchises across all market sectors.'

It had always been Malcolm's intention to retire once he had achieved his long held ambition to take the company public, and a UK Stock Exchange listing was achieved two years ago. Your appointment was part of his vision that the company would require different leadership as a public company.

It was made clear to you during the recruitment process that while the board believed that the company's strategy should be reviewed and refreshed, it was felt that the outcome of this review should acknowledge the existing values which had been instilled by Malcolm Sayles.

Prior to joining Motorsayles you had several years' experience as Chief Operating Officer of a distributor of electronic components. Before taking up that position your experience was mainly in product development and marketing.

Following your appointment with Motorsayles, as discussed during the recruitment process, you undertook a strategic review of the company. The purpose of this review was to allow you to become familiar with the specific issues affecting the retail motor trade, and to develop the company's strategy. It had been agreed with the Board of Directors that the findings from this review, and the existing values, would provide the basis for the development of the company's strategic plan for the next five years. You are due to meet with the Board of Directors in the near future, and you are now preparing a briefing paper with your analysis and proposals. This is due to be circulated to the board members for their consideration two weeks before the meeting. You have formed the view that an important part of the development process is to confirm that the directors, all of whom have been with the company for more than five years, clearly understand how their roles have changed due to the company's listing. Although they were fully briefed as part of the listing process, you took the view that it would be valuable to confirm that the change in role continues to be recognised.

Prior to presenting your recommendations to the board you plan to assess the company's performance since it achieved a listing. You have decided that this will be done most effectively by focusing on a small number of key measures (you have decided to focus on six measures), and ensuring that the significance of these is clearly understood by the board members.

Current Lines of Business

The company has two core business activities:

- the sale of new and used cars; and
- the provision of after-sales service.

Within the new and used car sales business, franchises are held for a range of manufacturers and these are managed in two business areas – volume manufacturers and specialist manufacturers. The company's portfolio of franchises includes all the main volume manufacturers, and a number of high quality marques. Because of the wide range of manufacturers which the company represents, it is possible to meet customers' requirements for a range of vehicle types. It has been Malcolm Sayles' proud boast that 'we can provide all the vehicles a customer will need, from the sales rep's motor to the chairman's Rolls'.

The after-sales business is also managed on the basis of two activities:

- servicing and repairs; and
- sales of parts and accessories.

You have noted that the ability to generate profit from the after-sales activities is directly dependent on the volume of vehicle sales.

Servicing has a high level of fixed costs, and the key operating objective is to achieve a high level of activity from routine servicing, repairs and warranty work. While customers are obliged to ensure that their vehicle is routinely serviced according to the manufacturer's schedule, they are not required to have this work carried out by the supplying dealer.

Parts and accessories sales provide opportunities for additional profit to be earned on the sale of vehicles. Due to the low profit per unit on vehicle sales, it can often be the case that more profit is generated from the sale of parts and accessories (for example, an upgrade in the in-car entertainment system or satellite navigation system) than is generated by the sale of the vehicle.

The core business is supported by two complementary activities: contract hire and vehicle finance.

The company's contract hire business offers a comprehensive package to customers, and also contributes to overall company performance by generating sales which are included in the overall calculation for volume bonuses.

The contract hire business offers customers a combination of certainty and flexibility. The certainty comes from a fixed price for the supply, routine maintenance and disposal of the vehicle, while the flexibility comes from the company's ability to change vehicles during the contract period, due to the range of manufacturers represented and the ability to dispose of the contract vehicle through the dealer network.

Most customers use some form of finance for their vehicle purchase. Such finance is provided by a number of companies. Most of these are subsidiaries of either the major banks or vehicle manufacturers.

As a registered financial intermediary, the company earns commission by arranging both finance and insurance for customers. The level of activity and profits from this line of business have reduced in recent years due to the impact of direct marketing by banks and building societies and the increasing use of the internet by customers. Nevertheless, it remains profitable and is seen as an important element in offering a complete service to customers.

Volume bonuses

The profit on the sale of an individual vehicle is very low for both volume manufacturers and specialist manufacturers. The overall profitability of vehicle sales is dependent on achieving the sales volume targets set by the manufacturer in order to earn volume bonuses. Such bonuses can be significant, and failure to achieve volume targets would have a detrimental effect on the company.

Staff

The company has low labour turnover, and staff are highly motivated. This is regarded as a key element in achieving the high levels of customer satisfaction which in turn lead to customer retention, and profitability.

Staff are encouraged to undertake structured training and each employee is appraised on an annual basis. During this appraisal, staff agree targets for the next six, twelve and eighteen months with their line manager.

Employee incentive scheme

One of the directors has suggested that the company should consider setting up an employee share ownership trust as an incentive to staff. He has commented that his understanding is that any investment in such a trust would be reported on the balance sheet under 'Fixed asset investments'. He went on to say that although this would have the short term effect of reducing the key ratio of return on capital employed, the long term benefit, in terms of employee motivation, would be far greater.

On checking the accounting treatment of such a trust, you have been advised that the correct treatment is to deduct any investment in the company's own shares from shareholders' funds.

Market outlook

While there has been strong demand for several years, there is evidence that market growth will not continue at the current level. The growth to date has been due, in large part, to strong consumer confidence, as a result of relatively low interest rates. The trade is also characterised by over-supply and it is expected that competition between manufacturers, particularly in the volume sector, will intensify.

Strategic choice

As noted above, the board continues to seek opportunities to acquire additional dealerships as well as growing existing outlets. Your view is that, while this may be possible, it is important to consider alternative strategies. You have also noted that the focus to date on growth has meant that little attention has been paid to ensuring that the company's structure is appropriate, and you have indicated to the board that as a listed company, this must be considered if the company is to meet the objectives of shareholders.

Financial and industry data

You have obtained the following data to assist your review:

Motorsayles plc
Profit and Loss Account for the year ended 31 March

		2006	2005
		£m	£m
Turnover	Continuing operations	1,199.64	1,009.24
	Acquired operations	98.72	51.11
		1,298.36	1,060.35
Cost of sales	Continuing operations	1,038.73	866.98
	Acquired operations	85.90	46.26
		1,124.63	913.24
Gross profit	Continuing operations	160.91	140.26
	Acquired operations	12.82	6.85
		173.73	147.11
Operating expenses (excl. goodwill amortisation)		136.31	115.62
Goodwill amortisation		0.62	0.75
Operating profit	Continuing operations	35.86	30.35
	Acquired operations	0.94	0.39
		36.80	30.74
Net interest charges		3.74	2.81
Profit on ordinary activities before tax		33.06	27.93
Tax		9.80	8.38
Profit on ordinary activities after tax		23.26	19.55
Dividends		7.36	6.62
Retained Profit for year		15.90	12.93
Earnings per share – basic (pence)		12.45	11.40
– diluted (pence)		11.90	10.95

Balance Sheet as at 31 March

	2006 £m	2005 £m
Fixed Assets Intangible	2.56	1.06
Tangible	144.29	123.84
	146.85	124.90
Current Assets Stocks	198.02	127.86
Debtors	62.87	57.25
Cash and Bank	19.41	36.42
	280.30	221.53
Creditors falling due within one year	217.04	187.76
Net Current Assets	63.26	33.77
Creditors falling due in more than one year	48.41	15.19
Provisions for liabilities	4.96	4.67
Net Assets	156.74	138.81
Capital and reserves		
Called up share capital (5p shares)	9.70	8.98
Share premium	38.86	37.55
Revaluation reserve	0.13	0.13
Profit and loss account	108.05	92.15
Equity shareholders' funds	156.74	138.81

Analysis of Turnover, Profit before Tax and Net Assets

	Turnover		Profit before tax		Net assets	
	2006 £m	2005 £m	2006 £m	2005 £m	2006 £m	2005 £m
Vehicle sales and after-sales	1,275.28	1,044.63	31.12	26.63	153.23	136.12
Contract hire and finance	23.08	15.72	1.94	1.30	2.82	2.69
	1,298.36	1,060.35	33.06	27.93	156.05	138.81

Number of vehicles sold

	Volume		Specialist	
	2006	2005	2006	2005
New	51,260	40,210	4,963	3,380
Used	48,750	44,990	4,875	2,510

Share price

Company	2006	2005
Start of year	140p	152p
Mid year	180p	145p
End of year	223p	140p

Average for a group of similar companies	2006	2005
Start of year	89p	124p
Mid year	105p	102p
End of year	128p	89p

Analysis of stock

	2006 £m	2005 £m
Vehicles for resale	160.83	99.52
Vehicles on consignment	14.61	11.67
Repurchase commitments	16.91	11.29
Parts and sundry stock	5.67	5.38
	198.02	127.86

Debtors

	2006 £m	2005 £m
Trade debtors	53.94	48.94
Prepayments	8.93	8.31
	62.87	57.25

Creditors falling due within one year

	2006 £m	2005 £m
Trade creditors	152.43	113.48
Finance lease obligations	16.38	12.78
Bank overdraft	–	22.62
Consignment stock loans	14.62	11.65
Repurchase commitments	8.24	6.09
Tax and VAT	9.63	6.84
Accruals and deferred income	15.74	14.30
	217.04	187.76

Creditors falling due in more than one year

	2006 £m	2005 £m
Finance lease obligations	6.96	10.15
Bank loans	32.76	–
Repurchase commitments	8.69	5.04
	48.41	15.19

Provisions for liabilities

	2006 £m	2005 £m
Deferred tax	4.07	3.74
Warranty provision	0.89	0.93
	4.96	4.67

Industry averages for 2006

Growth in sales (based on 2005 sales)	14.72%
Return on capital employed	16.87%
Profit margin	2.80%
Gearing (Debt/Equity)%	48.2%
Interest cover	6.22 times
Asset utilisation	6.57 times
Profit per unit	£329
Current ratio	0.96
Quick assets ratio	0.42
Debtors collection period	11.2 days
Creditors payment period	37.2 days
Stock turnover period	41.5 days

Required

Prepare the briefing paper for circulation to the board members. Your paper should:

(a) **Discuss:**

    (i) **the information needs of the company's shareholders now that it is a listed company as compared to the period when it was a private company with the majority of shares held by Malcolm Sayles and members of his family; and** (4 marks)

    (ii) **the implications of shareholders' information needs for the company's managers.** (4 marks)

(b) Based on Malcolm Sayles' expression of the company's strategy, the published financial statements and the industry averages.

    Required

    Assess the company's performance in the two years since it achieved a listing. (34 marks)

    (As noted in the introductory information provided, this assessment should be based on a maximum of six measures with the significance of each measure being clearly explained.)

(c) **Discuss the accuracy of the director's assessment of the impact of establishing an employee share ownership trust on the financial results, and indicate how the measures you have used to assess the company's performance would have been affected if such a trust had been in place in the past.** (8 marks)

(d) **Propose an updated statement of strategic intent and an appropriate mission statement.** (8 marks)

(e) **Discuss the factors which will influence the type of responsibility centres which the company should use, and propose a suitable organisational structure.** (12 marks)

(f) **Identify and justify six appropriate critical success factors for internal use in managing the company's performance.** (30 marks)

(100 marks)

2 Suggested approach

The entire project, covering both subject areas, Interpretation of Financial Statements and Performance Management, is set in the context of the Motorsayles plc information which you are provided with.

Start by reading through the information provided quickly so that you get an idea of what you will be dealing with in this project. Note that you are the new Chief Executive of Motorsayles plc.

Requirements

Now have a look at the requirements to see what is required of you. As Chief Executive you are to prepare a briefing paper to the board members. Therefore there is no need for any formal layout such as in a report.

The examiner often comments that the word count in candidates' projects does not always relate to the mark allocation. He has made it quite clear that the mark allocation is an accurate guide to the number of words required for each part of the project. Therefore it is worthwhile at this stage just calculating the approximate number of words required for each part of the project.

(a) (i) $4/100 \times 5{,}000$ =   200 words

     (ii) $4/100 \times 5{,}000$ =   200 words

(b) $34/100 \times 5{,}000$ =   1,700 words

(c) $8/100 \times 5{,}000$ =   400 words

(d) $8/100 \times 5{,}000$ =   400 words

(e) $12/100 \times 5{,}000$ =   600 words

(f) $30/100 \times 5{,}000$ =   1,500 words

Read through the individual requirements so that you have an idea of what areas are being tested in this project. One of the key elements of this project is that Motorsayles has moved from being a private company to a public listed company two years ago and the effect this will have on the company and its strategy.

Now go back to the information you have been given about Motorsayles plc and read through it very carefully bearing in mind the requirements that you have just read through. There is no need to do any calculations at the moment just take note of the financial information that you have been provided with.

Part (a)

There are two aspects to consider here. Firstly as Malcolm Sayles was heavily involved in the business when it was a private company then as the major shareholder he had all the information about the company to hand. This will not be the case for the new shareholders now that the company is listed.

Secondly as the major shareholder Malcolm knew what the shareholders' needs and objectives were. Again this will not be the case now that the shares are held by a wide variety of external shareholders.

Part (b)

The requirement here is very straightforward – to assess the company's performance in the two years since achieving the listing. However the complication is that you can only carry out this assessment using a maximum of six measures.

The examiner frequently asks candidates to choose only a small number of measures with which to assess a company and has commented that the purpose of providing a large number of ratios and then asking candidates to select just 6 was to "highlight the need to be selective and to ensure that ratios chosen would assist in assessing the performance".

Therefore the choice of your six performance measures is very important. You are told to base your assessment on Malcolm Sayles' expression of the company's strategy, the published financial statements and the industry averages. So to make your choice of ratios start by looking at the list of industry average ratios and referring back to Malcolm's strategy – "To grow the business through the acquisition of high quality dealerships, and the development of a range of franchises across all market sectors". So the key here would appear to be growth. Therefore this will affect your choice of ratios.

The other factor to consider is the fact that the company is now a listed company which has to consider the needs of its shareholders. This should also affect your choice of ratios.

Note that you are given a variety of information about the company including non-financial information and share price information which you may find useful.

Once you have chosen your six ratios then you are required to justify that choice with the significance of each ratio being clearly explained. You must however make sure that your justification is related to Motorsayles plc in particular rather than just a general justification. The examiner often comments that many answers read like extracts from a study text, and there are many occasions when answers are too generalised and not specific to the particular scenario set, in this case Motorsayles plc. You are given quite a lot of information about how the company operates and in particular the importance of the volume bonus in the car sales industry therefore try to use this information in your answer.

You will need to calculate a number of performance measures therefore it is worthwhile doing this first and putting them all into an appendix at the end of the briefing paper and you can then refer to the calculations throughout your assessment.

Part (c)

The first part of this section is to discuss the accuracy of the director's assessment of the impact of establishing a share ownership scheme. Your answer should discuss the impact on the employees as well as the impact on the financial results. Then relate this to the various performance measures used in the previous part of the project.

Part (d)

Before starting this section of the project it is worthwhile reading all of the background information through once more. Then think about any conclusions you may have drawn from the assessment of the business performance in part (b). Clearly the company is doing well so no radical change in strategy is required but perhaps a rather more subtle change.

There is really no right or wrong answer to this part of the project provided that what you write is consistent with the scenario and with the assessment you performed in part (b).

Part (e)

Again two parts to this section of the project – firstly to discuss the factors that would influence the choice of responsibility centres and secondly to propose a suitable organisation structure.

This part of the project takes you into the Performance Management part of the syllabus and requires a different way of thinking. Therefore it is probably worthwhile at this stage re-reading all of the information in the scenario whilst thinking about organisation structure rather than interpretation of financial statements.

Part (f)

In this final part of the project you are to consider critical success factors for the company. You are to identify six critical success factors (CSFs) and most importantly to justify them. These CSFs must of course be related to the objectives of the company. So go back to your answer to part (d) and make sure that any CSFs you choose are related to the strategic intent and mission statement in that part of your answer.

These CSFs are for internal use in managing company performance so as well as explaining and justifying the factors you must also state how they would be measured for performance management purposes.

3 Suggested answer

Briefing paper to board of directors of Motorsayles plc

(a) (i)   When the company was a private company the majority of the shares were held by Malcolm Sayles and his family. Malcolm also worked within the business and would have had access to all information about the business and would be constantly informed about key issues. At any point in time therefore the major shareholder would have all necessary information about the company to hand. As such Malcolm would have placed little reliance on the annual financial statements as they would not have provided him with any further information than that which was already available to him.

In contrast, now that the shares are more widely distributed after the listing of the company, the majority of shareholders will have no information at all about the day to day activities and results of the company. Therefore in terms of information needs the shareholders will rely on the formal methods of communication from the company about results and position particularly in the form of the annual financial statements.

A further aspect of this change in status of the company is that as the major shareholder, together with his family, Malcolm would know what the needs and objectives of the shareholders were. Now the company is listed it will be harder to know what the needs and objectives of the more diverse shareholders now are.

(ii)   Now that the company is listed there will be a requirement for the management team to keep the shareholders informed of the company results and financial position. As a listed company there are formal requirements for production of financial information specifically for shareholders. However, this need to communicate to external shareholders brings with it dangers of also communicating sensitive information to competitors. Therefore the management team will have to carefully consider how and what information is communicated.

In terms of the specific information needs of a public company's shareholders they will tend to concentrate on key figures such as earnings per share and the related price/earnings ratio. This will bring with it the temptation for the management to also concentrate on these limited figures with the objective of ensuring that they show the company in as good a light as possible to the shareholders. This could lead to a greater focus by management on short to medium term measures of performance and objectives rather than longer term.

(b)   In this part of the briefing paper I will be assessing the performance of Motorsayles plc based upon Malcolm Sayles' expression of company strategy - 'To grow the business through the acquisition of high quality dealerships, and the development of a range of franchises across all market sectors', the published financial statements for the last two years and a variety of industry average figures.

In order to focus on the key issues I will be using only six performance measures in this assessment and will start with an explanation of why I have chosen each of these performance measures for this assessment.

Growth in sales

As we have seen Malcolm's stated strategy was growth, both organically and by acquisition. Therefore growth in sales in both volume terms (ie units) and revenue terms is vital to the continuation of this strategy. Sales growth in this competitive industry is also vital in order to meet the manufacturers' volume targets and therefore earn the ever important volume bonuses.

Return on capital employed

The managers of Motorsayles plc have a duty to utilise the funds invested by the shareholders in order to achieve a healthy overall return on those funds. The return on capital employed measures the profit of the company compared to the overall funds invested and therefore this measures how well the investment by the shareholders is doing. Although the overall strategy is one of growth this must also be profitable growth. This will be of even more importance now that Motorsayles plc is a listed company. Although the shareholders in a private company may be prepared to accept short term falls in return in order to achieve longer term benefits this will not necessarily be the case for a listed company where the shareholders will expect a gradual rise in their returns over time.

Profit margin

The overall return on capital employed is dependent upon two factors - the profit margin that is earned on sales and how efficiently the assets at the disposal of the managers are being used, known as asset utilisation (see below). Therefore in order to fully appreciate any change in overall return to the shareholders we must also consider the profit margin that is being earned. As was mentioned above growth alone will not provide a satisfactory return to shareholders. It must be profitable growth.

Asset utilisation

The overall return to shareholders is partly due to how profitably the company trades but also with how efficiently the managers of the business use the assets of the company. This is measured by comparing the sales turnover to the capital employed to determine how much revenue is being made for each £ of capital employed.

Earnings per share

As Motorsayles plc is now a listed company earnings per share will become an important indicator of performance for the company. As the shareholders have little or no knowledge of the day to day operations of the company they will tend to use earnings per share as an indicator of the strength of performance of the company.

Price/earnings ratio

Although earnings per share compared from one period to the next is a good indicator of company performance it does not allow a comparison between one company and another. However if earnings per share is compared to the share price of the company, the price/earnings ratio, then comparisons can be made to other companies in the same sector. For shareholders in a listed company such as Motorsayles plc this will be an important indicator of the worth of their investment in the company.

ASSESSMENT

The calculations of various performance measures and ratios on which this assessment is based are included in an appendix at the end of this project.

Sales growth

The overall growth in turnover between 2006 and 2005 has been 22.4%. Comparing this to the industry average growth in turnover of 14.72% it would appear that Motorsayles plc has certainly achieved its strategic objective of growth. This growth in sales can be analysed further:

Growth in sales of continuing operations	18.9%
Growth in sales of acquired operations	93.2%

This would also indicate that the strategic objective of growth by acquisition as well as organically has been met.

However growth cannot only be considered in terms of turnover but also, very importantly in this industry where competition for sales is great, by considering growth in terms of volume of cars sold:

Volume cars	New	27.5%
	Used	8.4%
Specialist cars	New	46.8%
	Used	94.2%

There are no industry breakdowns with which to compare these figures but on the face of it this would appear to be very healthy volume growth particularly in the specialist car market. The only concern might be the lower volume increase for used volume cars which will need investigation.

Certainly therefore the strategic objective of growth both organically and by acquisition appears to have been achieved. However growth on its own is not enough and we need to assess whether this has been profitable growth.

Return on capital employed

The current year return on capital employed of 17.5% is slightly better than the industry average of 16.87%. However the return on capital employed has in fact decreased from 19.4% in 2005. Although Motorsayles plc are still ahead of the industry average this decrease must be investigated as it may be an indication that the growth that has been achieved may be at a peak and although growth is still possible it may not be profitable growth. So we will now consider the two elements of return on capital employed in order to analyse it further – the profit margin and asset utilisation.

Profit margin

Profit margins in the car sales industry tend to be very low indeed which is why volume of business is so important. The profit margin for Motorsayles plc has decreased from 2.90% in 2005 to 2.83% in 2006 although it remains slightly above the industry average of 2.80%. Although such a small decrease may not appear significant this does actually represent over £0.85m of additional profit which would have been earned if the profit margin had been maintained. This is perhaps further evidence that growth is not necessarily still the best strategy for the company.

Asset utilisation

Asset utilisation based upon capital employed has decreased from 6.68 to 6.18 which is a further reason for the decrease in return on capital employed. However if asset utilisation is measured using net assets rather than capital employed then it would appear to have increased. However this is probably due to the fact that a large bank overdraft (current liability) last year has been consolidated into a bank loan (long term liability) in 2006. It is not clear whether the industry average figure of 6.57 is based upon capital employed or net assets but as the figure is closer to the capital employed basis for Motorsayles plc it is assumed that it was based upon capital employed.

Therefore although Motorsayles plc's profit margin is still slightly higher than the industry average the efficiency with which the assets have been used has declined both during the year and compared to the industry average. These two factors in combination have led to the decline in return on capital employed for Motorsayles plc.

Earnings per share

Earnings per share, both basic and diluted, has increased by about 9% over the 2005 figures. Although this increase is not as high as the increase in sales it is still commendable.

Price/earnings ratio

As well as a considerable increase in earnings per share the price/earnings ratio has shown a considerable increase of almost 46% to now stand at 17.91. The share price has increased by 59% between the start and the end of 2006 compared to an industry average increase of just 43%. The shares in Motorsayles plc themselves have a low nominal value of just 5 pence but the large share premium balance indicates that they were issued at a value of about 25 pence per share therefore this has been a huge increase.

The P/E ratio is perhaps one of the most important indicators for a listed company and this does appear to show that the market has confidence in the company's ability to use the funds invested in it to obtain strong returns. The market, and therefore the shareholders, appear to have confidence in the company and are endorsing the company's plans and placing confidence in the directors to carry out those plans and achieve the goals of the company.

Conclusion

In comparison to last year it would appear that the company is still performing well although there has been a slight slip in profit margin and asset utilisation. Equally in terms of comparison with industry average figures Motorsayles plc appears to be outperforming the industry averages in most areas.

If the strategic objective of growth is considered then there has been considerable growth both in terms of sales revenue and sales volume which again is higher than average in the industry. As profits are dependent upon volume this is a good sign. However there are some indications that this goal of growth at all costs may need to be rethought. We can see both a reduction in profit margin and return on capital employed which although both are still above the industry average might indicate that such an aggressive growth strategy may need to be revisited and reconsidered.

For a listed company the overall strategic aim will be to maximise the wealth of the shareholders. In terms of this aim the reduction in return on capital employed is slightly disappointing. However the key performance indicator of earnings per share has shown a considerable increase as has the share price over the year. This indicates that in general terms the market is happy with the performance and direction of the company and of the directors who run the company.

(c)   It is clear from the background information on the company that the staff are a very important factor in the success of the company to date. We are told that the staff are highly motivated and there is low labour turnover. In any business involving selling to the public this is a very great asset indeed and one that should be nurtured.

When Motorsayles plc was a private company being run by Malcolm Sayles it is likely that much of this motivation and loyalty was due to the owner himself. It is often the case in a family run private company that one individual member of the family or management can motivate and keep the loyalty of the workforce single-handedly.

However when such a company becomes a listed company then the owners become anonymous shareholders to whom the workforce have no similar ties of loyalty. Therefore a method of trying to unite the goals of the workforce and the needs of the shareholders should be considered.

An employee share ownership trust could be the answer to this problem. The aim of a listed company will be to maximise shareholder wealth which in practice means maximising the share price. If the workforce are provided with a method for acquiring shares in the company then effectively this goal congruence is being achieved. The aim of the company over time is to increase the share price and by including the employees as shareholders as well then by working towards this corporate goal they will also be enhancing their own personal shareholding value.

In terms of the effect on the financial statements of such a scheme the correct accounting treatment for these shares is to deduct them from shareholders' funds in the balance sheet. This will have the effect of reducing the amount of capital employed. This will have little effect on the performance indicators used to assess the company earlier in this briefing paper other than to reduce the capital employed figure in the return on capital employed calculation and the asset utilisation calculation. This will mean that return on capital employed will increase with a corresponding increase in asset utilisation.

Whereas the potential effect of the employee share ownership trust is to increase return on capital employed this should not be the sole reason for recommending consideration of the scheme. What is potentially far more important is harnessing the goals of the employees into the same goals as the company in terms of maximisation of share price. Therefore such a scheme would certainly appear to be good for the company and will be investigated further with the aim of being put in place in the near future.

(d)   When we consider the assessment of performance of the company since its listing two years ago it is clear that Motorsayles plc continues to be successful and therefore there is no need for any major rethink in terms of strategies and aims. However the assessment of performance does indicate that maybe the period of aggressive growth is over and we will not be able to maintain that rate of profitable growth into the future.

If we combine with this the evidence that the market outlook is that general market growth due to consumer confidence will not continue at the current level then we need to consider where we go in the future. Rather than continue with our aggressive growth strategy we need to consolidate our position and maintain our profit margins. In particular we need to ensure that we consolidate the benefits of our growth achieved to date.

We are in a service related industry and rely totally upon our customers in a market which is characterised by over-supply and where the competition between manufacturers, particularly in the volume sector, will only intensify.

Therefore it is suggested that our strategic intentions should be as follows:

- to build upon customer loyalty and maximise repeat customers
- to maintain market share
- to maintain profit margins by maximising the volume bonuses available
- to maximise the profits achieved through value added products and services

We must become totally customer focused and aim to maximise our shareholders wealth by maximising customer satisfaction.

Based upon these strategic objectives the following Mission Statement has been drafted in order to start our discussions on this area.

Our customers are our first and foremost consideration. Customer satisfaction and repeat business is our reason for being in business. We aim to meet and exceed our customers' expectations in all areas of our service.

We will achieve this by:

- maintaining and improving our retail outlet services

- capitalising on our previous growth and thereby being able to offer customers a wide variety of vehicles in all price ranges

- listening to our customers

- communicating with our customers

- keeping our promises to our customers

- at every opportunity adding value for our customers

- driving down costs and maintaining quality and excellent value for money

- meeting and exceeding our customers' expectations

(e) The scenario indicates that little attention has in the past been paid to the company's structure and that the board must consider this if the company is to meet the objectives of shareholders. Before considering a possible organisational structure for Motorsayles plc we will firstly consider the typical factors which will influence the type of responsibility centres that are chosen for the company.

Objectives

The structure of the company must be capable of meeting the objectives of the shareholders which in turn are the strategic objectives of the business. It has already been considered that the company's objectives will be changing from growth at all costs to a period of consolidation of the growth that has taken place, maintenance of profitability and a customer centred approach. Therefore the structure that is chosen must be one that is capable of meeting these objectives. The responsibility centres that are chosen must be capable of providing a performance which moves towards achieving these objectives.

Comprehensive coverage

In line with what has been said about objectives above it is important that if a responsibility centre is chosen, and a manager is given charge of that responsibility centre then that manager must be responsible for all aspects of performance which contribute towards achieving the objectives of the company. In this way it will be possible to ensure that no important objectives are being disregarded.

Controllability

The factors of a business which are given to a manager who runs a responsibility centre must be controllable by that manager. All relevant factors must be capable of being influenced by the manager concerned. If there is a variable that can be controlled by one manager then that variable should be the responsibility of that manager and not included within another manager's responsibility centre.

Consistency

Not only must all relevant factors be included in the manager's responsibility but there must also be consistency between the objectives the company is seeking to achieve and the factors that the manager must control. This does not mean that there will not be conflicts between objectives and factors that a manager is responsible for as it is the manager's role to manage such conflicts. For example the aim of keeping costs down may be seen to conflict with the objective of customer satisfaction and added value but it is the manager's job to manage this conflict.

Timescale

The aim of the structure of the company is to put the company in a position to meet the objectives of the shareholders. It has already been noted that shareholders in a listed company are likely to have a shorter timescale for success than the owners of a private company may have had. Therefore the chosen structure must be able to allow managers to achieve the objectives of the company within an appropriate timescale.

Proposed structure

As one of our major objectives is to achieve high levels of customer satisfaction and repeat sales it would appear to make sense that each retail outlet throughout England and Wales operates on an individual basis but as part of a much larger nationwide organisation. Each of the retail outlets should be able to get close to their local customers and to build customer loyalty but with the added aspect of being part of a much larger company which can provide additional resources to meet customers' needs.

Therefore it is suggested that each retail outlet is run as a profit centre with a general manager responsible for achieving profit and customer satisfaction targets. Within each retail outlet there should be individual managers responsible for profit centres for sales of new vehicles, sales of used vehicles and after sales services. Other support services within the outlet such as administration and human resources should be run on a cost centre basis.

Above the retail outlet level in the organisational structure there should be three divisions which are investment centres. These would be volume vehicles, specialist vehicles and finance. Finance would include contract hire as well as vehicle finance. Each divisional manager will be responsible for achieving profit targets from the retail outlets and ensuring that the retail outlets are given the appropriate levels of investment in order to achieve the objectives of customer satisfaction. As these divisions are investment centres then the managers will also be responsible for the amount of capital investment made.

(f) Finally we need to consider how to measure performance internally within the company in line with the proposed organisational structure given above. Any assessment of performance must of course be directly related to our strategic aims of:

- building upon customer loyalty and maximise repeat customers
- maintaining market share
- maintaining profit margins by maximising the volume bonuses available
- maximising the profits achieved through value added products and services

In this initial discussion we will consider just six critical success factors for internal measurement of performance looking at how each will be measured and the justification for their use.

Volume bonuses achieved

This would be measured as the value of volume bonuses earned as a percentage of the total bonus available from the manufacturer.

It has been noted that only a very small unit profit is made on the sale of an individual new car. Therefore our achievement of our profit targets is dependent upon maximising the amounts earned from the manufacturer's volume bonuses available. The manufacturers set the volume bonus targets, although there is usually some scope for negotiation, and we must sell enough new cars to meet these targets and earn the bonuses.

As an add-on to this the more cars we sell the more we can make through more profitable areas such as the sale of accessories, servicing and the provision of finance.

Customer retention

This would be measured as the percentage of customers who purchased their previous vehicle from any Motorsayles plc retail outlet.

One of our strategic aims is to build upon customer loyalty and maximise repeat customers. Our ability to retain our customers therefore is a key critical success factor. As we are a nationwide company, and the proposed organisational structure (see above) stresses that aspect, we do not have to restrict ourselves to retaining customers within the same retail outlet. One of our major strengths is that we have a wide range of manufacturer dealerships therefore if a customer wishes to change their make of car we can still provide this albeit from a different retail outlet. Therefore the key is to ensure that every customer returns to us in one way or another for their next vehicle purchase. Given our network of retail outlets and wide range of manufacturers the only reason why a customer should feel the need to buy from one of our competitors would be if we have failed to give that customer satisfaction with our services.

Sales of accessories

This would be measured as the revenue from the sale of accessories as a percentage of total sales revenue.

Parts and accessories sales provide an opportunity for additional profit to potentially be earned on the sale of every vehicle. Due to the low profit per unit on vehicle sales it can often be the case that more profit is generated from the sale of parts and accessories than is generated by the sale of the vehicle itself. By selling parts and accessories such as in-car entertainment systems or satellite navigation systems our profitability can be improved. This will require the minimum of investment as it is unlikely that such accessories will need to be kept in stock as the lead time to acquire the vehicle should allow the time to acquire the accessories. It will be important therefore that the sales force are trained and motivated to maximise the sales of such accessories.

Speed of throughput

This would be measured in two ways:

- stock turnover ratio for both vehicles and parts
- index of time taken for service and repairs based upon manufacturer's standard time

Speed of throughput will be a key factor in achieving our required levels of customer satisfaction. This will apply to both sales and servicing. Therefore we need to assess the speed with which we provide a new vehicle to a customer and the speed with which we can provide replacement parts. This can be done by the measurement of stock turnover for both vehicles and parts.

If a customer has their car serviced or repaired clearly the quicker we can return the vehicle to the customer the more satisfied the customer will be. If we can minimise the disruption to customers by returning vehicles as quickly as possible then this will help us to achieve our customer satisfaction targets and retain our customers for the future.

Non-warranty services

This would be measured as the value of services carried out outside the requirements of the manufacturer's warranty terms as a percentage of our total servicing revenue.

Non-warranty servicing is where a customer chooses for Motorsayles plc to carry out their vehicle servicing even though they are not required to under the terms of the manufacturer's warranty. Such commitment to Motorsayles plc indicates levels of customer satisfaction as there is no requirement for the customer to come to us for this servicing. Therefore this measure should again show how we are achieving our goal of customer satisfaction.

New customers

This would be measured as the number of customers who did not buy their previous vehicle from Motorsayles plc. This would be measured as an absolute figure rather than a percentage so that it could be easily compared to target numbers on a periodic basis.

Although our focus is largely on the satisfaction and retention of existing customers rather than our previous strategy of unrestrained growth it is still important that we grow our customer base. Once we have attracted a new customer then of course we must also retain that customer for future business.

Appendix – Calculation of performance measures

	2006	*2005*
Growth in overall sales	1,298.36	1,060.35
	22.4%	
Return on capital employed		
Operating profit	36.80	30.74
Capital employed	156.74 + 48.41 + 4.96	138.81 + 15.19 + 4.67
	= 210.11	= 158.67
	17.5%	19.4%
Profit margin	36.80/1,298.36	30.74/1,060.35
	2.83%	2.90%
Asset utilisation	1,298.36/210.11	1,060.35/158.67
(based upon capital employed)	6.18	6.68
(based upon net assets)	1,298.36/156.74	1,060.35/138.81
	8.28	7.63
Price/earnings ratio	223/12.45	140/11.40
	17.91	12.28
Increase	45.8%	

4 Examiner's comments

Examiner's comments. At this sitting, the project was based on a case study on the retail motor industry. Because this allowed for a high level of integration between the two subject areas, there was only one question, which was broken down into six sub-parts. The sub-parts did not carry equal marks.

The requirements of the question may be summarised as follows:

(a) consider the information needs of shareholders, and the implications of these needs for managers

(b) assess the company's recent performance

(c) examine the impact of an employee share ownership trust on the financial results

(d) propose an appropriate strategy and mission statement

(e) propose an appropriate organisational structure

(f) identify and justify appropriate critical success factors (CSFs)

Overall performance was good with a number of candidates presenting very good answers.

In the main, answers that scored high marks were characterised by a logical thought process, comments that were rigorously linked to the specific requirements of the question, and ideas that were developed to provide analysis.

In contrast, candidates who did not obtain good marks, tended to restrict their comments to description, and did not answer the questions fully. The predominant tendencies in this regard were to ignore the requirement for the significance of each measure to be clearly explained, and failing to provide a clear justification for the CSFs identified and/or an indication of how the CSFs would actually be measured. This is considered further in the comments below on Parts (b) and (f) of the question.

Other reasons for candidates failing to obtain marks were:

- **Not answering questions in full**

  The most obvious example of this was the lack of justification for ratios selected as noted above. However, in Part (d), some candidates only gave either a statement of strategic intent or a mission statement, but not both as required by the question. Indeed, a few candidates took this omission further, and did not answer all the questions, omitting Part (d) entirely.

- **Not answering the question set**

  Some candidates discussed other (in some cases, unrelated) issues. This is considered further in the detailed question comments below.

There is continuing evidence that some candidates are not using the mark allocation as a guide to how much discussion is required. For example, Part (b) was worth 34 marks. This would represent about 1,700 words, 34% of the permitted 5,000. Many candidates wrote less than 1,000 words in this section, with some writing less than 300. It should, of course, be noted that while brevity is a useful skill in business, it is highly improbable that any candidate will obtain sufficient marks to pass if their answer is as far away from the benchmark as those referred to above. Equally, the material included in the answer must address the question, if any marks are to be gained.

Some submissions were characterised by poor proof-reading, with numerous typographical errors. This is unprofessional, and would not be acceptable in a commercial situation. In this instance, this did not lead to a lower mark, because no marks had been allocated to the overall quality of the material. However, candidates at future sittings should be aware that it is possible that marks will be allocated for the quality of the material submitted.

A new, and irritating, tendency was for a few candidates to use language that is more appropriate for use on a mobile phone SMS. For example, when citing sources a number of candidates referred to the study text by use of the term 'TxT'. This is not acceptable and is strongly discouraged.

Part (a)

There were some excellent answers to this part of the question, with some candidates obtaining full marks. However, some candidates made the mistake of not answering the question that was actually set, and instead provided material that although factually correct, was irrelevant to the question, and could not attract marks. There were three main examples of this.

The first is describing the workings of the stock market, and the rules for stock market listing. While it was acceptable to note that as a listed company, the directors are now required to comply with the rules of the stock market, this reference was sufficient. There was no need to provide an exhaustive list of the rules. Where such a list was provided, candidates had obviously simply copied this from a source document. In a project such as this, simply copying material will not attract marks. The project seeks to provide an opportunity for candidates to develop their analytical skills and demonstrate an awareness of how the material might be used by managers of the company on which the project is based.

The second was that in some cases, answers included a detailed discussion of corporate governance. In many cases this would have been good material – if required by the question. Because it was not relevant, no marks could be awarded.

Finally, some candidates described the legal differences between private companies and public companies. Once again this was not required by the question, and attracted no marks.

Part (b)

There were a number of extremely good answers to this part of the question, and again some answers attracted maximum marks. Such answers clearly indicated why the chosen measure was relevant for *this* company. In the main this was done by referring to the goals and strategy of the company.

However, as noted above, a number of candidates did not provide any justification for the measures chosen. This is particularly disappointing, because the need to explain why a measure was chosen has been referred to in reports for previous sittings, has been the topic of an article in the March 2004 issue of *finance matters* and was explicitly included in the requirement of the question.

Candidates should note that the wording of questions is the subject of much thought, discussion and debate. The wording that appears on the question paper should therefore be considered carefully when developing answers.

Candidates should also note that justification is not simply providing a general comment about the significance of a measure, such as 'gearing provides a measure of financial risk'. Although this is correct, it does not explain why the measure was chosen in this instance. A statement such as 'The company is seeking to grow, and it will therefore require additional funding. Care must be taken to ensure that unnecessary risk is not introduced as a result of the method of funding' is more appropriate and will attract marks because it links the analysis to the company's strategy and clearly shows why the measure is significant for *this* company.

In future, projects will require even more in-depth consideration of which measures should be used to assess performance, and will provide less (or perhaps very little) financial data in an effort to motivate candidates to discuss, rather than describe ratios.

Part (c)

Those candidates who read the question carefully and based their answers on the requirement scored good marks. This was achieved by considering how the accounting treatment of an ESOT would affect the measures discussed in Part (b). In many ways this was a very straightforward question.

Unfortunately, some candidates seem only to have read certain words in the question, and therefore produced material that was much more technical than was required. A number of candidates provided a detailed discussion of various UITF abstracts and traced the development of the accounting treatment of ESOTs. While this provided very interesting reading, it did not gain any marks, because it was not what was required by the question.

Once again the advice is – read the question carefully – and then answer *that* question.

Part (d)

In some respects, this question provided a blank canvas for candidates. It is pleasing to note that a good number of candidates accepted the challenge, and showed a clear link between the existing strategy, the company's current position, and the stated aspirations. This was done by careful selection of material from the case, and often led to full marks.

In contrast, those answers that were underdeveloped simply provided a statement of strategic intent and a mission statement which was not supported by any analysis. This approach did not maximise the number of marks gained.

Part (e)

Once again, the key to obtaining marks in this part of the question was to ensure that comments followed logically from the preceding analysis. Those candidates who did this, and clearly illustrated how responsibility centres could be used by Motorsayles and justified the types of responsibility centres to be used in the context of the company's strategy and goals, gained good marks.

Those candidates who simply described different types of responsibility centre, often by reproducing material from a textbook, did not gain marks.

With regard to the proposed organisational structure, where the structure was discussed and justified in terms of strategy and goals, candidates gained high marks. Those candidates who simply described a structure, or provided an organisational chart without any discussion or justification, predictably did not score high marks.

Part (f)

The requirement of this part of the question was to use the preceding analysis to identify the key factors that the company must control if it is to be successful. The greater the extent to which the CSFs chosen were justified, the more marks were obtained. Once again, a number of candidates rose to the challenge and obtained full marks.

Those candidates who did not score high marks tended to provide a list of possible CFSs that could have been taken from a textbook. The key point about CSFs is that they measure important outcomes for a specific company. As such, they must be closely aligned with the company's strategy.

It is perhaps this need to align strategy and CSFs which contributed to some candidates going down one of two incorrect paths.

The first of these was to discuss strategic objectives, rather than CSFs. CSFs are operational outcomes that can be tracked by staff at an operational level. The link to strategy is that achieving the identified operational outcomes will lead to achieving strategic goals.

A second mistake was to create a balanced scorecard, and to discuss the merits of the balanced scorecard. While a balanced scorecard will report the same outcomes that would be measured by CSFs, the question did not require a balanced scorecard to be developed. It is a matter of concern that some candidates chose to take this approach, as it indicates, at best, a lack of thought, and at worst, a replication of answers to previous projects. Neither of these approaches is likely to lead to success.

11

ACCA Live Project – Spring 2006: Module B

1 Spring 2006 Project: Module B

Diploma in Financial Management

PROJECT DB2, INCORPORATING SUBJECT AREAS
- FINANCIAL STRATEGY
- RISK MANAGEMENT

All questions are compulsory and MUST be answered

The project MUST be written in English.

The maximum word count (including appendices and tables but excluding references and bibliography) is 5,000.

The project MUST be TYPED in black ink, one-sided, double-spaced, using a minimum 12-point font size and a 1-inch margin at each side. HANDWRITTEN SUBMISSIONS WILL NOT BE ACCEPTED. The project must be submitted by post, electronic submissions are not acceptable.

The project should be submitted on A4 paper with your student number, project name, date and page number at the top of each page.

A project submission form MUST be completed for each project submitted and attached to the front of the project.

The Association of Chartered Certified Accountants

BPP)))
LEARNING MEDIA

Incorporating subject areas – Financial Strategy and Risk Management

This ONE question is compulsory and MUST be attempted

Centaur Communications plc

Centaur Communications plc is a large media business that is listed on the London Stock Exchange. The company runs its operations through two, wholly-owned subsidiaries – Centaur Magazines Ltd and Centaur Radio Ltd. To date, the two subsidiaries have been allowed considerable autonomy, with each being responsible for its own investment and financing decisions. Details of each subsidiary are set out below.

Centaur Magazines Ltd

Centaur Magazines Ltd is the larger of the two subsidiaries. The company owns several famous UK magazine titles, with each occupying a leading position in the particular market served. In recent years, the company has expanded into Europe and now owns leading magazine titles in Spain, Portugal and France. It believes that magazine sales in mainland Europe are likely to grow rapidly in the near future as the Euroland economies come out of recession. The company is committed to having an increasing presence in mainland Europe and, to this end, the following titles are about to be launched:

1.   *Tele mois* – a monthly TV listings magazine aimed at the French market;
2.   *Nouveau Homme* – a monthly men's magazine also aimed at the French market;
3.   *Hasta La Vista, Baby* – a weekly movie magazine aimed at the Spanish market.

The launch of these magazines is in line with the declared strategy of making the company the largest magazine publisher in Europe.

The most recent financial statements of Centaur Magazines Ltd are as follows:

Abridged profit and loss account for the year ended 31 January 2006

	£'000
Sales revenue	180,000
Operating profit	37,750
Interest payable	4,000
Net profit before tax	33,750
Corporation tax (20%)	6,750
Net profit after tax	27,000
Dividends proposed and paid	16,200
Retained profit for the year	10,800

Abridged balance sheet as at 31 January 2006

	£'000	£'000
Fixed assets		
Property, plant and equipment		27,400
Goodwill		45,000
Publishing rights and titles		49,600
		122,000
Current assets		
Stocks	2,500	
Trade debtors	58,500	
Other debtors	980	
Cash	20	
	62,000	
Creditors: Amounts due within one year		
Trade creditors	31,800	
Other creditors	6,200	
Bank overdraft	2,000	
	40,000	
		22,000
		144,000
Creditors: Amounts due beyond one year		
Loan capital		54,000
		90,000
Capital and reserves		
Ordinary shares of £1 each		20,000
Retained profit		70,000
		90,000

The subsidiary is committed to strong growth and sales are set to rise rapidly. A sales forecast for the next five years has been produced by the marketing director of Centaur Magazines Ltd, which is as follows:

Sales forecast for the year ended 31 January

Year	£'000
2007	206,000
2008	252,000
2009	312,000
2010	356,000
2011	382,000

The board of directors of Centaur Magazines Ltd is currently reviewing the amount of finance required to sustain its growth strategy. When considering this matter, the following key assumptions were made by the board members:

1. The parent company, Centaur Communications plc, will continue to receive the same percentage of profits in the form of dividends as it currently receives.

2. The current net profit margin (after tax) will be maintained for the foreseeable future.

3. The current debt/equity ratio will be maintained in order to maintain the same level of financial risk.

4. The current sales to capital employed ratio will also be maintained to ensure sufficient resources are available to sustain the level of sales.

5. Finance will be made available by the parent company to cover any shortfall in funds that cannot be covered by additional loan capital.

A plan covering the next five years, which sets out the financing requirements, is to be presented to the board of directors of the parent company, Centaur Communications plc, with a view to obtaining any additional finance that may be required.

Centaur Radio Ltd

Centaur Radio Ltd operates a number of commercial radio stations, all of which were acquired ten years ago when the parent company was seeking to diversify its interests. The main radio stations operated are:

– Yoof-2day – consisting of two analogue stations and ten digital stations with more than two million listeners throughout the UK. It is targeted at 15–24 year olds and plays indie, dance and Hip Hop music.

– Wrinkly Rock – consisting of six analogue and five digital stations with more than four million listeners in South East of England, South West England, Wales and Scotland. It is targeted at 35–54 year olds and plays hits from rock and pop legends of the 1960s, 1970s and 1980s.

– Radio Ga-Ga – consisting of four analogue and eight digital stations with more than one million listeners in Southern England and Wales. It is targeted at those in the 50+ age range and plays easy-listening music.

The most recent financial statements of Centaur Radio Ltd are as follows:

Abridged profit and loss account for the year ended 31 January 2006

	£'000
Sales revenue	75,000
Operating profit	7,500
Interest payable	–
Net profit before tax	7,500
Corporation tax	–
Net profit after tax	7,500
Dividends proposed and paid	4,500
Retained profits for the year	3,000

Abridged balance sheet as at 31 January 2006

	£'000	£'000
Fixed assets		
Property, plant and equipment		8,500
Goodwill		65,000
		73,500
Current assets		
Debtors	12,500	
Cash	500	
	13,000	
Creditors: Amounts due within one year		
Trade creditors	18,900	
Other creditors	3,600	
	22,500	(9,500)
		64,000
Capital and reserves		
£1 Ordinary shares		20,000
Retained profit		44,000
		64,000

Although the commercial radio stations are now making profits, the board of directors of the parent company, Centaur Communications plc, has been dissatisfied with their performance. None of the radio stations enjoy a leading position in the particular markets served and it seems that a considerable investment of time and resources would be required to improve their market position.

The board of directors of Centaur Radio Ltd has been asked by the parent company to come up with a five-year plan that will establish each radio station as a leading player in the market served. In response, the marketing director of Centaur Radio Ltd believes that, if sufficient resources were made available, the following sales could be achieved:

Sales forecast for the year ended 31 January

Year	£'000
2007	80,000
2008	87,000
2009	98,000
2010	107,000
2011	116,000

To achieve these sales, the following additional investment would be required:

Additional investment requirements

	Additional fixed assets	Additional working capital
Year ended 31 January	£'000	£'000
2007	12,700	5,300
2008	12,800	5,500
2009	13,700	5,200
2010	5,200	5,100
2011	2,500	4,420

The additional investments in fixed assets will be written off over a ten-year period using the straight-line method of depreciation. Depreciation charges are currently £830,000 a year, and have totalled the same amount for each of the past ten years. The additional depreciation resulting from the additional investments could be offset by savings elsewhere and so net profit margins are not likely to be affected.

When drawing up the plans for presentation to the board of the parent company, the directors of Centaur Radio Ltd will use a slightly different method of establishing its future annual cash flows and financing needs than that used by Centaur Magazines Ltd. It will also use the following key assumptions:

1.   The parent company, Centaur Communications plc, will continue to receive the same percentage of profits in the form of dividends as it currently receives.

2.   The current operating profit margin will be maintained for the foreseeable future.

3.   As a result of heavy tax losses in earlier years, no taxation will be paid by the company during the five-year period.

Although the board of directors of Centaur Communications plc will consider the plans to be presented by the board of Centaur Radio Ltd, it is by no means certain that they will be accepted. Committing funds to both the future growth of magazine sales and to the future growth of the commercial radio stations will place a considerable strain on resources. Furthermore, the commitment to the radio subsidiary is wavering. Some members of the board of Centaur Communications plc argue that the magazine business has far better long-term prospects and that the radio stations are really a distraction from its core operations.

Astrid Ltd

The board of Centaur Communications plc has recently been approached by Astrid Ltd, a venture capital business. During lengthy discussions, the venture capitalist offered to pay 12 times the current operating profits to acquire Centaur Radio Ltd. This unexpected offer brought the discussion concerning the future of the radio business to a head. However, a final decision on the future of the subsidiary was deferred until the board had the opportunity to consider the five-year plan being drawn up by the directors of Centaur Radio Ltd.

The offer made by Astrid Ltd was based on its own background research and on information provided by the directors of Centaur Communications plc during their discussions. The venture capitalist believes that it would be possible to work the existing assets of Centaur Radio Ltd harder and, as a result, much more modest levels of investment would be needed than those planned by the directors of the company. Nevertheless, it was believed that sales growth could still be achieved with the introduction of a more able and committed management team. The following sales forecast was produced by Astrid Ltd for the radio subsidiary.

Sales forecast for the year ended 31 January

Year	£'000
2007	78,000
2008	82,000
2009	88,000
2010	95,000
2011	104,000

To achieve these sales, Astrid Ltd believes that the following additional investment would be required:

Additional investment requirements

Year ended 31 January	Additional fixed assets £'000	Additional working capital £'000
2007	3,800	1,000
2008	4,300	800
2009	5,600	200
2010	3,400	400
2011	3,400	100

The additional investments in fixed assets will be written off over a ten-year period using the straight-line method of depreciation. Astrid Ltd also believes that it would be possible to maintain the existing operating profit margin as additional depreciation charges would be offset by cost savings elsewhere.

The offer by Astrid Ltd was made subject to appropriate due diligence investigations. Assuming these are satisfactory, the venture capitalist proposes to invest £48·6 million in order to acquire 90% of the ordinary share capital. A team of managers, appointed from outside Centaur Radio Ltd, will be expected to invest £5·4 million to acquire the remaining 10% of the ordinary shares. The remaining funds are expected to be raised by Centaur Radio Ltd using a bank loan with an annual rate of interest of 6%. However, the financing arrangement just described may be altered if necessary. If the buyout proposal is accepted, Centaur Radio Ltd will be kept as a private limited company for five years, after which time it will be turned into a public company and floated, either on the Alternative Investment Market (AIM) or on the main market of the London Stock Exchange. Similar radio companies command a price/earnings ratio of around 14 times and it is believed that Centaur Radio Ltd would eventually be floated at this figure. When the company is floated, Astrid Ltd will realise the investment by selling its shares.

During the period leading up to the flotation, no dividends will be paid and all available cash generated by the company will be used to repay the outstanding loan. Any loan amounts still outstanding at flotation will be paid off by Astrid Ltd and the management team from the proceeds of the sale of their shares. Astrid Ltd has a cost of capital of 21% and uses the internal rate of return (IRR) method to assess investment opportunities.

The accumulated tax losses will be available for Astrid Ltd and will be sufficient to ensure there will be no tax liability on the projected profits.

Required

(a)   Based on the assumptions mentioned by the directors of each company, calculate the annual financing requirements for each of the next five years, for:

    (i)   Centaur Magazines Ltd; and

    (ii)   Centaur Radio Ltd.   (24 marks)

(b)   Comment on the assumptions of the respective directors and upon the results of the calculations in (a) above and state, with reasons, which of the approaches used to establish the financing requirements for each company you would recommend.   (10 marks)

(c)   Identify and discuss the issues that the board of directors of Centaur Communications plc should consider before making a final decision concerning the divestment of Centaur Radio Ltd.   (10 marks)

(d)   Prepare a report for Astrid Ltd, which:

    (i)   evaluates the viability of the proposed investment in Centaur Radio Ltd using IRR; and

    (ii)   demonstrates how the IRR of the proposed investment might be improved without changing the underlying assumptions (made by Astrid Ltd) regarding sales, operating profits, the acquisition or disposal price of the company.   (28 marks)

(e)   Assuming the bid for Centaur Radio Ltd is accepted, identify and discuss:

    (i)   the information that Astrid Ltd may gather when carrying out a due diligence investigation on Centaur Radio Ltd; and

    (ii)   the factors that may be taken into account when deciding between AIM and the main market of the London Stock Exchange for the eventual flotation of Centaur Radio Ltd.   (28 marks)

Notes

In answering the case study questions:

1.   All key workings must be shown and key assumptions must be clearly stated.
2.   Calculations should be to the nearest £'000.
3.   Ignore inflation.

(100 marks)

2 Suggested approach

Start by reading all of the information in the scenario through quite quickly. There is no need to take note of any of the numbers at this stage – the point of this read through is to familiarise yourself with the scenario and the information provided.

Then read quickly through the requirements so that you have an idea of what is being asked of you for this project. Bearing this in mind read through the scenario again but this time more carefully and try to relate the information in the scenario to each of the requirements of the project.

Part (a)

Take care with the calculations here. Even though you are being asked to calculate the same figures for each company, ie the funding requirements each year, the calculation is different for each subsidiary as the information you are given is different.

For Centaur Magazines Ltd you are given the sales for each year and from this you can work out the net profit after tax. By then calculating the dividend payment to the holding company you can find the retained profit for the year. The total equity will be the brought forward equity figure each year plus the retained profits for that year and from this figure the maximum amount of loan capital can be calculated. Finally the total capital employed required can be found as 80% of the sales figure and the shortfall each year between equity plus loans and the capital employed can be calculated.

For Centaur Radio Ltd again you are given the sales figure from which you can calculate operating profit. As you need to work out the operating cash flows from the operations the next step is to add back the depreciation charge for the year. This is made up of the existing depreciation plus depreciation on the new fixed assets. Remember when calculating the depreciation charge that the additional depreciation charge is based upon the cumulative investment in new fixed assets. Finally deduct the additional working capital required and this will leave you with the operating cash flow for the year. This must be compared with the cash required for the new fixed assets to find any surplus or deficit.

Part (b)

You are now effectively asked to compare and contrast the two methods of calculating the funding requirements from part (a). You are to comment on the assumptions made by the two sets of directors and upon the results of the calculations. You are then required to state which of the two methods you would recommend and give your reasons.

Aim for about 500 words for this section (10/100 × 5,000).

Part (c)

In this part we move onto the prospective sale of the investment in Centaur Radio Ltd. You are required to identify and discuss the issues which the board of Centaur Communications plc should consider concerning the potential sale of Centaur Radio Ltd. At this stage it would be worthwhile reading through the material again so that you fully understand all the issues relating to Centaur Radio Ltd.

Aim for about 500 words for this section (10/100 × 5,000).

Part (d)

Note first of all for this part that you are to prepare a report for Astrid Ltd. Therefore this must be in report format.

Read through all of the information provided about the Astrid Ltd offer bearing in mind that the requirements of the report are to do with the internal rate of return. Concentrate initially on part (i) of this section, the evaluation of the proposed investment in Centaur Radio Ltd using IRR. Once this has been done then you can consider what to do for part (ii) of this section.

For part (i) think carefully about the cash flows for Astrid which will be part of the internal rate of return calculation. These are the initial purchase price of the company and the proceeds of the eventual flotation. However in order to calculate the proceeds from the eventual sale it is necessary to determine how much of the loan which Centaur Radio Ltd will be taking out will still be outstanding at the time of the flotation. This is turn is dependent upon the cash flows produced by Centaur Radio Ltd each year until the flotation.

You can use the same format for calculating the cash flows from Centaur Radio Ltd that you used in part (a) however there is an additional cash flow which is the loan interest which must be calculated on the amount of the loan outstanding at the start of each year. Until you have included this figure in your cash flow calculation you will not know how much is available to repay the loan and therefore how much will be outstanding at the start of the following year.

For part (ii) you will need to think quite carefully to determine what the examiner is after here. You are told that you are to demonstrate how the IRR can be improved (made to be a higher figure) without changing either sales, operating profit, the acquisition price or the disposal price. If you go back to your calculations from part (i) you will see that the only other figure (assuming that the fixed asset and working capital investment remain the same) which can change is the amount of loan finance. So what the examiner wants you to do is demonstrate that if the gearing of the company is increased then this will benefit the shareholders. You will now have to re-work your figures with an increased loan amount of say £50 million.

Part (e)

The first part of this section is about the due diligence process and the second part is about the advantages and disadvantages of a listing on the main market of the Stock Exchange compared to a listing on the Alternative Investment Market.

Both requirements are very straightforward but it is likely that you may have to do a little bit of research before you can find enough to write about as the mark allocation indicates about 1,400 words for the whole of this section.

3 Suggested answer

(a)   (i)   **Financing requirements for Centaur Magazines Ltd**

			Year ended 31 January		
	2007	2008	2009	2010	2011
	£'000	£'000	£'000	£'000	£'000
Sales	206,000	252,000	312,000	356,000	382,000
Net profit after tax 15% × sales	30,900	37,800	46,800	53,400	57,300
Dividends (60% × net profit after tax)	18,540	22,680	28,080	32,040	34,380
Retained profit	12,360	15,120	18,720	21,360	22,920
Equity (opening bal + retained profit)	102,360	117,480	136,200	157,560	180,480
Maximum loans (equity × 60%)	61,416	70,488	81,720	94,536	108,288
	163,776	187,968	217,920	252,096	288,768
Capital employed (80% × sales)	164,800	201,600	249,600	284,800	305,600
Funding required	1,024	13,632	31,680	32,704	16,832

(ii)   **Financing requirements for Centaur Radio Ltd**

			Year ended 31 January		
	2007	2008	2009	2010	2011
	£'000	£'000	£'000	£'000	£'000
Sales	80,000	87,000	98,000	107,000	116,000
Operating profit (10% × sales)	8,000	8,700	9,800	10,700	11,600
Add: depreciation (W)	2,100	3,380	4,750	5,270	5,520
	10,100	12,080	14,550	15,970	17,120
Working capital	(5,300)	(5,500)	(5,200)	(5,100)	(4,420)
Operating cash flows	4,800	6,580	9,350	10,870	12,700
Capital expenditure	(12,700)	(12,800)	(13,700)	(5,200)	(2,500)
Cash surplus/(deficit)	(7,900)	(6,220)	(4,350)	5,670	10,200
Dividend (60% × p'fit)	(4,800)	(5,220)	(5,880)	(6,420)	(6,960)
Funding required	(12,700)	(11,440)	(10,230)	(750)	-

Working – depreciation

	Year ended 31 January				
	2007	*2008*	*2009*	*2010*	*2011*
	£'000	£'000	£'000	£'000	£'000
Cumulative investment in fixed assets	12,700	25,500	39,200	44,400	46,900
Existing depreciation charge	830	830	830	830	830
Additional depreciation	1,270	2,550	3,920	4,440	4,690
Total depreciation	2,100	3,380	4,750	5,270	5,520

(b) Regarding the assumptions made by the directors of Centaur Magazines Ltd the first and most obvious one is that they expect turnover to more than double between 2006 and 2011. Although they are committed to strong growth and believe that sales are set to rise rapidly this does seem to be a very optimistic position.

As the relationship between sales and profits is assumed to remain the same as currently then this means that profits are also set to more than double over the period. In a similar vein the relationship between total capital employed and sales is assumed to remain the same therefore net assets are also assumed to more than double.

A further issue with the assumptions made is that in three of the five years the dividend paid is more than the finance required. If some of the dividend were forgone then no finance would be required.

Moving onto the assumptions made by the directors of Centaur Radio Ltd sales are assumed to increase by 55% over the current period figure by 2011. Although this seems to be a large increase it may not be enough to satisfy the parent company. The increase in sales over the period from 2006 to 2011 is estimated to be £41 million but to achieve this it is estimated that an investment of £73 million is required.

There might also be a problem with the assumption that the additional depreciation charges will have no effect on the net profit margin as they will be offset by savings elsewhere. There are no details of these cost savings and as the depreciation charges are considerable, particularly towards the end of the period being considered this would seem to be surprising. More information about these cost savings is therefore required.

In all periods until 2010 there is not enough cash in the company to pay the dividend to the parent company. Therefore if the dividend is paid this will just serve to increase the amount of funding required from the holding company.

Regarding the approaches adopted in (i) and (ii) for establishing the funding requirements of each subsidiary, the approach in (i) provides more approximate figures than that in approach (ii). The approach with Centaur Magazines Ltd relies very heavily on the maintenance of the current relationships between sales, capital employed, loan capital etc. Such assumptions may not be realistic or reliable particularly where new strategies are being adopted. It also ignores any possible economies of scale particularly when a business is growing. This approach is also heavily dependent upon the profit figure which includes the non-cash charge of depreciation which should be added back to profit when determining cash funding requirements.

The approach taken with Centaur Radio Ltd however is much more precise. It does not rely so much on past relationships and makes realistic estimates of fixed asset investment and the investment in working capital that is likely to be required. It also adds back the depreciation to give a more realistic figure for the actual cash funding required each year. Therefore it is this approach which provides the most reliable information.

(c) Centaur Communications plc is a large, listed media business which runs its operations currently through two wholly-owned subsidiary operations, Centaur Magazines Ltd and Centaur Radio Ltd.

Centaur Radio Ltd operates a number of commercial radio stations all of which were acquired ten years ago. The reason for the initial investment in Centaur Radio Ltd was that Centaur Communications plc was seeking to diversify its interests. As with the other subsidiary, Centaur Radio Ltd has always been allowed considerable autonomy with each subsidiary being responsible for its own investment and financing decisions.

Centaur Communications plc is now considering an offer from Astrid Ltd to purchase Centaur Radio Ltd. However there are a number of factors that the board of Centaur Communications plc must consider before making a final decision about the divestment of Centaur Radio Ltd.

Although Centaur Radio Ltd has not been as successful as the board hoped and although some of the board believe that the magazine business has far better long-term prospects than the radio stations the directors must consider that the initial investment in Centaur Radio Ltd was in order to diversify their operations. If Centaur Radio Ltd is sold then the only operation that they will have remaining is that of the magazine business. With no diversification at all it can be argued that the company will be more at risk and particularly with a view to a hostile takeover.

In 2006 Centaur Radio Ltd accounted for 42% of the equity of the two subsidiaries and provided 28% of the retained profits of the two subsidiaries. The sale of Centaur Radio Ltd will considerably reduce the size and operations of the group. Therefore the directors of Centaur Communications plc must seriously consider their strategic objectives before any final decision is made.

The board should also consider whether there are any less drastic options than sale of the radio stations business. To date Centaur Radio Ltd has been allowed considerable autonomy with its own investment and financing decisions. Astrid Ltd clearly believes that the investment in Centaur Radio can be more efficiently used and that a more able and committed management team could be effective. Centaur Communications plc should therefore consider whether an internal restructuring and replacement of the management team may be a better move than divestment. Although the five year plan shows a need for financial support from the parent company until 2010 if, as Astrid Ltd believes, the company could be turned around with less but more efficient investment then the radio subsidiary could be self-financing before the magazine subsidiary.

Finally if it is decided by the board that the sale of Centaur Radio Ltd is its strategic objective then it may be better to consider selling the company through a competitive bidding process rather than just accepting the first offer from Astrid Ltd in order to maximise its sale proceeds.

(d)   **Report**

To: The directors of Astrid Ltd
From: Accountant
Date: June 06
Subject: Proposed purchase of Centaur Radio Ltd

(i)   In the first part of this report I have been asked to calculate the internal rate of return (IRR) of the investment by Astrid Ltd in Centaur Radio Ltd. The cash flows involved in the IRR calculation are the initial purchase price of the company and the proceeds of the eventual flotation. However in order to calculate the proceeds from the eventual sale it is necessary to determine how much of the loan which Centaur Radio Ltd will be taking out will still be outstanding at the time of the flotation. This is turn is dependent upon the cash flows produced by Centaur Radio Ltd each year until the flotation.

Therefore we will start with calculation of the cash that will be available to repay the loan taken out by Centaur Radio Ltd each year.

Cash available to repay loan

	2007	2008	2009	2010	2011
	£'000	£'000	£'000	£'000	£'000
Sales	78,000	82,000	88,000	95,000	104,000
Operating profit					
(10% × sales)	7,800	8,200	8,800	9,500	10,400
Add: depreciation (W1)	1,210	1,640	2,200	2,540	2,880
	9,010	9,840	11,000	12,040	13,280
Working capital	(1,000)	(800)	(200)	(400)	(100)
Operating cash flows	8,010	9,040	10,800	11,640	13,180
Loan interest (W2)	(2,160)	(2,037)	(1,875)	(1,675)	(1,281)
Capital expenditure	(3,800)	(4,300)	(5,600)	(3,400)	(3,400)
Cash to pay off loan	2,050	2,703	3,325	6,565	8,499

Year ended 31 January

Internal rate of return

Cash flows are for Astrid Ltd:

Initial cost	£48,600,000
Proceeds (W3)	£119,468,000

At 20%:

	£'000
Proceeds (£119,468 × 0.402)	48,026
Initial cost	48,600
Net present value	(574)

At 19%:

	£'000
Proceeds (£119,468 × 0.419)	50,057
Initial cost	48,600
Net present value	1,457

$$\text{IRR} = 19\% + \frac{1,457}{1,457 + 574} \times 1\%$$

$$= 19.7\%$$

Working 1 – depreciation

Year ended 31 January

	2007	2008	2009	2010	2011
	£'000	£'000	£'000	£'000	£'000
Cumulative investment in fixed assets	3,800	8,100	13,700	17,100	20,500
Existing depreciation charge	830	830	830	830	830
Additional depreciation	380	810	1,370	1,710	2,050
Total depreciation	1,210	1,640	2,200	2,540	2,880

Working 2 – loan interest and capital repayments

Initial amount of loan:

	£'000
Purchase price (12 × £7,500)	90,000
Less: contribution by shareholders (£48,600 + 5,400)	(54,000)
Loan required	36,000

	Year ended 31 January				
	2007	*2008*	*2009*	*2010*	*2011*
	£'000	£'000	£'000	£'000	£'000
Loan at start of year	36,000	33,950	31,247	27,922	21,357
Interest (loan × 6%)	2,160	2,037	1,875	1,675	1,281
Loan at start of year	36,000	33,950	31,247	27,922	21,357
Cash to repay loan	(2,050)	(2,703)	(3,325)	(6,565)	(8,499)
Loan at end of year	33,950	31,247	27,922	21,357	12,858

Working 3 – Proceeds of sale available for Astrid Ltd

	£'000
Proceeds (14 × £10,400)	145,600
Less: loan to be repaid (W2)	(12,858)
Proceeds available to shareholders	132,742
Proceeds available to Astrid Ltd	
(90% × 132,742)	119,468

(ii) **Improving the IRR**

In this part of the report I will demonstrate how the IRR of this investment for Astrid Ltd can be improved by Centaur Radio Ltd becoming a more highly geared company by taking out a higher loan and therefore requiring less initial investment from Astrid Ltd.

We will assume for this demonstration that the amount of loan finance taken out by Centaur Radio Ltd is £50 million.

Initial purchase cost for Astrid

	£'000
Purchase price (12 × £7,500)	90,000
Loan by Centaur Radio	(50,000)
Required from shareholders	40,000
Required from Astrid Ltd	
90% × 40,000	36,000

Cash available to repay loan

	Year ended 31 January				
	2007	*2008*	*2009*	*2010*	*2011*
	£'000	£'000	£'000	£'000	£'000
Sales	78,000	82,000	88,000	95,000	104,000
Operating profit					
(10% × sales)	7,800	8,200	8,800	9,500	10,400
Add: depreciation (W1)	1,210	1,640	2,200	2,540	2,880
	9,010	9,840	11,000	12,040	13,280
Working capital	(1,000)	(800)	(200)	(400)	(100)
Operating cash flows	8,010	9,040	10,800	11,640	13,180
Loan interest (see below)	(3,000)	(2,927)	(2,819)	(2,676)	(2,342)
Capital expenditure	(3,800)	(4,300)	(5,600)	(3,400)	(3,400)
Cash to pay off loan	1,210	1,813	2,381	5,564	7,438

Loan interest and capital repayments

	Year ended 31 January				
	2007	*2008*	*2009*	*2010*	*2011*
	£'000	£'000	£'000	£'000	£'000
Loan at start of year	50,000	48,790	46,977	44,596	39,032
Interest (loan x 6%)	3,000	2,927	2,819	2,676	2,342
Loan at start of year	50,000	48,790	46,977	44,596	39,032
Cash to repay loan	(1,210)	(1,813)	(2,381)	(5,564)	(7,438)
Loan at end of year	48,790	46,977	44,596	39,032	31,594

Proceeds of sale available for Astrid Ltd

	£'000
Proceeds (14 × £10,400)	145,600
Less: loan to be repaid (see above)	(31,594)
Proceeds available to shareholders	114,006
Proceeds available to Astrid Ltd	
(90% × 114,006)	102,605

Internal rate of return

At 20%

	£'000
Proceeds 102,605 × 0.402	41,247
Cost	36,000
Net present value	5,247

At 23%

	£'000
Proceeds 102,605 × 0.355	36,425
Cost	36,000
Net present value	425

Therefore with the increased level of gearing the IRR of the investment has increased from 19.7% to just over 23%. This means that the IRR is now above the cost of capital of Astrid Ltd. However due to the increased gearing of the investment this will make it more risky and it might therefore be necessary to compare it to a higher figure for cost of capital to account for this risk.

(e)   (i)   Due diligence is the term used to describe the various processes that the potential purchaser of another business will go through when considering buying it. It could be considered as a method of managing the risks that the business faces when buying another business. The types of information that Astrid Ltd may gather during this process will be many and varied.

As a typical starting point the board of Astrid Ltd will want to find as much financial information about Centaur Radio Ltd as possible. They will want information about the financial performance, financial position and financial possibilities. As a starting point this will include the most recent and probably past audited financial statements. The directors would also wish to review budgets for the operations, financial forecasts used for management purposes, details of any major expenses, details of any major capital commitments, details of any contingent liabilities and details of all significant accounting policies.

Astrid Ltd's directors will then consider in detail the assets of the business. They will be concerned with the quality of the assets which will include evidence of ownership rights. They will also be interested in the current market values of the major assets and their current condition. It is likely that they may wish to carry out valuations of any major assets.

In a business such as radio the directors of Astrid Ltd will probably also be interested in the technology which Centaur Radio Ltd has available and how up-to-date it is, its fitness for purpose, usability and its maintainability.

A further potentially important asset that Centaur Radio Ltd may have is its staff and directors. The directors of Astrid Ltd will wish to inspect any employment agreements with directors and employees, find details of any terms for compensation for loss of office, any incentive schemes and details of any disputes. This area will be of particular importance for

Astrid Ltd as they are likely to wish to replace the management team with a more effective one.

The board will also require information regarding any major contracts or agreements that Centaur Radio Ltd has. This will include any credit agreements and any lease agreements. The board will also wish for information about the relationship that Centaur Radio Ltd has with its bank and any other financial institutions with which it deals.

As this due diligence exercise is about determining and managing risks the directors will need to know of any litigation or disputes with any third parties such as suppliers or customers or government agencies such as HM Revenue and Customs or regulators such as Ofcom.

In more general terms the directors of Astrid Ltd will also want to find information about the competitive environment within which Centaur Radio Ltd works and also the regulatory environment. They will want to know the details of Centaur Radio Ltd's main competitors, the reputation that Centaur Radio Ltd has in the marketplace and who are the main market drivers. They will also need to know of any relevant regulations governing the radio industry and their implications for how they will affect their management of Centaur Radio Ltd.

(ii) The aim of Astrid Ltd is to keep Centaur Radio Ltd as a private limited company for five years after which time it will be turned into a public company and floated either on the Alternative Investment Market (AIM) or on the main market of the London Stock Exchange. Therefore the directors of Astrid Ltd will have to consider which market is most suitable for the flotation for Centaur Radio Ltd.

The main advantages of the main market of the London Stock Exchange concern profile and the ability to raise additional finance. On the main market of the Stock Exchange Centaur Radio Ltd will have a higher financial profile than on the AIM and this may be helpful in its dealings with suppliers, customers and potential lenders. If Centaur Radio Ltd wishes to raise finance in the future in order to expand then this will often be easier with a listing on the main market as this is dominated by large institutional investors.

However for a smaller company such as Centaur Radio Ltd there are also a lot of advantages to a flotation on the Alternative Investment Market. AIM specialises in smaller companies and to that end it attracts investors that are actively seeking to invest in the smaller company. Sometimes it may appear that such smaller companies are overlooked if they are listed on the main market. However it is of course possible for a smaller company to switch to the main market in future years as it grows and expands.

There are also fewer conditions imposed on a company seeking a quotation on AIM rather than the main market. On AIM there is no minimum trading record required whereas for the main market there is a minimum of three years. There is also no minimum requirement for the proportion of shares to be held by the public whereas for the main market there is a minimum of 25%. There is also no requirement for a company on AIM to seek prior approval from shareholders for substantial acquisitions and disposals whereas for the main market prior approval must be sought.

Finally a listing on the main market can be more expensive than the flotation costs on AIM as on the main market flotation fees can be as much as 10% of the amount raised in an initial public offering.

4 Examiner's comments

Examiner's comments. Overall, the performance of candidates was satisfactory and this was reflected in the pass rate.

The technique displayed by the vast majority of candidates was satisfactory. It was pleasing to see that most made an attempt at each part of the question, thereby enhancing their chances of success. Most candidates also answered the questions posed and showed key workings and key assumptions, as required. Although these are basic points, too often they have been a source of problems in the past.

The main weakness displayed by candidates was the failure to adopt a more critical, more thoughtful approach to answering narrative parts of the question. Many candidates would have gained higher marks by relating points made much more closely to the information contained within the case study. Answers were often too broad and generalised.

SPECIFIC COMMENTS

The case study on which the project question was based concerned Centaur Communications plc, which has two wholly-owned subsidiaries – Centaur Magazines Ltd and Centaur Radio Ltd.

Part (a) carried 24 marks out of 100 marks for the whole project and required candidates to calculate the annual financing requirements of each subsidiary over the forthcoming five years. Overall, the standard of answers for this part was satisfactory.

The annual sales provided the starting point for calculating the financing requirements of each company as other key items were often expressed as a percentage of sales. Most candidates were familiar with the approach required to undertake the financing requirements for Centaur Magazines Ltd and marks were generally high. However, candidates sometimes struggled with the financing calculations for Centaur Radio Ltd, which required a slightly different approach. It involved adjusting the annual operating profits for depreciation and working capital in order to derive the annual operating cash flows. Even those who recognised the approach to take often experienced difficulties with the calculations, particularly with respect to the depreciation charge. The cumulative effect of new investments on the depreciation charge was not always properly considered and the depreciation charge for existing investments was often omitted.

Part (b) carried 10 marks and required candidates to comment on the financing requirements of each subsidiary and on the assumptions underpinning the financing calculations. It also required comments on the different approaches used to calculate the financing requirements for each subsidiary. Although most candidates gained some marks for their efforts, the general standard of answers was not high.

A key problem was a failure to take a more critical look at the figures and the underlying assumptions. It was useful to examine, for the five-year period, the level of sales, profits, and the net assets needed for each subsidiary. Significant differences between the two subsidiaries could be found. The assumption that, for Centaur Radio Ltd, additional depreciation charges would have no effect on the net profit margin is highly questionable. Given the size of these charges, it implies huge cost savings in other areas.

The comparison between the two approaches to determining the financing requirements was almost always poorly attempted and, in some cases, not attempted at all. A good answer would have considered the extent to which each approach is dependent on the continuation of existing relationships between key figures. In addition, the degree to which key figures, such as depreciation, are specifically taken into account could have been mentioned.

Part (c) carried 10 marks and required candidates to identify and discuss the issues that should be considered before a final decision concerning the divestment of Centaur Radio Ltd is made. Most candidates made a reasonable attempt at this part. However, more marks would often have been gained if greater account were taken of the information contained within the case study. Too often, the points made were rather general and did not relate closely o the information available. The size of the proposed divestment was very large in relation to the size of the company as a whole and this has important ramifications for the future financial health of the company and the process that it would have to go through in order to undertake the divestment.

Part (d) carried 28 marks and required candidates to evaluate, from the perspective of a venture capital company, the viability of the proposed purchase of Centaur Radio Ltd using the internal rate of return (IRR) method. It also required a suggestion as to how the IRR could be improved without changes to the key assumptions regarding sales, profits, and the acquisition and disposasl price of the subsidiary. Most candidates had an understanding of how to answer the first element of this part, although they often struggled with particular calculations. Determining the loan interest charges and loan repayments often proved the most troublesome.

The suggestions made concerning how to improve the IRR were often not worth many marks. The key was to use the benefits of financial gearing in order to enhance the returns to shareholders. This point was not widely mentioned and some candidates even suggested reducing financial gearing in order to boost IRR returns.

Part (e) carried 28 marks and required a discussion of the due diligence process and the factors to be taken into account when deciding between AIM and a main market listing on the London Stock Exchange. Although most candidates obtained reasonable marks for this part, the main problem was (again) a failure to discuss the issues within the context of the case study information. Too often, broad generalisations were made that did not consider the specific issues relating to Centaur Radio Ltd. A good answer would have tried to discuss the competitive and regulatory environment within which the company operates as well as possible technological issues.

ACCA Live Project – Autumn 2006: Module A

Note. we reproduce in this chapter the questions that were set in the Autumn 2006 Module A Project, however we do not reproduce the supplement that was also supplied, containing the financial statements of Compass Group.

You will need to download this from the ACCA's website:

www.accaglobal.com/students/study_exams/qualifications/ diploma_fm/module_a/project_da2/projects/da2_2006_aug

If you do not have internet access please contact our Customer Services department on 020 8740 2211 for hard copy.

1 Autumn 2006 Project: Module A

Diploma in Financial Management

PROJECT DA2, INCORPORATING SUBJECT AREAS
- INTERPRETATION OF FINANCIAL STATEMENTS
- PERFORMANCE MANAGEMENT

All questions are compulsory and MUST be answered

The project MUST be written in English.

The maximum word count (including appendices and tables but excluding table of contents, references and bibliography) is 5,000.

The project MUST be TYPED in black ink, one-sided, double-spaced, using a minimum 12-point font size and a 1-inch margin at each side. HANDWRITTEN SUBMISSIONS WILL NOT BE ACCEPTED. The project must be submitted by post, electronic submissions are not acceptable.

The project should be submitted on A4 paper with your student number, project name, date and page number at the top of each page.

A project submission form MUST be completed for each project submitted and attached to the front of the project.

The Association of Chartered Certified Accountants

BPP
LEARNING MEDIA

Incorporating subject areas – Interpretation of Financial Statements and Performance Management

All questions are compulsory and MUST be attempted

1 Background

You are employed as a loans officer in a financial institution. One of the cases you are dealing with is Exfood, a UK based limited liability company. The company provides outsourced catering services to a range of customer groupings in the UK, Europe and North America.

Exfood has grown steadily and is now seeking to undertake a major expansion, and your organisation has been approached with a view to providing finance.

At the request of your departmental manager, you are required to assess the performance of Exfood and consider its expansion plans. You have obtained the summarised financial information in appendix 1 for this purpose.

You have also obtained the extracts from the financial statements of Compass plc which are in appendix 2.

You have chosen Compass because this is a key company in the industry, and you believe this will provide a useful benchmark against which to assess both the past performance and future plans of Exfood.

The management team of Exfood have stated that their objectives for the expansion are to achieve profitable growth, combined with a positive cash flow, thereby increasing shareholder value.

They believe that these objectives will be achieved by identifying key growth markets as well as gaining customers in existing markets, through offering unrivalled customer service and value for money.

Although the company completed an acquisition in the last month of the 2006 financial year, the management team do not envisage further acquisitions forming part of the growth strategy. They have given two reasons for this view.

The first is that they believe that significant opportunities for organic growth exist and that these can be exploited by constantly improving the service to customers. As growth is achieved, the company will be better placed to improve profit margins due to economies of scale, and improved supply chain management.

The second reason is that they are concerned that the requirement under IFRS for an annual impairment review of purchased goodwill may lead to increased volatility in earnings.

Required

Prepare a report to the Lending Committee of your institution, which:

(a) **Identifies five ratios or other measures, derived from the financial statements, which would be of most significance for your institution in assessing the performance of Exfood, and explains why these are significant for your assessment.** (11 marks)

(b) **Assesses the performance of Exfood, using relevant ratios and other measures, including those you have identified in (a).**

This assessment is to be carried out using Compass plc as a benchmark, in the context of the information referred to in the reports of the Chairman, Chief Executive and Financial Director of Compass plc with regard to the business environment and market conditions, and should also suggest possible reasons for any differences in the performance of the two companies.

(26 marks)

(c)   Assesses the view of the directors that the need to carry out an annual impairment review of purchased goodwill may lead to increased volatility in earnings, by:

(i)   explaining how purchased goodwill arises;
(ii) explaining the nature of impairment; and
(iii) explaining why earnings may be more volatile.   (13 marks)

(50 marks)

2   Background

Your lending manager has indicated that if a decision is taken to advance funds to Exfood, it is likely that your institution will take a close interest in the ongoing performance of the company. This will mean that internally generated management information will be made available to your institution. He has also questioned the validity of using Compass as a benchmark for the assessment carried out in question 1.

You have been asked to consider these points and make a presentation to the Lending Committee.

Required

Prepare a presentation* to the Lending Committee, which:

(a)   **Evaluates the suitability of Compass plc as a benchmark for the performance of Exfood.**
                                                                                              (11 marks)

(b)   **Identifies and explains the measures of shareholder value which may be used by Exfood, and recommends a specific measure for use by the company.**   (11 marks)

(c)   **Discusses how improved supply chain management may assist Exfood to achieve the stated objectives.**   (9 marks)

(d)   **Identifies and, in the context of the company's stated objectives, justifies critical success factors (CSFs) which could be used to manage performance.**   (13 marks)

(e)   **Provides specific measures for the CSFs you have identified in (d).**   (6 marks)

(50 marks)

*Your presentation should include suitable visual aids and a text of the speech you would make when delivering the presentation.

(100 marks)

Appendix 1

Summarised financial information for Exfood Ltd

	2006	2005
Summary Income Statement	$'000	$'000
Revenue	248,180	180,560
Cost of Sales	216,840	157,420
Gross Profit	31,340	23,140
Expenses	27,000	19,500
Operating profit	4,340	3,640
Other income	80	80
Profit before interest	4,420	3,720
Interest paid	240	180
Profit before tax	4,180	3,540
Tax	1,180	1,140
Profit for year	3,000	2,400
Dividends paid	1,400	640
Retained Profit	1,600	1,760

Summary Balance Sheet

	2006	2005
	$'000	$'000
Fixed Assets		
Tangible non-current assets	5,800	3,960
Intangible non-current assets	860	–
	6,660	3,960
Current Assets		
Inventories	3,420	1,380
Trade receivables	29,200	22,520
Bank	11,640	4,120
Prepayments	6,100	5,520
	50,360	33,540
Current Liabilities		
Trade payables	28,680	19,400
HP and other loans	2,860	1,860
Tax	1,500	1,280
Accruals	14,360	7,780
	47,400	30,320
Non-current liabilities		
HP and other loans	1,700	860
Total net assets	7,920	6,320
Equity		
Share capital	1,460	1,460
Share premium	220	220
Retained profit	6,240	4,640
	7,920	6,320

2 Suggested approach

The entire project, covering both subject areas, Interpretation of Financial Statements and Performance Management, is set in the context of the Exfood and Compass plc information which you are provided with.

Start by reading through the information provided quickly so that you get an idea of what you will be dealing with in this project. The project, as you will see, is clearly split into two parts – the first dealing with Interpretation of Financial Statements and question 2 dealing with Performance Management.

Note that you are a loans officer in a financial institution.

Requirements

Now have a look at the requirements to see what is required of you. For question 1 you are asked to prepare a report to the Lending Committee of your institution therefore this must be in report format. For question 2 you are to prepare a presentation which must include suitable visual aids and the text of the speech that you would make when delivering the presentation. The examiner noted in his comments on this project that a surprising number of candidates ignored the reporting format stated in the question so make sure that you do prepare a report and a presentation for the two respective questions.

General considerations before you start

The examiner, in his comments on this project, gave some helpful general insight into why candidates are not necessarily scoring as high marks as they might do in these projects so it is worth considering some of these general comments before starting.

One of the most common reasons for candidates not scoring highly is that answers are often descriptive or contain little analysis. Even where an attempt at analysis is made it is often left underdeveloped. Questions that the examiner suggests candidates ask themselves before starting the project are 'why am I writing this?' and 'how does this develop the discussion?'.

In terms of the development of discussion the examiner also comments upon the mark allocations and number of words. The maximum number of words for the project is 5,000 but in extreme cases projects are presented with less than 2,500 words. The examiner has commented on how a candidate submitting a project of only 2,500 words can realistically expect to obtain enough marks to pass. To quote the examiner 'this limit of 5,000 has been set to encourage candidates to carry out a reasonably in-depth analysis of the material. However it would be incorrect to assume that a pass can only be obtained by using the maximum number of words.'

The examiner often comments that the word count in candidates' projects does not always relate to the mark allocation. He has made it quite clear that the mark allocation is an accurate guide to the number of words required for each part of the project. Therefore it is worthwhile at this stage just calculating the approximate number of words required for each part of the project. You do not necessarily have to write the exact amount of words per part of the project but use the word count as a feel for the depth of analysis that is required.

Question 1

(a) 11/100 x 5,000   =   550 words

(b) 26/100 x 5,000   =   1,300 words

(c) 13/100 x 5,000   =   650 words

Question 2

(a) 11/100 x 5,000   =   550 words

(b) 11/100 x 5,000   =   550 words

(c) 9/100 x 5,000   =   450 words

(d) 13/100 x 5,000   =   650 words

(e) 6/100 x 5,000   =   300 words

Read through the individual requirements so that you have an idea of what areas are being tested in this project. Remember that you are a loans officer providing information to the Lending Committee of your financial institution. The question they will be asking is 'should we be lending money to this business and why?'.

Now go back to the information you have been given about Exfood and Compass plc and read through it very carefully bearing in mind the requirements that you have just read through. There is no need to do any calculations at the moment just take note of the financial information that you have been provided with.

Question 1

Remember that a report format is needed for this which must cover all three parts of the question. Any detailed calculations should be in an Appendix at the end of the report.

Part (a)

For this part you must identify just five ratios or other measures which would be of most significance for your institution in assessing the performance of Exfood and explain why these measures are significant.

Before starting think back to the examiner's comments about analysis. He has made the point that 'when selecting ratios for use in an appraisal of performance candidates should ensure that they have carefully thought about why the appraisal is being carried out and how the needs of the party carrying out the appraisal can be met. In simple terms, if candidates constantly ask themselves 'why?' and 'how?' the quality of answers would improve'.

As with many projects you are given a limit (5 in this case) on the number of ratios that you are to select. This is done for a purpose, to ensure that you do think about why you are performing the analysis and what may or may not be useful in this particular scenario.

It is worth noting the examiner's full comments on the analysis in both parts (a) and (b) here.

'Too many candidates provide what might be termed a general analysis of performance and therefore scored low marks. It may be helpful to reiterate what is meant by a general analysis. Such answers tend to simply choose a number of ratios, calculate the results for these ratios and note that performance is better or worse than the comparator. This is not the kind of analysis which is being sought. Further development of the answer is required. This can be done by explaining why a particular ratio has been chosen. In particular the explanation should clearly state the significance of the ratio in this case. An attempt to signal this was made in the wording of the question: candidates were specifically asked to choose ratios '*which would be of most significance for your institution'*. The need for development was further emphasised by the requirement to explain 'Why these ratios are significant for your assessment.' The key point is that the assessment was to be carried out for a particular purpose. Perhaps this can be illustrated by referring to the kind of comment offered with regard to return on capital employed. Many candidates chose this ratio, and explained their choice by noting that the ratio measured the company's success in obtaining a return on the funds invested. This is absolutely correct, but could be copied from any textbook. Consequently, it did not attract any marks. What was required was a comment to explain why (in this case) a lender would be Interested In thls ratlo'.

Bearing all of this in mind now turn to the financial statements of Exfood and in a draft Appendix to your report calculate a number of ratios for Exfood to get a feel for what has changed over the last two years. You may not use all of these ratios but as an initial starting point this can be useful.

Once you have calculated a few basic ratios you will get a feel for the fact that profitability and return on capital employed have reduced slightly although asset turnover has improved slightly. Liquidity has generally reduced and gearing increased but interest cover is still healthy. One of the most significant changes has been the large increase in the percentage of profits paid out as dividends and therefore consequently a large decrease in the amount that has been retained for future investment.

Then think about the type of ratio that a potential investor of loan capital would be concerned about and try to find the 5 most significant ratios or measures in this context.

Make sure that you explain and justify each of the chosen performance measures but at this stage no analysis is required, eg there is no need to discuss the fact that gross profit margin has decreased or that gearing has increased. All that is required is an explanation of why each of these performance measures is appropriate from the perspective of a financial institution which is considering investing loan capital in the company.

Part (b)

For this part of the report you are required to now assess the performance of Exfood and in particular to use Compass plc as a benchmark. Return to the operating and financial review of Compass plc and read this through very carefully as it gives a lot of information about results, business environment, market conditions etc.

Now return to your appendix and calculate the same ratios that you did for Exfood for Compass plc as well. This is not quite as easy as it sounds as you are provided with very different information for the two companies. The financial statements of Exfood are summarised and simplified whereas those for Compass plc are the full published financial statements. Therefore it will not always be possible to match like with like but you should be able to get a feel for similarities and differences.

Part (c)

This part of the question requires specific technical knowledge and as there are no time limits to this project then there is no excuse for any technical errors. Therefore if necessary make sure that you revise thoroughly the accounting requirements for purchased goodwill and impairment before embarking on this part of the project.

Note that the question specifically applies to purchased goodwill therefore do not discuss internally generated goodwill. The examiner notes his disappointment that a number of candidates did do this despite the requirements being quite clear.

The information that you are given for this question also clearly refers to IFRS therefore any discussion of the accounting treatment must be based upon the requirements of IFRS. The examiner noted that he was surprised at how many candidates discussed amortisation of goodwill and referred to UK GAAP.

Structure your answer to this part carefully as you have to explain how purchased goodwill arises, explain the nature of impairment and how impairment reviews may lead to earnings becoming more volatile.

Question 2

In question 2 we now move onto the Performance Management element of the syllabus.

Most importantly however this part of the project requires you to prepare a presentation with visual aids plus the script of your speech which you would deliver in the presentation. Visual aids have been asked for in a number of Module A assessments now and the examiner has made it clear that marks are allocated to them and therefore marks are lost if they are not prepared. In fact the preparation of visual aids can help you to plan your answer as most visual aids will be lists of the key topics to be considered or breakdowns of points within a topic. They will then need to be padded out with the full speech but can be a good starting point for your answer.

Part (a)

The best approach here is to consider the advantages of using Compass plc as a benchmark and the disadvantages so that all aspects are covered. The examiner commented that good marks were scored when this approach was taken but where there was simply a generalised discussion of the nature of benchmarking scores were low.

Part (b)

This part asks for you to identify and explain measures of shareholder value which may be used by Exfood. It also asks you to recommend a specific measure for use by the company. So have a think first of all, or refer to your study text, about measures of shareholder value.

Again make sure that your comments are specific and related to the scenario not generalised. Also note that you are asked to come to a conclusion and recommend a measure.

Part (c)

For this part you need to be knowledgeable about supply chain management so a good starting point might be to re-read your Study Text on this area. However beware of simply regurgitating the Study Text material as the examiner has made it quite clear that this will not earn marks. You must ensure that you discuss specific aspects of the supply chain and how these relate to the business of Exfood.

Part (d)

Here you have to both identify and justify critical success factors for Exfood in the context of the company's stated objectives. Therefore as a starting point consider these stated objectives:

- profitable growth
- positive cash flows
- increase in shareholder value
- identify key growth markets

- gain customers in existing markets
- offer unrivalled customer service and value for money

The examiner has stated that the key to gaining good marks here is to ensure that the CSFs and performance measures were clearly linked to the objectives of Exfood.

Now you have to think of critical success factors to measure the level of achievement of these objectives. Try reading through the operating and financial review of Compass plc again as this may give you some ideas about possible CSFs and also performance measures for these CSFs for part (e).

Part (e)

Finally you are required to provide specific measures for the CSFs that you have identified in part (d). These have to be specific to each CSF and with a clear explanation of how they would be measured.

Remember that CSFs are not measured by a large number of measures. The whole point about CSFs is that they are very tightly focused so you do not need a long list of measures.

3 Suggested answer

Question 1

REPORT

To:	**The Lending Committee**
From:	**Loans Officer**
Date:	**X – X – 20XX**
Subject:	**Exfood**

This report will cover a number of aspects concerning Exfood, a UK based limited liability company. The company provides outsourced catering services to a range of customer groupings in the UK, Europe and North America.

Exfood has grown steadily and is now seeking to undertake a major expansion. This is the reason that they have approached us with a view to us providing the finance for this expansion. The management team of Exfood have stated that their objectives for the expansion are to achieve profitable growth, combined with a positive cash flow thereby increasing shareholder value. They believe that these objectives will be achieved by identifying key growth markets as well as gaining customers in existing markets, through offering unrivalled customer service and value for money.

From our perspective I have written this report covering three aspects of Exfood and its expansion plans.

(a) I have identified 5 ratios or performance measures derived from the financial statements which would be of most significance to us in assessing the performance of Exfood. I will also explain why these particular measures are significant for our assessment.

(b) Having obtained the financial statements of Compass plc, a key company in this industry, I have been able to use their performance measures as a benchmark against which I have assessed the performance of Exfood and its plans for the future.

(c) Finally the directors of Exfood have made it clear that they intend to concentrate their growth strategy on organic growth rather than any further acquisitions partly due to their concerns about impairment losses on purchased goodwill leading to increased volatility of earnings. In the final part of this report I will consider aspects of this concern.

(a) Key financial ratios

In an appendix to this report I have calculated a number of financial ratios and performance measures for Exfood based upon their 2006 and 2005 financial statements. However in order to clearly quantify the analysis I will be concentrating on only five key ratios which in this section of the report will be explained and justified.

In our position as a potential lender of funds to Exfood for an expansion project our major concerns are with the long term stability and growth of the company and their ability to repay our interest charges when due and the capital amount loaned to them as and when that falls due.

In general terms we will be concerned that Exfood continues as a profitable company which is able to make the most of the opportunities that face it. For this reason the **gross profit margin** has been selected in order to measure the underlying profitability of the core business of Exfood. We would expect to see a constant or even improving gross profit margin as evidence of strength of the company performance in order to give us confidence in the future performance of the company.

One of our major concerns will be that the company has enough funds to be able to pay our interest charges as and when they fall due. We can consider this from both an income statement aspect and from a balance sheet liquidity aspect.

The **interest cover** shows how many times the current interest charge in the income statement is covered by the profits before interest that are therefore available to make interest and tax payments and any payouts to shareholders. A high interest cover shows that the company is earning plenty of profits out of which interest payments can be met.

However we are not just concerned about profitability but also about the liquidity of the company and the availability of the cash to make our interest payments and any capital repayments that may fall due. Therefore we will also be considering the **quick (or acid test) ratio.** This figure compares the current assets that are fairly easily converted into cash such as receivables and the bank balance to the current liabilities that the company must also pay in the fairly near future. This will give us an indication of the liquidity levels of the company and their ability to find the cash for our payments as and when they fall due.

As was noted above we are also concerned about the long term stability of the company both in terms of its profitability but also in terms of its capital structure. Therefore we will be considering the **gearing ratio** which as the percentage of loan finance to equity finance will give us some indication of the long term stability of the company and its ability to continue in business during the period of our loan.

Finally we will be considering the **dividend payout ratio** which measures the proportion of the final profits each year which are paid out as dividends to the shareholders. The importance to us of this performance measure is that although we would expect to see a reasonable level of payments to shareholders we would not wish to find that profits and cash available to repay the company's commitments to us are in fact being disproportionately diverted to the equity shareholders.

(b)   Assessment of the performance of Exfood

This assessment of the performance of Exfood has been performed not just by taking into consideration the performance measures calculated from Exfood's own financial statements but also by comparing Exfood's performance measures to similar measures for Compass plc which is a key company in this industry and which should provide a useful benchmark in order to assess the past performance and future plans of Exfood.

We will start with an overview of the performance of Exfood during the 2006 financial year. We know that Exfood has grown steadily over the years but in the current year turnover was 37.5% higher than in the previous year and operating profit was 19% higher. This growth is all organic as there was only one acquisition during the year and this was in the last month of the year and therefore would have had little impact on the income statements. This position is in line with the objectives of the company which is to achieve profitable, organic growth in order to increase shareholder value.

However even though there is definitely growth we must also consider how profitable this growth has been given that operating profit, although higher than last year, is still increasing at a lower rate than the rate of increase in turnover. If we consider the gross profit margin, the actual trading margin, then there has only been a very slight decrease from 12.8% to 12.6% in the current year. This is mirrored in the figures for net profit margin (using profit before interest and tax) which has again fallen from 2.0% to 1.8%.

This decline in profitability has partly been offset by a slight improvement in asset turnover, the efficiency with which the business uses its overall assets, but has still led to a decrease in return on capital employed from 51.8% to 46.0%. Therefore it would appear that the growth that has been noted has been at the slight expense of profitability.

From our perspective as a potential lender to Exfood we are concerned about their ability to pay interest when due and any capital repayments of the loan as and when they fall due. The safety of our repayments can be considered from the income statement perspective by looking at interest cover, the amount of times that the current interest figure is covered by the profits available for payments of interest, tax and dividends. Although the amount of interest payable in 2006 has increased by a third over the previous year the interest cover is still very respectable at 18.4 times. We do not have any available cash flow information but from a profit perspective it would appear that there are plenty of profits to cover additional interest payments.

Allied to the interest cover is the measure of capital gearing. This is a comparison of the amount of debt in the capital structure to the amount of equity. Although this has increased significantly during the 2006 financial year the ratio of debt to equity is still only 21.5% and therefore it would appear that additional loan capital should not be a problem for the company.

As lenders we will also of course be concerned about the liquidity of the business. Despite its profitability there must also be cash available for payment of interest and repayment of capital. We have no cash flow information about Exfood but can look at liquidity from the balance sheet perspective. Both the current ratio and the quick (acid test) ratio have declined from last year and are both seemingly quite low however we will return to this when considering Compass plc later in this report.

Finally as potential providers of capital to this company we will be interested in the amount of profits which are being paid out to the shareholders of the company. The dividend payout ratio measures the proportion of the available profits after tax which have been paid out to the ordinary shareholders as their annual dividend. This has increased significantly from 26.7% to 46.7% over the last two years. This means that not only is less profit being retained to reinvest in the business but also large amounts of cash are having to be found in order to pay the dividend.

Having looked at Exfood in isolation we will now compare, wherever possible, to the position shown by the financial statements of Compass plc which is a key company in the industry. Before we look at any comparisons however a number of factors must be considered. The Exfood financial statements are for the financial year 2006 whereas the financial statements of Compass plc are for the year to 30 September 2005. We do not know exactly when Exfood's year end is but there is obviously a considerable time difference which may mean that the company's financial statements reflect slightly different market and economic conditions. Secondly we only have summarised financial statements for Exfood but full financial statements for Compass plc so it is difficult to tell if the ratios that are being compared are in fact truly comparable. Finally bear in mind that there is a considerable difference in size between Exfood and Compass plc. If we consider their respective turnovers Compass plc is approximately 100 times bigger than Exfood (assuming $2 = £1$).

One of the major factors of Exfood's performance that has been noted is the growth in turnover. Moreover the management of Exfood aim to achieve their objective of profitable growth through organic growth rather than acquisition by identifying key growth markets as well as gaining customers in existing markets through offering unrivalled customer service and value for money. Compass plc has also experienced growth in turnover, although similar reductions in profit levels, and their operating and financial review makes it quite clear that the markets, in particular the UK market, still offer significant opportunities for profitable growth. Exfood operates in the UK, Europe and North America and so is similar to Compass plc with the absence of Compass's strong new business opportunities in the 'Rest of the World'.

With regards to profitability Compass plc seem to have similar problems to Exfood in that profitability levels have fallen. This is particularly the case in the UK where one suspects that Exfood has its core business. These cost pressures referred to in Compass plc's report have not always been able to be transferred to the customer and it is suspected that this is also the case for Exfood. It was also noted in Compass plc's report that trading in Continental Europe 'remains difficult with little or no growth in the major markets' which will also be affecting Exfood. It would seem therefore that the decrease in profitability seen in Exfood's financial statements, and mirrored in those of Compass plc, are due to cost increases which both companies are facing in this particular type of market. However the market itself would appear to be buoyant with scope for growth.

One concern noted earlier about the Exfood figures was that of liquidity. If we compare Exfood to Compass plc it would appear that Exfood is in a stronger position than Compass plc. Compass plc has interest cover of only 5.5 times compared to 18.4 times for Exfood and Compass also has a much higher level of gearing at 113.4%. We were concerned about Exfood's low current and quick ratios but Compass plc has even lower measures for these liquidity ratios but still has free cash flow of £348 million up from £246 million last year. This would indicate that businesses in this type of market can operate successfully with these seemingly low liquidity levels with no major problems.

In conclusion we may have had some concerns about the profitability levels and liquidity levels of Exfood when considering their financial statements in isolation. However when the information provided in the operating and financial review and financial statements of Compass plc is also considered these concerns are put to rest. The fall in profitability appears to have affected the market generally due to increased costs which cannot as yet be passed onto the customer. However there would appear to be plenty of scope for the type of growth which Exfood's management envisage. Similarly with liquidity levels, when those of Exfood are compared to those of Compass plc, it would appear that there are no major problems here.

In conclusion, on the basis of the limited information available, it would appear that a loan to Exfood for its expansion purposes would be a sound investment.

(c)   Purchased goodwill can potentially arise when one company acquires an interest in another company. This may be a controlling interest where the acquired company becomes a subsidiary or the purchase of an interest which gives the acquiring company significant influence over the acquired company in which case it is known as an associated company. In either situation the fair value of the consideration given for the shareholding is compared to the fair value of the share of net assets of the company that has been acquired. If the fair value of the consideration exceeds the fair value of the net assets acquired then purchased goodwill has been created.

This purchased goodwill is an asset of the acquiring company and under IFRS should appear in the balance sheet under non-current assets and be described as an intangible non-current asset. According to IFRS this asset of purchased goodwill is not amortised (in the same way as tangible non-current assets are depreciated) but instead each year an impairment review must be carried out to determine whether there has been any impairment in the value of the purchased goodwill.

Any impairment of purchased goodwill is determined by comparing the carrying amount of the asset in the balance sheet to its recoverable amount. Therefore impairment is a fall in the value of the asset so that its recoverable amount is now less than its carrying value in the balance sheet. An impairment loss is the amount that the purchased goodwill must be written down by in order for it to appear in the balance sheet at its recoverable amount. Therefore impairment is not a bookkeeping entry such as depreciation on tangible non-current assets but is an entry that has to be made due to an actual impairment of the asset usually due to external circumstances.

As we have seen an impairment takes place when the recoverable amount of the asset is lower than its carrying value. The recoverable amount is defined as:

* the higher value of:

    –   the asset's fair value less costs to sell, and
    –   its value in use.

An asset's fair value less costs to sell is the amount net of selling costs that could be obtained from the sale of the asset. However when we are considering purchased goodwill this is not an asset that could be sold on any open market. Therefore the consideration of any impairment means that the carrying value in the balance sheet must be compared to the value in use of the asset.

The value in use of an asset is defined as the present value of the estimated future cash flows generated by the asset. For an asset such as purchased goodwill in most cases it will not be possible to determine the estimate of the future cash flows of the purchased goodwill itself as these are impossible to define and calculate. Instead the recoverable amount of the asset's cash generating unit should be determined. A cash generating unit is the smallest identifiable group of assets for which independent cash flows can be identified and measured. For purchased goodwill therefore this cash generating unit is usually the shareholding to which it relates. Therefore the present value of the future cash flows of the acquired company should be calculated and compared to the carrying value of the assets of the company and any shortfall will be the amount of impairment loss. This impairment loss is firstly allocated to any assets of the acquired company that have been obviously damaged or destroyed and then to the write down of any purchased goodwill relating to the shareholding.

If an impairment loss has been incurred then the purchased goodwill must be written down in the balance sheet to its recoverable amount as calculated in the impairment review. The amount of this write-down in value is a charge to the income statement. It can therefore be argued, as the directors of Exfood are arguing, that having purchased goodwill on the balance sheet may lead to volatility in earnings. If it is anticipated that the value in use of the acquired company will fall below the value at which its assets are held in the balance sheet then there will be additional charges to the income statement. However if the acquired company is thriving and successful then there is less chance that any such impairment losses will have to be recognised.

Appendix

Exfood – ratios

	2006	2005
Growth in turnover from 2005 to 2006	37.5%	
Gross profit margin	12.6%	12.8%
Net profit margin (before interest and tax)	1.8%	2.0%
Return on capital employed	46.0%	51.8%
Asset turnover	25.8	25.2
Interest cover	18.4 times	20.7 times
Dividend payout ratio	46.7%	26.7%
Current ratio	1.06 : 1	1.11 : 1
Quick (acid test) ratio	0.99 : 1	1.06 : 1
Gearing ratio (debt to equity)	21.5%	13.6%

Compass plc – ratios

	2005	2004
Growth in turnover from 2004 to 2005	7.9%	
Operating profit margin	5.7%	6.8%
Return on capital employed	5.7%	6.4%%
Interest cover	5.5 times	3.8 times
Dividend payout ratio	51.3%	111.1%
Current ratio	0.76 : 1	0.74 : 1
Quick (acid test) ratio	0.67 : 1	0.64 : 1
Gearing ratio (debt to equity)	113.4%	107.4%

Question 2

Good morning ladies and gentlemen. Most of you may know that I am one of the loan officers for this institution and I am here this morning to consider the proposal that we are to loan money to Exfood, a limited liability UK company, which provides outsourced catering services to a range of customer groupings in the UK, Europe and North America.

Exfood has grown steadily and is now seeking to undertake a major expansion. This is the reason that they have approached us with a view to us providing the finance for this expansion. The management team of Exfood have stated that their objectives for the expansion are to achieve profitable growth, combined with a positive cash flow thereby increasing shareholder value. They believe that these objectives will be achieved by identifying key growth markets as well as gaining customers in existing markets, through offering unrivalled customer service and value for money.

I have already prepared for you a report which assesses the performance of Exfood particularly in comparison to a key company in this industry, Compass plc, but in this presentation I would like to consider further aspects of the performance of Exfood that may be useful in your final decision as to whether to provide the loan finance that we have been approached for.

(a)

Visual aid 1 – Compass plc

Advantages

- similar type of business
- key company in the market place
- striving to be a benchmark company

Disadvantages

- different year ends
- size
- geographical areas
- comparison of figures

We have used the financial statements of Compass plc as a benchmark which as Compass plc appears to have a very similar business in similar parts of the world and is a key player in the market would seem to be sensible. Compass plc is also a company which seeks to be a benchmark for others and is therefore striving for the excellence that is required in a benchmark.

However there are some problems with this comparison. The Compass financial statements are for the year ending 30 September 2005 whereas those for Exfood are for the financial year 2006 although we do not know the actual year end date in 2006. This timing difference may have an effect in that the figures in the two sets of financial statements reflect different market and economic conditions.

A further obvious problem in comparison is that of size. Based upon turnover Compass plc is approximately 100 times larger than Exfood and as such will enjoy economies of scale not available to Exfood. As a key company in the industry it is also likely that Compass plc has more influence on its environment than would be possible for Exfood.

Although there are similarities in geographical areas of business between the two companies we do not know how similar these are. For example in Compass plc the more profitable North American market accounts for 32% of group turnover. Although we know that Exfood operates in North America we do not know whether the proportion of business is similar to that of Compass plc. We also note that even though Exfood operates in the UK, Europe and North America it does not have the rest of the world operations that Compass plc has which is proving to be a profitable growth area.

Finally given the limited information available it is not known how comparable the figures being calculated are. For Exfood we only have very limited summarised financial statements whereas we have the full financial statements of Compass plc.

(b)

Visual aid 2

What is shareholder value?

In this part of this presentation we will be considering measures of shareholder value which may be used by Exfood.

As a starting point therefore we should consider what is meant by shareholder value.

The shareholder value concept is that a company has as its main objective the aim of maximising the wealth of Its shareholders and should therefore develop strategies for increasing shareholder value. So what exactly is shareholder value?

Shareholder value can be viewed as the returns received by the owners of a company, the shareholders. These returns come in the form not only of cash returns of dividends but perhaps even more importantly in terms of the increase in the value of their shares.

The management team of Exfood have stated that their objectives for their expansion are to achieve profitable growth, combined with positive cash flows, thereby increasing shareholder value. Therefore we must now consider how to measure shareholder value in terms of Exfood.

Visual aid 3

- **How is shareholder value measured?**
- **profit**
- **earnings per share**
- **return on assets**
- **economic value added**

There are a variety of methods of measuring shareholder value and we will now consider each in turn.

We have seen that shareholder value is about maximising the return to the shareholders either in the form of dividends paid or an increase in share value. Therefore profit will be a key factor in the measurement of shareholder value. Profits can be either paid out to the shareholders in the form of dividends or re-invested in the company to earn profitable growth for the future. Shareholders will tend to have expectations of what profits may be and if actual profits are less than expected then this may lead to a fall in share value and therefore in shareholder value. Therefore targets will normally be set for annual growth in profits.

Earnings per share is a key factor in the measurement of shareholder value. As the name implies this figure is the amount of earnings for every share in issue. Even if new shares are issued in order to raise more capital to invest profitably then the existing shareholders must be convinced that this additional capital has been worthwhile in that their earnings per share have increased. Therefore one of the market's key elements of measurement of performance and enhancement of shareholder value is a target for earnings per share each year or a figure for growth in earnings per share each year.

In order for profits to be earned capital must be invested. However overall performance can only be judged by comparing the size of the profit made in terms of the size of the investment. Therefore the overall performance of the assets of the company can be measured either by return on the assets employed or the return on investment measure. Both of these measures compare the profits made to the book value of the assets used in the earning of these profits.

Profits and returns on assets are based upon accounting measures of profitability and asset values. It can be argued that accounting values are not reliable guides to economic value. Economic value added (EVA®)is a measure of performance that addresses this problem. Adjustments are made to expense and asset values in order to convert reported accounting profits into a measure that represents the economic value added for shareholders during the period.

On balance EVA® is probably the performance measure most closely linked to changes in shareholder value and as such is the better measure of performance than the other measures which are based upon accounting profits and values.

(c)

Visual aid 4

Supply chain management

What is the supply chain?

What is supply chain management?

Application to Exfood

The supply chain is the network of suppliers, manufacturers and distributors that is involved in the process of moving the goods/services for a customer from the materials stage to the customer itself.

Supply chain management views all of the buyers and sellers in the supply chain as part of a continuum, and the aim should be to look at the supply chain as a whole and seek to optimise the functioning of the entire chain.

So let us now consider how this concept of supply chain management can be applied to Exfood to assist them in achieving their objective of profitable growth.

One of the problems faced in this market is an increase in costs which can potentially start to erode profitability. By focusing on its supply chain management Exfood could reduce these costs without any loss of value or quality to its customers. For a company like Exfood the main area to consider will be its suppliers of foodstuffs. During 2006 approximately $216 million of foodstuffs were sourced by the company over a wide range of geographic areas. Exfood should seek to establish mutually beneficial relationships with these suppliers and encourage them to match Exfood's own high standards of food safety, working conditions, trading practices, health and safety and environmental protection. Together with its suppliers Exfood must also ensure that these supplies of foodstuffs are nutritious, safe and from sustainable sources.

(d)

Visual aid 5

Objectives of Exfood

- profitable growth
- positive cash flows
- increase in shareholder value
- identify key growth markets
- gain customers in existing markets
- offer unrivalled customer service and value for money

We now move on to a consideration of the critical success factors (CSFs) that Exfood could use to manage performance. However before we can do this we must consider the stated objectives of the management of Exfood as listed on this slide.

From this point we can then determine CSFs that will help to meet these stated objectives.

Visual aid 6

Critical success factors

- Quality of produce
- Customer satisfaction
- Cost control
- Employee quality
- Market share
- New markets

These are the critical success factors for Exfood which are the key areas of the business which must all go right if Exfood is to achieve its stated objectives.

Quality of produce

If Exfood is to provide high levels of customer satisfaction and value for money then key to this must be the quality of the food that it produces. This in turn will be largely dependent upon the quality of the ingredients and products that are used in the catering.

Customer satisfaction

As this is a customer focused business then in order to retain customers and to gain new customers through reputation Exfood must ensure high levels of satisfaction amongst its current customers.

Cost control

One of the aims of the business is profitable growth therefore there must be strict control over the cost of the inputs.

Employee quality

As a service industry dealing directly with the end customer it is vital that the company employs and keeps in employment only the best employees.

Market share

As growth is to be organic Exfood must keep and increase its market share of the markets in which it currently operates by gaining new customers.

New markets

A further stated aim of the company is to identify key growth markets. For example there is said to be large growth in the education, sports and leisure and health markets.

The company may also consider expanding into new geographical markets.

(e)

Visual aid 7		
Performance measures		
• Quality of produce	-	levels of wastage
• Customer satisfaction	-	client retention level
• Cost control	-	gross profit margin
• Employee quality	-	staff retention levels
• Market share	-	new business wins in current markets
• New markets	-	new business wins in new markets

Quality of produce can be measured by the levels of wastage or rejected produce from individual suppliers. This will help to determine the best suppliers or to improvements in quality from suppliers.

Customer satisfaction can be measured by the percentage of customers retained from one year to the next.

Cost control can be measured by monitoring of gross profit margins.

Employee quality and satisfaction can be measured by staff retention or staff turnover levels. The higher the retention levels the better quality of staff.

Growth in market share can be measured by the number and turnover value of the new clients in an existing market each period.

Expansion into new markets can be measured by the number and turnover value of new clients in new markets – this will be either new areas such as education or sports and leisure or new geographical markets.

4 Examiner's comments

Examiner's comments. The project covers both Subject Area 1 (Interpretation of Financial Statements) and Subject Area 2 (Performance Management). At each sitting, an attempt is made to ensure that marks are divided equally between the two subject areas. This was the case at this sitting.

It is invariably the case that, in terms of the proportion of successful candidates, overall performance in the project is better than the performance in the exam. It has been noticeable that the number of candidates achieving very high marks has been reducing in recent sittings. As there appears to be a small number of reasons for this, it seems appropriate to make some observations as to why this is the case.

These general comments will then be developed in the consideration of candidate performance in each of the questions.

Perhaps the most common reason for candidates not scoring highly is that answers are often descriptive, or contain little analysis. In some cases, even when the answer includes analysis, this has been left underdeveloped.

In the most extreme cases, some candidates present projects of less than 2,500 words. Given that the limit is 5,000 words, one is left to reflect how such candidates can realistically expect to obtain sufficient marks to achieve a pass. The limit of 5,000 words has been set to encourage candidates to carry out a reasonably in-depth analysis of the material. However, it would be incorrect to assume that a pass can only be obtained by using the maximum number of words, For example, on occasions, those candidates who are able to express themselves succinctly by discussing relevant issues in the correct context have obtained almost 60% for a submission of around 4,000 words. The key issues, as already noted, are context and development of comments. Therefore, candidates are reminded that it is essential that they should prepare a number of drafts of their work and critically review these to ensure that the context for comments is set out, and that observations are justified and explained.

It is also interesting to note that, in general, the performance in the elements of the project that relate to performance management is better than in the elements that relate to interpretation of financial statements. It seems that there are two reasons for this. The first is probably related to the fact that the DipFM is intended for practising managers who wish to develop their skills of financial awareness and financial literacy. By definition this will mean that candidates come to the qualification with some managerial competences. It is therefore natural that it will be more straightforward to apply these competences, than the newly acquired financial competences. The second is almost certainly linked to the issue of context, and a related misunderstanding as to what is expected in answers. An attempt to address this matter was an article in *finance matters* entitled 'Ratios – a place for everything?'. The point to note is that when selecting ratios for use in an appraisal of performance, candidates should ensure that they have carefully thought about why the appraisal is being carried out, and how the needs of the party carrying out can be met. In simple terms, if candidates constantly ask themselves 'why?' and 'how?', the quality of answers would improve.

The matter of the number of words must also be considered in another context. Marks are not awarded for effort, but for outcome. It is probably the case that, when the results are released, a number of candidates (both successful and unsuccessful) find themselves thinking 'I put a lot of work into that. I spent hours going through the material, and I wrote 4,998 words. Why did I not get more marks?'

The reason is because it is too late to ask 'why?'. This should have been done before the work was submitted. This might be best explained by noting how some candidates do not obtain the maximum advantage from their use of references and personal experience. Many candidates who provide such references (to writers or personal experience) do not take the next step of explaining why the reference is relevant. While such references can be valuable, no marks are awarded unless the reference is used to develop the point which is being made. If candidates were to ask themselves 'why am I writing this?' or 'how does this develop the discussion?' this weakness may be less apparent.

A further general point is that there continues to be a surprising number of candidates who ignore the reporting format stated in the question. Question 1 required a report format to be used, and Question 2 required a presentation. Even more surprising is the fact that even though more work is required to present an answer in the form of a presentation, some answers were in the correct format for Question 2, but not for Question 1. Candidates who ignore the opportunity to pick up such easy marks can only be described as extremely careless.

QUESTION 1

Parts (a) and (b) of this question required an analysis of the performance of the company. As information about a competitor had been provided, it was expected that this would be used to provide a benchmark. Most candidates attempted to make appropriate use of the competitor information to carry out a comparative analysis. Those candidates who developed their comments and provided some analysis scored well on these two parts. Such analysis tended to attempt to explain differences or similarities in performance or to suggest additional research which could be carried out.

However too many candidates provided what might be termed a general analysis of performance, and therefore scored low marks. It may be helpful to reiterate what is meant by 'a general analysis'. Such answers tend to simply chose a number of ratios, calculate the results for these ratios, and note that performance is better (or worse) than the comparator. This is not the kind of analysis that is sought. Further development of the answer is required. This can be done by explaining why a particular ratio has been chosen. In particular, the explanation should clearly state the significance of the ratio in this case. An attempt to signal this was made in the wording of the question: candidates were specifically asked to choose ratios *'which would be of most significance for your institution'*. The need for development was further emphasised by the requirement to explain 'why these (ratios) are significant for your assessment'.

The key point is that the assessment was to be carried out for a particular purpose.

Perhaps this can be illustrated by referring to the kind of comment offered with regard to return on capital employed. Many candidates chose this ratio, and explained their choice by noting that the ratio measured the company success in obtaining a return on the funds invested. This is absolutely correct, but could be copied from any textbook. Consequently, it did not attract any marks. What was required was a comment to explain why (in this case) a lender would be interested in this ratio.

In Part (b), the tendency to provide a general analysis led to comments that simply noted how the ratio had changed since the previous period or compared to the competitor. The need here is to explain:

- why the change may be important for the specific analysis being carried out

- what further information may be relevant

- what might explain the change.

The last of these points is probably the most difficult, as no specific information is likely to be available. For that reason, those candidates who can make realistic suggestions as to why the change may have occurred will score good marks. The greater the extent to which such suggestions are backed up by reference to the material provided, the higher the marks which will be obtained.

Part (c) required candidates to consider the impact of the accounting treatment of goodwill. Answering the question required specific technical knowledge. It is the need for such technical knowledge that led to this issue being tested in the project rather than the exam. The fact that candidates have time to carry out research while developing project answers makes it disappointing that a number of answers were technically incorrect. It was also disappointing that a number of candidates discussed internally generated goodwill, even though the question specifically referred to purchased goodwill.

The question also emphasised the need to answer in the context of IFRS by clearly referring to impairment. This built on the reference to IFRS in the background material. It is therefore surprising that a number of answers discussed amortisation of goodwill and referred to UK GAAP. This can only be explained by a less than careful reading of the question and a failure to carry out research to obtain relevant technical knowledge.

QUESTION 2

The requirements of this question tested candidates' application of a number of aspects of performance management.

The progression from Part (a) to Part (e) was intended to provide a clear structure for candidates to follow. In many cases, the structure was used and very good marks were scored.

As before, the main reason why candidates did not score good marks was a lack of application. This is best illustrated by considering each part of the question in turn.

Part (a) involved a critical appraisal of the suitability of the chosen benchmark. The best answers were those which considered both the reasons why Compass was a suitable benchmark and the reasons why it may not be – and provided a logical conclusion to the discussion. Answers that merely discussed the nature of benchmarking and how it could be used in general terms did not score good marks.

The use of measures of shareholder value was tested in Part (b). Once again, good marks were obtained by those candidates who ensured that comments were related to the target company, as well as provided – and justified – a specific measure. Discussion of all the measures of shareholder value included in a textbook with no final recommendation did not gain many marks. To repeat a common theme in this report, the fact that some candidates did not ensure that their comments were specific and applied, or did not provide a final recommendation is more than a little surprising, as this was specifically and explicitly required by the wording of the question.

Exactly the same comment can be made with regard to Part (c) which covered supply chain management. General discussion of supply chain management, and reproduction of a diagram taken from a textbook did not gain many marks. Those candidates who discussed specific aspects of the supply chain and how these related to the business of Exfood were well rewarded.

The final to parts of the question required candidates to draw their preceding discussion together to present specific performance measures. This was set in the context of critical success factors (CSFs). An encouraging number of candidates scored very good marks. The key to obtaining good marks was to ensure that the performance measures were clearly linked to the objectives of Exfood, and that the specific means of measuring the CSF was provided. An example of this is 'customer satisfaction'. It goes without saying that for any customer focused organisation, this is an important measure. What is almost as obvious but often overlooked, is that it is notoriously difficult to measure. Those answers that considered aspects of customer satisfaction in the context of Exfood, and then proposed logical – and specific – means of measuring such aspects, obtained good marks. Conversely, those candidates who did not move from the general and omitted to provide specific measures did not.

A further point to note is that in any organisation, CSFs are not measured by a large number of measures. The whole point about CSFs is that they are very tightly focused. Therefore some candidates weakened their answers by providing a long list of measures.

SUMMARY

To summarise, candidates can improve their marks by:

- Reading the question carefully and noting the requirement to set answers in context.

- Fully explaining the significance of all measures of performance in the context of the specific company.

- Constantly asking themselves 'how?' and 'why?' For example:

    - How does this measure help in assessing performance?

    - Why am I using it?

    - How can the results be interpreted?

    - Why has the measure changed?

    - Why is the measure different between the two companies?

    - How might changes in the company's activities or practices have affected the measure?

ACCA Live Project – Autumn 2006: Module B

1 Autumn 2006 Project: Module B

Diploma in Financial Management

PROJECT DB2, INCORPORATING SUBJECT AREAS
– FINANCIAL STRATEGY
– RISK MANAGEMENT

All questions are compulsory and MUST be answered

The project MUST be written in English.

The maximum word count (including appendices and tables but excluding table of contents, references and bibliography) is 5,000.

The project MUST be TYPED in black ink, one-sided, double-spaced, using a minimum 12-point font size and a 1-inch margin at each side. HANDWRITTEN SUBMISSIONS WILL NOT BE ACCEPTED. The project must be submitted by post, electronic submissions are not acceptable.

The project should be submitted on A4 paper with your student number, project name, date and page number at the top of each page.

A project submission form MUST be completed for each project submitted and attached to the front of the project.

The Association of Chartered Certified Accountants

Incorporating subject areas – Financial Strategy and Risk Management

All questions are compulsory and MUST be attempted

Burrator plc

Burrator plc was founded in 1996 by four academics from the University of Oxbridge and was floated on the London Stock Exchange in 2000. The company uses biochemistry and biotechnology to develop new treatments and dressings for severe wounds such as leg ulcers, burns and scars. Despite a promising start, the company experienced financial difficulties in 2002. Large losses, caused by high research and development costs, and a weak product pipeline led to a share price collapse. For a while it seemed that the company would go into liquidation, however, it was eventually taken over in 2003 and became a wholly-owned subsidiary of a large pharmaceutical company – Kes Pharmaceuticals plc.

Abridged versions of the group financial statements of Kes Pharmaceuticals plc (including Burrator plc) and the separate financial statements of Burrator plc for the most recent year are shown below.

Income statements for the year ended 30 June 2006

	Group results (incl. Burrator plc)	Burrator plc results
	£m	£m
Revenue	2,835	26
Cost of sales	(695)	(9)
Selling, general and administration expenses	(1,373)	(5)
Research and development expenses	(185)	(5)
Operating profit	582	7
Interest charges	(42)	–
Profit (loss) before taxation	540	7
Corporation tax (20%)	(108)	(1)
Profit (loss) attributable to shareholders	432	6

Balance sheets as at 30 June 2006

	Group financial position (incl. Burrator plc)		Burrator plc financial position	
	£m	£m	£m	£m
Non-current assets		1,470		20
Current assets	1,345		12	
Less Current liabilities	810		5	
Net current assets		535		7
Total assets less current liabilities		2,005		27
Less Non-current liabilities		620		–
		1,385		27
Equity				
£1 Ordinary shares		500		10
Retained profit		885		17
		1,385		27

Soon after the takeover, it became apparent that a mistake had been made as Burrator plc did not fit comfortably with the overall aims and objectives of the parent company. The directors of Kes Pharmaceuticals plc had failed to appreciate fully the nature of Burrator plc's business and the problems and issues that it posed. In January 2006 it was therefore decided that Burrator plc should be demerged soon after the end of the financial year to 30 June 2006. To prepare for this event, a new board of directors was appointed for Burrator plc and financial guarantees were made to ensure that the company could survive as a separate entity for a reasonable period. To ensure long-term survival, it was agreed that the newlydemerged company should immediately seek a listing on the Alternative Investment Market (AIM) in order to raise the profile of the company and attract investor interest. Shareholders in Kes Pharmaceuticals plc will own all of the shares of the demerged company and an appropriate number of shares in Burrator plc will be allocated to each shareholder.

A public announcement of the demerger will soon take place and this is expected to be welcomed by major institutional shareholders of Kes Pharmaceuticals plc. In the past, they have expressed doubts as to whether the acquisition of Burrator plc would enhance shareholder value and saw the acquisition as a distraction from the core business of the parent company. The finance director of Kes Pharmaceuticals plc therefore believes that the market will view the demerger as a signal that the parent company is returning to its core business activities and he expects a 5% increase in the P/E ratio, based on the pre-demerger group earnings of Kes Pharmaceuticals plc, once the announcement takes place. The current P/E ratio of the company is 10 times.

The advanced wound management sector, within which Burrator plc operates, is still in the early stages of development. The total global market size is approximately £800 million per year as at 30 June 2006 and it is expected to grow at a rate of between 8 and 10% each year up to, and including, 2013, as an ageing population drives demand. Thereafter, the market is expected to stabilise at the level achieved by the end of 2013. The main customers are Accident and Emergency and Surgical departments of hospitals in the UK and USA, which account for around 60% of the total market size. The concentration of demand in these countries is mainly due to the fact that other countries impose tight regulatory requirements for advanced wound management treatments and/or governments are not prepared to pay for such treatments.

To date, Burrator plc has failed to develop a strong pipeline of new treatments and dressings and the failure rate for new products has been higher than in many comparable biotechnology companies. Furthermore, two of the most successful treatments developed by the company came to the end of their useful lives during the year to 30 June 2006 and thereafter only two remaining treatments seem certain of generating revenues. These are:

Derova – a transparent dressing that can be easily removed. This polyurethane-based product requires less frequent dressing changes than conventional wound dressings and hastens the healing process by ensuring that essential proteins produced by the body are not absorbed by the dressing.

Polova – a temporary covering for burns. This tissue-engineered product acts as a skin substitute, providing protection for the wound and reducing pain.

It is estimated that each product has four years' life remaining and the share of the total market that each are expected to achieve over this period are set out below.

	Share of total market size for years ended 30 June			
	2007	*2008*	*2009*	*2010*
Product				
Derova	2.0%	1.5%	1.0%	0.5%
Polova	3.2%	2.4%	1.0%	0.4%

In the advanced wound management sector, high levels of scientific and technological expertise are the critical success factors. Hence, strong links with leading universities are essential. Although the company was founded by academics, links with universities have been fairly weak. However, considerable effort has been invested in strengthening these links and Burrator plc has recently signed agreements with two leading universities, resulting in three new products in the development pipeline. These are:

AN113 – an impregnated dressing. This product, which contains an amorphous hydrogel, loosens damaged tissue and helps to moisten wounds in order to encourage healing.

AN144 – a plaster with a special polymembrane. This plaster contains cell tissues from the patients own skin thereby accelerating the healing process and avoiding rejection by the host.

AN175 – a moistening dressing for chronic wounds. This dressing relies on super-absorbent technology to ensure that sufficient moisture is retained to promote healing but excess moisture produced by the body is absorbed.

If the above treatments receive regulatory approval, the following estimates have been made concerning the market share of each product over their ten-year life.

Expected market share for the year ended 30 June

Product	2007	2008	2009	2010	2011	2012	2013– 2017
AN113	–	1.5%	1.8%	2.0%	2.0%	2.5%	2.5%
AN144	–	0.2%	1.2%	2.4%	3.0%	3.6%	3.6%
AN175	–	0.1%	1.0%	1.8%	2.2%	2.4%	2.4%

Burrator plc does not have a sales and marketing division that is capable of dealing with the demands of a global market. Thus Burrator plc, which had not been taken over when the two existing treatments were first developed, had signed a licensing agreement with a large pharmaceutical company for the marketing and distribution of the treatments. This agreement gave Burrator plc a royalty of 30% of the sales proceeds from each treatment. It is quite common for biotechnology companies operating in the sector to do this and the company will shortly sign licensing agreements with another large pharmaceutical company relating to the treatments that are currently being developed. These will provide a royalty on future sales of each treatment, the amount of which will depend on the particular stage of development that has been reached.

A treatment must successfully complete three phases of clinical trials in order to obtain regulatory approval and, when negotiating licensing agreements, the more developed the treatment, the higher the royalty that can be expected. The trial phase reached and expected royalty for each treatment are as follows:

1. *AN113* is undergoing Phase I trials (which is the earliest point at which trials can be carried out on humans). Royalty payments will be 20% of sales, with a 100% contribution towards all future development costs.

2. *AN144* is undergoing Phase II trials. Royalty payments will be 40% of sales with a 100% contribution to all future development costs.

3. *AN175* is undergoing Phase III trials. Royalty payments will be 60% of sales with 100% contribution towards any remaining development costs.

The estimated total development costs for each product up to the launch are as follows:

Product	Total development costs up to launch
AN113	£2.6m
AN144	£2.2m
AN175	£1.4m

Industry data show that the chances of a treatment, at a particular trial phase, successfully completing all trial phases and receiving regulatory approval are as follows:

1. For treatments undergoing Phase I trials – 10%
2. For treatments undergoing Phase II trials – 30%
3. For treatments undergoing Phase III trials – 70%

If each treatment successfully completes the three phases of clinical trials, they will all be ready to launch at some point during the year to 30 June 2008.

Burrator plc outsources the manufacture of the treatments and dressing to traditional textile-dressings' manufacturers, specialist pharmaceutical companies and specialist chemical companies. Following the re-negotiation of contracts with suppliers and the reduction in administrative costs, the future total costs incurred by the company (excluding development costs) are estimated to be 45% of the expected value of the royalty payments received during each year. The company has no financial commitments beyond the year ended 30 June 2017.

In preparation for the AIM listing, the new board of directors of Burrator plc has been giving consideration to corporate governance issues. The board is convinced that good corporate governance will instil confidence among investors in the company and this may, in turn, lower the cost of capital. As part of its review of corporate governance procedures, it has decided to introduce an annual appraisal for each board member and has also decided to appoint two non-executive directors as the board currently has none. The board is clear as to the criteria that should be applied when appraising executive directors but has yet to decide what criteria should be applied to non-executive directors. It has therefore decided to seek advice on this issue.

Recently, the board of directors of Burrator plc identified a similar company that is currently listed on AIM. Kilmar plc operates within the advanced wound management sector and has been listed on AIM for the past three years. The abridged financial statements of the company for the year ended 30 June 2006 are shown below.

Income statement for the year ended 30 June 2006

	£m
Revenue	46
Cost of sales	(15)
General and administration expenses	(10)
Research and development expenses	(11)
Operating profit	10
Interest charges	(1)
Profit before taxation	9
Corporation tax (20%)	(2)
Profit (loss) attributable to shareholders	7

Balance sheet as at 30 June 2006

	£m	£m
Non-current assets		29
Current assets	28	
Less Current liabilities	15	
Net current assets		13
Total assets less current liabilities		42
Less Non-current liabilities (Loan capital)		15
		27
Equity		
£1 Ordinary shares		10
Retained profit (loss)		17
		27

The ordinary shares of Kilmar plc have a current market value of £5.40 per share and the equity beta is 1.7. Returns to the market are 10.5% and the risk-free rate is 3.2%. The loan capital is irredeemable and currently trading at £120 per £100 nominal value. The corporation tax rate is 20%.

Required

(a) Evaluate the proposal for the demerger of Burrator plc. In carrying out this evaluation you should:

   (i) Provide an estimate of the average cost of capital for Burrator plc. (10 marks)

   (ii) Suggest a value for each share in Burrator plc that could be used as a basis for the company's flotation on AIM, assuming that global demand for advanced wound dressings is:

      (1) at the lower end of expectations;
      (2) at the higher end of expectations. (27 marks)

   (iii) Derive a value for each share in Burrator plc using an alternative valuation method to that used in (ii) above in order to test the validity and reliability of your earlier valuations and comment on your findings. (8 marks)

   (iv) Recommend an appropriate allocation of shares in Burrator plc to the shareholders of Kes Pharmaceuticals plc and, using the most conservative share value derived from your answers to (ii) and (iii) above, assess the likely effect of the proposed demerger on the wealth of an institutional shareholder holding 100,000 shares in Kes Pharmaceuticals plc. (11 marks)

   (56 marks)

(b) Prepare a briefing paper for the board of directors of Burrator plc setting out the criteria that may be used in the annual appraisal of a non-executive director. (16 marks)

(c) Prepare a report for the board of directors of Burrator plc which identifies and assesses the key risks faced by the company after the demerger and which explains how these risks may be managed. (28 marks)

Notes

In answering the case study questions:

1. All key workings must be shown and key assumptions must be clearly stated.
2. The estimate derived in (a)(i) should be to the nearest percent.
3. Workings in (a)(ii) and (a)(iii) should be in £ millions and to one decimal place.
4. Ignore inflation.
5. Assume that corporation tax is paid in the year to which it relates.

   (100 marks)

2 Suggested approach

The case study that this project is based upon concerns a biotechnology company Burrator plc, which is a wholly-owned subsidiary of a large pharmaceutical company. Burrator plc is about to be demerged and the questions are based around the proposed demerger.

Start by reading through the information that is given in the case study. Do not get bogged down in the detailed numerical information but try to get a feel for what is going on and the information you have been given.

Now turn to the requirements and read through these. All of part (a) is fairly numerical but parts (b) and (c) are discursive on the appraisal of a non-executive director and management of risks in Burrator plc.

Now that you have an idea of what the requirements are read through all of the information in the case study again.

Part (a) (i)

You are asked to calculate the cost of capital for Burrator plc. You are expected to recognise that you can use the relationship between a geared company's beta and that of an ungeared company in order to do this as you are given relevant information about Kilmar plc.

Once you have realised how you are going to approach this go back to your Study Text to check on the correct formulae to use. You don't want to make a silly mistake by getting part of the formulae wrong.

Now before you start all the calculations in part (a) make sure that you have read the notes at the end of the requirements regarding roundings etc.

Part (a) (ii)

There are a variety of methods in theory of calculating share values and you are provided with a lot of information in the case study. Bear in mind that this part of the project is worth 27 marks and given the wealth of information that you are given about demand etc together with the fact that you are asked to suggest values under two different assumptions regarding global demand this should lead you in the right direction using future sales and discounted cash flows.

However the examiner did note that in some cases candidates were unable to grasp the approach needed and resorted to simple valuation models such as the dividend growth model to calculate a share value.

Once you have determined your overall approach you now need to read through the information in the case study again but this time taking note of all of the figures and details that you have been given.

Part (a) (iii)

In this part you are asked to derive a share value for Burrator plc using an alternative valuation method. Have a good look at the information that you have been given and see what the alternatives are. You are given Burrator plc's balance sheet so a net asset valuation is possible but this is a fairly meaningless valuation method as the balance sheet is based on depreciated historical cost and particularly in a business such as that of Burrator may not include vital assets such as know-how and employee value.

However as an alternative you are in a position to calculate the P/E ratio of Kilmar, a similar listed company, which should give a good indication of whether the share value in part (ii) is a reasonable figure.

Part (a) (iv)

The requirement here is to use the most conservative share value calculated in parts (ii) and (iii) and recommend how the shares in Burrator should be allocated and assess the effect on a shareholding of 100,000 shares in Kes.

To do this you firstly need to calculate the EPS of Kes and from that calculate its current market value based on the stated P/E value of 10. After the demerger the P/E ratio is estimated to increase so again calculate the market value of 100,000 shares based on this new P/E value plus the value of the shares in Burrator.

Part (b)

For this part of the project you are required to set out the criteria that may be used in the annual appraisal of a non-executive director. At this stage you may want to go back to the Study Text to remind yourself of the role and responsibilities of a non-executive director.

However bear in mind that the examiner commented that this part of the project was generally not answered well. He commented that 'Too often a rather mechanical approach was adopted, whereby candidates simply listed the attributes required of a non-executive director, based either on the Combined Code or some other authoritative source. There was no real attempt to clearly specify the criteria for assessment or to take account of the particular needs of the company. To gain higher marks, most candidates had to address the question posed in a more thoughtful manner.'

Note also that what is required is a briefing paper for the board of directors so no formal presentation is required.

You should be aiming for about 800 words (16/100 × 5,000) for this part.

Part (c)

For the final part of the project we move onto the Risk Management section of the syllabus. You are asked to identify, assess and explain how to manage the key risks faced by the company after the demerger. The examiner noted that although risks were generally well identified there were more problems with the assessment and management of those risks. As has been commented many times by the examiner many answers were 'rather superficial and failed to take account of the information provided in the case study'.

As this section does not really relate to anything that you have done so far in this project it is probably worth taking the time at this stage to re-read through the case study making notes on any areas of risk that you consider to be relevant. When you think you have identified the key risks then consider how you would assess them and then about how they could be managed.

Note that for this part your answer must be in the form of a report to the board of directors so make sure that it is in report format. Given the mark allocation of 28 marks aim for about 1,400 words (28/100 × 5,000).

3 Suggested answer

(a)   (i)   Kilmar plc is a similar company to Burrator plc and we are given Kilmar's beta as 1.7. However Kilmar plc is a geared company and Burrator is an ungeared company so we have to calculate the ungeared beta of Kilmar plc using the following formula:

$$\beta a = \beta e \, (E/E+D(1-t)$$

Where:

βa = asset beta (or ungeared beta)
βe = equity beta = 1.7
E = proportion of equity in the capital structure
D = proportion of debt in the capital structure
t = Corporation tax rate

Market values in Kilmar:

Equity =	10m × £5.40 =	£54m
Debt =	£15m × £1.20 =	£18m
		£72m

Proportions in capital structure:

Equity =	54/72 =	75%
Debt =	18/72 =	25%

$$\beta a = \beta e \, (E/E+D(1-t))$$

$$\beta a = 1.7 \, (75/75 + 25(1-0.2))$$

$$= 1.7 \times 75/95$$

$$= 1.342$$

Therefore the beta of Burrator plc can be estimated as 1.342 and used in the CAPM to estimate the cost of equity (cost of capital) in Burrator plc.

279

$$Ke = 3.2 + 1.342(10.5 - 3.2)$$
$$= 13\%$$

(ii)   (1)   **At the lower end of the expectations – using 8% for global market growth**

	2007	2008	2009	2010	2011	2012	2013 – 17
Global market £m	864.0	933.1	1,007.8	1,088.4	1,175.5	1,269.5	1,371.1
Derova							
Derova market share %	2.0	1.5	1.0	0.5			
Derova sales £m	17.3	14.0	10.1	5.4			
Derova royalty (30%) £m	5.2	4.2	3.0	1.6			
Polova							
Polova market share %	3.2	2.4	1.0	0.4			
Polova sales £m	27.6	22.4	10.1	4.4			
Polova royalty (30%) £m	8.3	6.7	3.0	1.3			
AN113							
Market share %		1.5	1.8	2.0	2.0	2.5	2.5
Sales £m		14.0	18.1	21.8	23.5	31.7	34.3
Royalty (20%) £m		2.8	3.6	4.4	4.7	6.3	6.9
AN144							
Market share %		0.2	1.2	2.4	3.0	3.6	3.6
Sales £m		1.9	12.1	26.1	35.3	45.7	49.4
Royalty (40%) £m		0.8	4.8	10.4	14.1	18.3	19.8
AN175							
Market share %		0.1	1.0	1.8	2.2	2.4	2.4
Sales £m		0.9	10.1	19.6	25.9	30.5	32.9
Royalty (60%) £m		0.5	6.1	11.8	15.5	18.3	19.7

From these workings the forecast net cash flows for Burrator plc can be calculated:

	2007 £m	2008 £m	2009 £m	2010 £m	2011 £m	2012 £m	2013 – 17 £m
Derova	5.2	4.2	3.0	1.6			
Polova	8.3	6.7	3.0	1.3			
AN113 – 10%		0.3	0.4	0.4	0.5	0.6	0.7
AN144 – 30%		0.2	1.4	3.1	4.2	5.5	5.9
AN175 – 70%		0.3	4.3	8.3	10.9	12.8	13.8
	13.5	11.7	12.1	14.7	15.6	18.9	20.4
Costs – 45%	6.1	5.3	5.4	6.6	7.0	8.5	9.2
	7.4	6.4	6.7	8.1	8.6	10.4	11.2
Tax (20%)	1.5	1.3	1.3	1.6	1.7	2.1	2.2
Net cash flows	5.9	5.1	5.4	6.5	6.9	8.3	9.0
Discount factor 13%	0.885	0.783	0.693	0.613	0.543	0.480	1.689
Present value	5.2	4.0	3.7	4.0	3.7	4.0	15.2

Total present value   =   £39.8m

Notes:

- development costs have been ignored as they are all fully reimbursed

- discount factor from time 7 (2013) to time 11 (2017) is cumulative discount factor to time 11 of 5.687 minus cumulative discount factor to time 6 of 3.998 = 5.687 – 3.998 = 1.689

    There are 10 million shares in Burrator plc therefore the estimated value of a share is £39.8/10 = £3.98

(2) **At the higher end of the expectations – using 10% for global market growth**

	2007	2008	2009	2010	2011	2012	2013 – 17
Global market £m	880.0	968.0	1,064.8	1,171.3	1,288.4	1,417.2	1,559.0
Derova							
Derova market share %	2.0	1.5	1.0	0.5			
Derova sales £m	17.6	14.5	10.7	5.9			
Derova royalty (30%) £m	5.3	4.4	3.2	1.8			
Polova							
Polova market share %	3.2	2.4	1.0	0.4			
Polova sales £m	28.2	23.2	10.7	4.7			
Polova royalty (30%) £m	8.5	7.0	3.2	1.4			
AN113							
Market share %		1.5	1.8	2.0	2.0	2.5	2.5
Sales £m		14.5	19.2	23.4	25.8	35.4	39.0
Royalty (20%) £m		2.9	3.8	4.7	5.2	7.1	7.8
AN144							
Market share %		0.2	1.2	2.4	3.0	3.6	3.6
Sales £m		1.9	12.8	28.1	38.7	51.0	56.1
Royalty (40%) £m		0.8	5.1	11.2	15.5	20.4	22.4
AN175							
Market share %		0.1	1.0	1.8	2.2	2.4	2.4
Sales £m		1.0	10.6	21.1	28.3	34.0	37.4
Royalty (60%) £m		0.6	6.4	12.7	17.0	20.4	22.4

From these workings the forecast net cash flows for Burrator plc can be calculated:

	2007 £m	2008 £m	2009 £m	2010 £m	2011 £m	2012 £m	2013 – 17 £m
Derova	5.3	4.4	3.2	1.8			
Polova	8.5	7.0	3.2	1.4			
AN113 – 10%		0.3	0.4	0.5	0.5	0.7	0.8
AN144 – 30%		0.2	1.5	3.4	4.7	6.1	6.7
AN175 – 70%		0.4	4.5	8.9	11.9	14.3	15.7
	13.8	12.3	12.8	16.0	17.1	21.1	23.2
Costs – 45%	6.2	5.5	5.8	7.2	7.7	9.5	10.4
	7.6	6.8	7.0	8.8	9.4	11.6	12.8
Tax (20%)	1.5	1.4	1.4	1.8	1.9	2.3	2.6
Net cash flows	6.1	5.4	5.6	7.0	7.5	9.3	10.2
Discount factor 13%	0.885	0.783	0.693	0.613	0.543	0.480	1.689
Present value	5.4	4.2	3.9	4.3	4.1	4.5	17.2

Total present value = £43.6m

Notes:

- development costs have been ignored as they are all fully reimbursed

- discount factor from time 7 (2013) to time 11 (2017) is cumulative discount factor to time 11 of 5.687 minus cumulative discount factor to time 6 of 3.998 = 5.687 – 3.998 = 1.689

There are 10 million shares in Burrator plc therefore the estimated value of a share is £43.6/10 = £4.36

(iii)   The price/earnings ratio of Kilmar plc can be calculated as an alternative method of estimating a share value for Burrator plc.

Earnings per share	=	£7m/10m
	=	£0.70
P/E ratio	=	£5.40/£0.70
	=	7.7

Applied to Burrator plc

Earnings per share	=	£6m/10m
	=	£0.60
Value per share	=	£0.60 × 7.7
	=	£4.62

(iv)

Number of shares in Kes Pharmaceuticals	=	500m
Number of shares in Burrator	=	10m

Share allocation

1 share in Burrator for every 50 (500/10) shares held in Kes Pharmaceuticals

Earnings per share of Kes Pharmaceuticals	=	£432m/500m
	=	£0.864
Value of one share in Kes Pharmaceuticals before demerger	=	10 × £0.864
	=	£8.64
Value of shareholding	=	100,000 × £8.64
	=	£864,000
P/E ratio of Kes Pharmaceuticals after demerger	=	10 × 1.05
	=	10.5
Value of one share in Kes Pharmaceuticals after demerger	=	10.5 × £0.864
	=	£9.07
Value of shareholding	=	100,000 × £9.07
	=	£907,000
Value of shareholding in Burrator (100,000/50 × £3.98)	=	£7,960
Total wealth of shareholders	=	£907,000 + £7,960
	=	£914,960

This compares to £864,000 before the demerger which indicates that shareholder wealth will increase.

(b)   **Briefing paper – Criteria to be used in the annual appraisal of a non-executive director**

Burrator plc currently has no non-executive directors but a decision has been made to appoint two non-executive directors to the board. As with the executive directors these non-executive directors must be appraised on an annual basis. The purpose of this briefing paper is to consider the criteria that may be used in the annual appraisal of a non-executive director. Therefore we must consider what it is we expect of our non-executive directors and how we can assess their performance in the light of our expectations.

The non-executive directors appointed will presumably have some knowledge of the specialist type of business environment in which Burrator plc operates. However they will need to acquire a degree of knowledge about the specific operations, circumstances and market placing of Burrator plc.

Criteria - Has the director attended an induction course regarding the specific ways in which Burrator plc operates and the factors affecting its operations?

Has the director identified any further skills or knowledge that he believes are necessary to keep up with changes in the industry and business world?

Has the director attended any other relevant training programmes?

How much time and effort has the director invested in understanding the business and the issues that face it?

How much time each month does the director devote to Burrator plc compared to his roles and duties for other companies?

Non-executive directors have a significant role to play during board meetings. Their role is to constructively challenge and help develop proposals on strategy, to scrutinise the performance of management in meeting agreed goals and objectives and to monitor the reporting of performance. The executive directors run the business on a day-to-day basis but the role of the non-executive directors is to bring their knowledge and experience to board meetings and to provide an objective and independent view.

Criteria - What is the attendance record at board meetings for the director?

Has the director been willing to prepare thoroughly for board meetings?

From the minutes of the board meetings has the director contributed regularly to discussions at board meetings?

Has the director used his experience and knowledge in dealing with problems, particularly those concerning strategy and risk management?

From the minutes has the director regularly challenged the assertions and assumptions made by the executive directors in support of particular plans and strategies?

Has the director shown his independence of mind and judgement during board meetings particularly if under pressure from executive directors?

Has the director been persistent in following up any unresolved issues?

One of the important roles of a non-executive director is to sit on a variety of other important committees of the company as well as attending board meetings. The nomination committee should be largely made up of non-executive directors. This committee should lead the process for board appointments and make recommendations to the board. It will also be involved in dealing with succession problems.

The remuneration committee for a small company should have two members who are independent non-executive directors. The remuneration committee has responsibility for setting remuneration for all executive directors and the chairman.

The audit committee for a small company should have two members who should be independent non-executive directors. The main roles and responsibilities of the audit committee are to monitor the integrity of the financial statements, to review the internal financial controls and internal control and risk management systems and to maintain relations with the company's external auditor.

Criteria - How many meetings of the nomination committee, remuneration committee and audit committee has the director attended?

Has the director been absent from any of these meetings?

Is the director's financial knowledge sufficient for him to perform his role on the audit committee?

Has the director maintained his independence during the period under review?

Has the director added value to any meetings of the nomination committee, remuneration committee or audit committee?

Although non-executive directors only work for the company for part of their time they are expected to not only contribute effectively to the running of the company but also to be a part of the management team.

Criteria - Has the director shown the ability to work as part of the team when necessary?

Has the director built effective relations with the other members of the board of directors and the senior management team?

Given any other duties outside of his non-executive directorship of Burrator plc has the director the time to give Burrator plc the input that is required?

(c) **REPORT**

To: Board of directors of Burrator plc
From: Accountant
Date: X – X – 20XX
Subject: Key risk analysis

In this report I consider the position of Burrator plc after the proposed demerger and I identify and assess the key risks faced by the company. I also consider how these risks may be managed.

Most of the risks faced by the company will be classified as business risks which are the risks of loss due to changes in the competitive environment or to trends that damage the operating economics of a business. In particular in this type of business two areas of business risk will be important – legal risk and reputational risk. Other risks that the business faces could be classified as process risk which is the risk that the organisation's processes may be ineffective or inefficient.

In terms of assessing risk this will be done by considering both the impact of the event or risk and the probability of its occurrence.

Finally when considering the management of risk there are basically four options:

- risk avoidance which means not carrying out the activity at all
- risk reduction
- risk sharing eg insurance
- risk acceptance or retention.

Business risks

If we first consider the economic and competitive environment in which we operate the advanced wound management sector is still in the early stages of development and there is uncertainty about the likely level of growth in the global market size. This is general business risk that we must accept unless we were to move away and operate in a different market sector. A further risk that we face but have little choice but to accept is that we rely heavily on governments maintaining or increasing healthcare expenditure. We already know that our market is limited by governments that are not prepared to pay for such treatments.

We have had problems in the past caused by failing to develop a strong pipeline of new treatments and dressings and the failure rate for new products has been higher than in many comparable biotechnology companies. This leads to two major business risks:

- the risk of development of more effective and/or cheaper products by competitors

- failure to develop new products which successfully complete all trial phases and receive regulatory approval

Such risks are sometimes also known as process risks as it would appear in the past that our processes have not been rigorous enough to ensure the success of our products. Without effective products then the company runs the risk of the business failing all together therefore the impact of these risks is very high and this combines with a reasonable probability that this could happen to ensure that these are key risks indeed. We must consider our processes and in particular our quality standards and attempt to maintain the highest possible quality of operations in order to be competitive.

Allied to this are two other risks which must be considered:

- failure to maintain strong links with research-based institutions and universities
- failure to attract and retain key staff.

High levels of scientific and technological expertise are critical success factors in the advanced wound management sector therefore strong links with the universities and technology based institutions is vital. We must maintain and strengthen these links as a key element of our strategy and may consider appointing one of the directors to be responsible for this important area.

In more general terms we must ensure that we recruit and retain the right calibre of staff. We have a new board of directors with the experience and abilities to run the company but our assessment of current staff and our recruitment procedures must be rigorous to ensure strength in this area. We should also consider whether our terms and conditions are comparable with those of our competitors in order to ensure that we are in a position to employ the best scientific and technological brains.

We must also consider the risks attached to our manufacturing, marketing and supply procedures. In common with much of the industry our company does not have a sales and marketing division that is capable of dealing with the global market. Therefore we enter into licensing agreements with large pharmaceutical companies for the marketing and distribution of our treatments. With regard to our manufacturing of the products we outsource the manufacture of the treatments and dressings to traditional textile-dressings' manufacturers, specialist pharmaceutical companies and specialist chemical companies.

This could be viewed as a way of reducing the risks attached to manufacture, marketing and sales but we must always strive to ensure that the quality of manufacture and marketing of these suppliers is of the highest level.

Reputational risk

In terms of reputational risk we have two areas to consider of potentially high risk:

- product liability arising from adverse reactions to our products or complaints from customers

- loss of reputation arising from design defects or ineffective products.

It would be possible to avoid these risks by not operating in a sector such as we do but that would of course mean that we would have no business. Therefore the answer is either to share the risk, reduce it or as a last resort accept it. By sharing the risk we mean insurance against negligence by employees or outsourced manufacturers and we should look into the possibility of any form of insurance that might be possible. Reduction of such risks should come about naturally if, as mentioned earlier in this report, we strive to maintain the highest quality in our research and manufacture of our products.

Legal risks

We must also consider legal risks:

- failure to comply with laws and regulations governing the testing and approval of products
- infringement of patents

These could be regarded as compliance matters and are of very great importance. The impact of either of these risks is high and therefore we must ensure that we minimise the risk of either taking place. A compliance officer should be appointed so that we are confident that all laws and regulations are acceded to and competitors' patent rights are not infringed. This is particularly important as the market is largely in the UK and US and if there were problems in either of these countries then our potential market would be much diminished.

I hope that this information has been useful and that we can use this information to drive forward our risk management processes and systems.

4 Examiner's comments

Examiner's comments. The pass rate for this sitting was satisfactory, with the majority of candidates producing projects of a good standard. In this sitting, marks were more widely dispersed than in previous sittings. Candidates tended to score either high marks or low marks with relatively few marginal candidates. The main weakness displayed by candidates was the failure to adopt a more thoughtful approach to the issues raised. In previous reports it has been mentioned that any principles or points raised should take account of the particular circumstances that are set out in the case study. Failure to do this results in answers that are too broad and superficial.

SPECIFIC COMMENTS

The case study upon which the question was based concerned a biotechnology company, Burrator plc, which is a wholly-owned subsidiary of a large pharmaceutical company. Burrator plc is about to be demerged and the questions posed were based around the proposed demerger.

Part (a) was divided into four sub-parts. Part (a)(i) carried 10 marks out of 100 marks for the whole project and required candidates to calculate the average cost of capital for Burrator plc.

To answer Part (a), the ungeared beta of a similar company had to be calculated. This could then be used in the CAPM formula to calculate the cost of equity capital for Burrator plc. This part was often answered well with many candidates gaining full marks. In some cases, however, candidates had no clear idea as to how the problem should be approached and so scored low marks. In other cases, candidates were able to identify the approach required but were unable to identify the approach required but were unable to apply the formula in the correct manner. In particular, the correct weighting of debt and equity when calculating the ungeared beta proved problematic.

Part (a)(ii) carried 27 marks and required candidates to suggest a value for the shares in Burrator plc based on both the lower end and the higher end of expectations concerning future market demand for its products.

This sub-part required candidates to calculate future sales from each of the company's products and then to forecast the future discounted net cash flows arising from the company's operations. Once again, this part was often answered well with the majority of candidates adopting an appropriate approach to the problem. However, a number of candidates came unstuck on specific technical points. In particular, candidates experienced problems in taking account of the probability of success of those products still in the pipeline and the treatment of development costs of the new products, which were fully reimbursed. In some cases, candidates were unable to grasp the approach needed and resorted to simple valuation models, such as the dividend growth model, to calculate a share value. Given the wealth of information available concerning future market demand, market share, costs etc, any approach used should have taken this information into account.

Part (a)(iii) carried eight marks and required candidates to value the shares of Burrator plc using an alternative approach in order to test the reliability of the share value figure derived in Part (a)(ii).

Most candidates employed the price-earnings approach to share valuation and used the P/E ratio of a similar listed company to undertake the valuation. This is a forward-looking valuation method and was an appropriate choice. Some candidates, however, chose to use the net assets approach to share valuation, rather than the P/E ratio method. While this approach could be used, it has serious limitiations and is much less likely to provide a suitable means of testing the reliability and validity of the DCF-based measure used in Part (a)(ii). Overall, marks awarded for this sub-part were high.

Part (a)(iv) carried 11 marks and required candidates to recommend an allocation of shares in Burrator plc for shareholders in the parent company and to assess the effect of the demerger on the wealth of a large shareholder in the parent company.

To answer this sub-part, the EPS of the parent company had to be calculated and the market value of a share, before and after the proposed demerger, and taking into account the shareholdings in the newly-demerged company, could then be compared. This part was answered well by most candidates and marks were generally high.

Part (b) carried 16 marks and required a briefing paper setting out the criteria that may be used in the annual appraisal of a non-executive director of Burrator plc.

This part was rarely answered well. Too often a rather mechanical approach was adopted, whereby candidates simply listed the attributes required of a non-executive director, based either on the Combined Code or some other authoritative source. There was no real attempt to clearly specify the criteria for assessment or to take account of the particular needs of the company. To gain higher marks, most candidates had to address the question posed in a more thoughtful manner.

Part (c) carried 28 marks and concerned the identification, assessment and management of risks of Burrator plc.

Most candidates made a reasonable attempt to this part, although the identification of risks posed fewer problems than the ways in which they may be assessed and managed. Once again, the main weakness in the answers provided was the failure to adopt a more thoughtful approach to the issues and to tailor the answer to the company's situation. Too often, answers to this part were rather superficial and failed to take account of information provided in the case study.

Mathematical tables

MATHEMATICAL TABLES

Present value table

Present value of 1, ie $(1+r)^{-n}$

where r = discount rate

n = number of periods until payment

Periods					Discount rates (r)					
(n)	1%	2%	3%	4%	5%	6%	7%	8%	9%	10%
1	0.990	0.980	0.971	0.962	0.952	0.943	0.935	0.926	0.917	0.909
2	0.980	0.961	0.943	0.925	0.907	0.890	0.873	0.857	0.842	0.826
3	0.971	0.942	0.915	0.889	0.864	0.840	0.816	0.794	0.772	0.751
4	0.961	0.924	0.888	0.855	0.823	0.792	0.763	0.735	0.708	0.683
5	0.951	0.906	0.863	0.822	0.784	0.747	0.713	0.681	0.650	0.621
6	0.942	0.888	0.837	0.790	0.746	0.705	0.666	0.630	0.596	0.564
7	0.933	0.871	0.813	0.760	0.711	0.665	0.623	0.583	0.547	0.513
8	0.923	0.853	0.789	0.731	0.677	0.627	0.582	0.540	0.502	0.467
9	0.914	0.837	0.766	0.703	0.645	0.592	0.544	0.500	0.460	0.424
10	0.905	0.820	0.744	0.676	0.614	0.558	0.508	0.463	0.422	0.386
11	0.896	0.804	0.722	0.650	0.585	0.527	0.475	0.429	0.388	0.350
12	0.887	0.788	0.701	0.625	0.557	0.497	0.444	0.397	0.356	0.319
13	0.879	0.773	0.681	0.601	0.530	0.469	0.415	0.368	0.326	0.290
14	0.870	0.758	0.661	0.577	0.505	0.442	0.388	0.340	0.299	0.263
15	0.861	0.743	0.642	0.555	0.481	0.417	0.362	0.315	0.275	0.239

	11%	12%	13%	14%	15%	16%	17%	18%	19%	20%
1	0.901	0.893	0.885	0.877	0.870	0.862	0.855	0.847	0.840	0.833
2	0.812	0.797	0.783	0.769	0.756	0.743	0.731	0.718	0.706	0.694
3	0.731	0.712	0.693	0.675	0.658	0.641	0.624	0.609	0.593	0.579
4	0.659	0.636	0.613	0.592	0.572	0.552	0.534	0.516	0.499	0.482
5	0.593	0.567	0.543	0.519	0.497	0.476	0.456	0.437	0.419	0.402
6	0.535	0.507	0.480	0.456	0.432	0.410	0.390	0.370	0.352	0.335
7	0.482	0.452	0.425	0.400	0.376	0.354	0.333	0.314	0.296	0.279
8	0.434	0.404	0.376	0.351	0.327	0.305	0.285	0.266	0.249	0.233
9	0.391	0.361	0.333	0.308	0.284	0.263	0.243	0.225	0.209	0.194
10	0.352	0.322	0.295	0.270	0.247	0.227	0.208	0.191	0.176	0.162
11	0.317	0.287	0.261	0.237	0.215	0.195	0.178	0.162	0.148	0.135
12	0.286	0.257	0.231	0.208	0.187	0.168	0.152	0.137	0.124	0.112
13	0.258	0.229	0.204	0.182	0.163	0.145	0.130	0.116	0.104	0.093
14	0.232	0.205	0.181	0.160	0.141	0.125	0.111	0.099	0.088	0.078
15	0.209	0.183	0.160	0.140	0.123	0.108	0.095	0.084	0.074	0.065

Annuity table

Present value of an annuity of 1, ie $\dfrac{1-(1+r)^{-n}}{r}$

where r = discount rate

  n = number of periods

Periods					Discount rates (r)					
(n)	1%	2%	3%	4%	5%	6%	7%	8%	9%	10%
1	0.990	0.980	0.971	0.962	0.952	0.943	0.935	0.926	0.917	0.909
2	1.970	1.942	1.913	1.886	1.859	1.833	1.808	1.783	1.759	1.736
3	2.941	2.884	2.829	2.775	2.723	2.673	2.624	2.577	2.531	2.487
4	3.902	3.808	3.717	3.630	3.546	3.465	3.387	3.312	3.240	3.170
5	4.853	4.713	4.580	4.452	4.329	4.212	4.100	3.993	3.890	3.791
6	5.795	5.601	5.417	5.242	5.076	4.917	4.767	4.623	4.486	4.355
7	6.728	6.472	6.230	6.002	5.786	5.582	5.389	5.206	5.033	4.868
8	7.652	7.325	7.020	6.733	6.463	6.210	5.971	5.747	5.535	5.335
9	8.566	8.162	7.786	7.435	7.108	6.802	6.515	6.247	5.995	5.759
10	9.471	8.983	8.530	8.111	7.722	7.360	7.024	6.710	6.418	6.145
11	10.37	9.787	9.253	8.760	8.306	7.887	7.499	7.139	6.805	6.495
12	11.26	10.58	9.954	9.385	8.863	8.384	7.943	7.536	7.161	6.814
13	12.13	11.35	10.63	9.986	9.394	8.853	8.358	7.904	7.487	7.103
14	13.00	12.11	11.30	10.56	9.899	9.295	8.745	8.244	7.786	7.367
15	13.87	12.85	11.94	11.12	10.38	9.712	9.108	8.559	8.061	7.606

	11%	12%	13%	14%	15%	16%	17%	18%	19%	20%
1	0.901	0.893	0.885	0.877	0.870	0.862	0.855	0.847	0.840	0.833
2	1.713	1.690	1.668	1.647	1.626	1.605	1.585	1.566	1.547	1.528
3	2.444	2.402	2.361	2.322	2.283	2.246	2.210	2.174	2.140	2.106
4	3.102	3.037	2.974	2.914	2.855	2.798	2.743	2.690	2.639	2.589
5	3.696	3.605	3.517	3.433	3.352	3.274	3.199	3.127	3.058	2.991
6	4.231	4.111	3.998	3.889	3.784	3.685	3.589	3.498	3.410	3.326
7	4.712	4.564	4.423	4.288	4.160	4.039	3.922	3.812	3.706	3.605
8	5.146	4.968	4.799	4.639	4.487	4.344	4.207	4.078	3.954	3.837
9	5.537	5.328	5.132	4.946	4.772	4.607	4.451	4.303	4.163	4.031
10	5.889	5.650	5.426	5.216	5.019	4.833	4.659	4.494	4.339	4.192
11	6.207	5.938	5.687	5.453	5.234	5.029	4.836	4.656	4.486	4.327
12	6.492	6.194	5.918	5.660	5.421	5.197	4.988	4.793	4.611	4.439
13	6.750	6.424	6.122	5.842	5.583	5.342	5.118	4.910	4.715	4.533
14	6.982	6.628	6.302	6.002	5.724	5.468	5.229	5.008	4.802	4.611
15	7.191	6.811	6.462	6.142	5.847	5.575	5.324	5.092	4.876	4.675

Index

Note: **Key Terms** and their page references are given in **bold.**

REVIEW FORM

BPP Learning Media always appreciates feedback from the students who use our books. We would be very grateful if you would take the time to complete this feedback form, and return it to the address below.

Name: _____   Address: _____

_____

How have you used this Text?
(Tick one box only)

☐ Home study (book only)

☐ On a course: college _____

☐ With 'correspondence' package

☐ Other _____

Why did you decide to purchase this Text?
(Tick one box only)

☐ Have used complementary Study Text

☐ Have used BPP Learning Media Texts in the past

☐ Recommendation by friend/colleague

☐ Recommendation by a lecturer at college

☐ Saw advertising

☐ Other _____

During the past six months do you recall seeing/receiving any of the following?
(Tick as many boxes as are relevant)

☐ Our advertisement in *ACCA Finance Matters*

☐ Our brochure with a letter through the post

Which (if any) aspects of our advertising do you find useful?
(Tick as many boxes as are relevant)

☐ Prices and publication dates of new editions

☐ Information on Text content

☐ Facility to order books off-the-page

☐ None of the above

Your ratings, comments and suggestions would be appreciated on the following areas

	Very useful	Useful	Not useful
Introductory section	☐	☐	☐
Chapter introductions	☐	☐	☐
Key terms	☐	☐	☐
Quality of explanations	☐	☐	☐
Case examples and other examples	☐	☐	☐
Live projects – questions	☐	☐	☐
Live projects – suggested approaches	☐	☐	☐
Live projects – answers	☐	☐	☐
List of key terms and index	☐	☐	☐

	Excellent	Good	Adequate	Poor
Overall opinion of this Text	☐	☐	☐	☐

Do you intend to continue using BPP Learning Media Products?   ☐ Yes   ☐ No

Please note any further comments and suggestions/errors on the reverse of this page

Please return to: Pippa Riley, BPP Learning Media Ltd, FREEPOST, London, W12 8BR or e-mail pippariley@bpp.com

REVIEW FORM (continued)

Please note any further comments and suggestions/errors below

REVIEW FORM (continued)

Please note any further comments and suggestions/errors below